#TellEveryone

#TellEveryone

#TellEveryone

#TellEveryone

#TellEveryone

#TellEveryone

#TellEveryone

#TellEveryone

#TellEveryone

#TellEveryone

#TellEveryone

#TellEveryone

#Tell

#TellEveryone
#TellEveryone
#TellEveryone
#TellEveryone
#TellEveryone
#Tell

Why We Share & Why It Matters ✕

#TellEveryone
#TellEveryone
#TellEveryone
#TellEveryone
#TellEveryone
#TellEveryone

Alfred_Hermida

ANCHOR CANADA

Published by Anchor Canada, a division of Penguin Random House Canada
Limited, in 2016. Originally published in hardcover by Doubleday Canada,
a division of Penguin Random House Canada Limited, in 2014.
Distributed in Canada by Penguin Random House Canada Limited, Toronto.

Anchor Canada with colophon is a registered trademark.

www.penguinrandomhouse.ca

Library and Archives Canada Cataloguing in Publication Data
is available upon request

ISBN 978-0-385-67958-9
eBook ISBN 978-0-385-67957-2

Cover and text design by Five Seventeen
Printed and bound in the USA

10   9   8   7   6   5   4   3   2   1

Penguin
Random House
ANCHOR CANADA

For Rachel, the light that never goes out

Contents

Introduction

▲

THIS IS A STORY ABOUT US. IT IS A STORY ABOUT HOW WE ARE making sense of the world at a time of remarkable change in the circulation of news, information and ideas. Our ability to share so much online, so often, so quickly with so many is rewriting the rules of the media game. Social media is transforming how we discover, learn and understand the world around us. But this is not a story about technology. People are not hooked on YouTube, Twitter or Facebook but on each other. Tools and services come and go; what is constant is our human urge to share.

Our enhanced capacity to share our experiences, emotions and opinions affects what we know and how we know it, requiring that we develop new skills to turn the rapid flow of information all around us into knowledge. Whenever I get asked to comment on how Facebook is making us lonelier or Twitter is full of falsehoods, I tend to spend the first ten minutes explaining that it isn't quite so black and white. For me, this is a dramatic illustration of the gulf between our view of social media and our understanding of it.

Every new form of communication brings with it a perennial angst about what it is doing to our brains. We are not the first to feel that everything is changing too quickly around us, and we won't be the last. Throughout history, communication technologies have been catalysts of societal and cultural change that upset the status quo. Even in ancient Greece, Socrates was wary of books, as he feared they would undermine thinking and learning.

We can't help it. We are creatures of habit. We are comfortable in the cozy embrace of the familiar. Our views of a new form of communication tend to be shaped by personal history and experience. We fall back on tried and tested approaches that worked in the past. As Marshall McLuhan said, "We look at the present through a rear-view mirror. We march backwards into the future." I want us to be able to march forward into the future, equipped with the appropriate skills and expertise to make good decisions. New opportunities to create and share knowledge spark new ways of thinking and doing for those who are equipped with the skills and knowledge to take advantage of those new opportunities.

Social media is so easy to use from a technical point of view that its ease masks how radically the platform changes the way we communicate. In the space of a decade, the marketplace of ideas has been turned on its head. In the past, politicians and businesses would compete for the attention of journalists to try to get their message across to a mass audience. That audience was used to getting its news at set times of the day in neatly packaged formats, like newspapers produced by professionally trained journalists. Now politicians and businesses are reaching out directly to voters and consumers, bypassing the media.

The news is a constant buzz in the background, available at any time, on any device, in just about any place, and is produced by both professionals and the audience itself.

Every generation that has lived through a period of media upheaval has faced the same issues. In the Middle Ages, it took about two hundred years for people to trust what was written on parchment over the oral recollection of witnesses. Before there was a written record of who owned property, villagers would turn to the elders to end disputes. When written records were first introduced, people treated them with suspicion. They asked some of the same questions we ask of what we read on Twitter: How do I know this document is accurate and reliable? How do I know it is not a forgery? It took a shift in mindset for communities to trust a piece of paper over the vague memory of the oldest person in the village.

The development of written records led to new ways of thinking and doing business in the Middle Ages, just as social media is doing in the twenty-first century. The marketplace of ideas is being reshaped by the volume, visibility, speed and reach of social media. It is easier to get a message out there, but also much harder to be noticed when so many are sharing so much so quickly. A hundred hours of video are uploaded to YouTube every minute, an average of 5,700 messages are sent on Twitter every second and more than a billion people are regularly sharing stories, links, photos and videos on Facebook.

For me, one of the most vivid examples of how social media has upended established ways of thinking about news and information was the Arab Spring of 2011. I felt a personal affinity with the revolutions, as I was based in Tunisia and Egypt in the early 1990s while working for BBC News. The contrast between now and then starkly illustrates how social media helps to shift power away from the state and into the hands of its citizens.

THE POWER OF KNOWLEDGE

In the 1990s, Egypt banned street protests, and any such attempts were quickly repressed. I was reporting on one such incident when I was tear-gassed by accident. Lawyers had gathered at the headquarters of the bar association in Cairo, dressed in their black gowns with white bands around their necks. Despite the ban, they planned to march peacefully to the presidential palace in protest of the suspicious death—in custody—of a fellow lawyer.

The lawyers were depending on the media to get their message out. Back then, there were no cell phones in Egypt. Internet access was restricted, as well as slow and unreliable at the best of times. Together with a handful of other journalists, I was standing behind a wall of riot shields and batons outside the compound of the bar association. For safety reasons, journalists covering protests are advised to stay behind the police to avoid being caught between the two sides.

The moment the lawyers tried to set foot outside the compound, the security forces fired tear gas. There are no YouTube videos that captured the sight of gowned lawyers coughing as they retreated into the building. So many canisters were fired that some of the tear gas started wafting back towards a row of police equipped with batons but not gas masks.

The first thing I noticed was an intense tingling sensation in my nostrils. The next few moments are a vivid but fragmented memory. A sudden realization that the stinging sensation was tear gas. The sight of police haphazardly running towards my colleagues and me. Pausing to help up a fellow journalist who had stumbled and was having trouble breathing. Kindly Egyptians who opened a storefront to let us in. Wet towels handed round to lessen the effect of the gas.

None of this was filmed on a cell phone. There were no tweets, no Facebook posts or images on Flickr. It took up a few column inches in the Western media, but Egyptians didn't hear about it. It remains a footnote in the thirty years of authoritarian rule in Egypt. As I followed the protests in Tahrir Square from Vancouver in 2011, I couldn't help but be amazed at the difference between now and then. The story of a people fed up with a corrupt president was being broadcast live on twenty-four-hour news channels and simultaneously unfolding across social media. The revolution was televised, tweeted and Facebooked.

As did so many in the West, I followed the ups and downs of the weeks of protest, often described by the people at the heart of it all. Social media was more than a megaphone for Egyptians denied a voice for so long. It helped to tip the scales away from the machinery of repression and in favour of disaffected Egyptians drawn together by a sense of injustice. Facebook, a service born in the dorms of Harvard as a way for college students to keep in touch, was an instrument of revolution. Twitter, named for its original meaning as a short burst of inconsequential information, was a channel of dissent.

Facebook was not intended to be a way for people to post links to news stories they consider worth reading. YouTube was not created to empower activists to broadcast videos of police beating up protesters. Twitter was not developed as a way to break news of devastating natural disasters. Yet social media has turned into a collection of spaces to share stories of triumph or ignominy, of joy or sorrow, of delight or distraction. Spaces where a video featuring cute kids can make headlines or chasten a multinational corporation, where 140 characters can reveal the truth or propel a rumour at lightning speed.

These technologies have insinuated themselves into the fabric of everyday life as they tap in to our innate nature as social animals. We love to talk, exchange views and argue. What we collectively call social media are a range of technologies, services and activities designed to enhance both communication and the formation of social ties on an unprecedented scale.

The renaissance in sharing harks back to an era when news was exchanged and discussed in marketplaces and coffeehouses, and then further spread by pamphlet, letter and word of mouth. Back then, sharing news would happen in private, in conversations at work or in the home; these acts of sharing were ephemeral and largely lost to future generations. Such conversations are now taking place in public on social networks, where they are recorded and archived and visible to all. The pulse of the planet is laid bare, revealing what has captured the attention of millions at any moment.

STRANGERS NO MORE

As I was researching this book, a gunman let loose in a packed movie theatre in Aurora, Colorado, killing twelve people. During that weekend in July 2012, I followed the news reports alongside the snippets coming through on social media. While researching how people heard the news of the tragedy, I felt I got to know one of the victims better than others because of how much she shared publicly. Jessica Ghawi was an aspiring sports broadcaster who lived life out loud online. As with so many of her generation who have never known a world before the Internet, the red-headed self-declared Texan spitfire openly recorded the twists and turns of her life in digital social spaces.

The twenty-four-year-old was prolific on social media, writing about her odd love for both hockey and grammar on her Twitter account, where she described herself as "Southern. Sarcastic. Sass. Class. Crass. Grammar snob." She came across as a smart and sharp young woman. A few days before she was killed, she told everyone about her delight at being a godmother, playfully warning that the "poor kid doesn't know what he's in for." In another, she posted a photo of herself all dishevelled, mockingly adding, "This picture is proof I belong as number 1 on the *Maxim* Hot 100 list, right?" One video on YouTube, of her first interview in 2010 with a professional athlete Chris Summers shows her tottering onto the ice in high heels, struggling to keep her balance and falling down numerous times.

Being able to find out so much about a stranger so easily was unsettling. Even more disconcerting was to read her blog and learn that she had escaped unscathed during a shooting at the Eaton Centre shopping mall in Toronto a month earlier.

"I was reminded that we don't know when or where our time on Earth will end," she wrote. "Every second of every day is a gift. After Saturday evening, I know I truly understand how blessed I am for each second I am given." I had also researched the Eaton Centre shooting for this book, so reading her blog gave me a chill.

That night in July, her Twitter account documented her final moments, conveying her excitement at making it to a midnight premiere of the Batman epic *The Dark Knight Rises*. In her last messages, posted minutes before the screening, she teased another friend about missing out on the movie. After her death, Jessica's family and friends connected online to express their sorrow and raise funds for a sports journalism scholarship in her name. The Jessica Redfield Ghawi Scholarship was launched in February 2013 to provide $10,000 to female journalism students who aspire to become sports journalists. "We know this scholarship will allow her dreams to live on through others who live life as vibrantly as she did," said Jessica's brother Jordan Ghawi.

News of this appalling crime was brought much closer to home by all the traces that Jessica Ghawi left behind online. Jessica was no longer a stranger to me or others who read about her in the news. Reading such personal details about her made her loss seem more terrible and vivid. It was a striking example of how social media can jolt the way we feel about something happening far away and make us care.

In less than a decade, social media is one of those things that has become part of the fabric of society. It is also something about which everyone has an opinion. At some point in a dinner party, someone tends to malign social media for being full of updates about lunch or photos of pets. Life is full of froth. It is the mundane that makes us human. The seemingly inconsequential tidbits we share help to forge social bonds and bring us closer together. Every day, minute and second, millions are sharing fragments that reflect the experiences, hopes and fears of us all. Together we are writing the story of us.

#The News Now
#The News Now
#The News Now
#The News Now
#The News Now
#The News Now
#The News Now
#The Ne
#The Ne

CHAPTER ONE

#The News Now

ONE FRIDAY NIGHT, MORGAN JONES WAS UP LATE, LOST IN *Oblivion*. The eighteen-year-old was in his bedroom in Denver, immersed in the fantasy role-playing video game. He was pulled out of the magical realm when he noticed a Facebook update from a local TV station about a shooting at a movie theatre. What Morgan did next, over the early hours of July 20, 2012, would propel him into the limelight, leading to interviews in *The New York Times*, in the *Denver Post,* on National Public Radio and many other media outlets. It also drew attention to how an online forum, where anyone could post just about anything, could rival the mainstream media as the go-to source for the latest about one of the worst shootings in recent U.S. history.

The website was Reddit, and the mass shooting took place at a sold-out midnight screening of *The Dark Knight Rises* in Aurora, Colorado. A man in a SWAT outfit, later identified by police as James Eagan Holmes, set off tear gas and started firing into the crowd. Twelve people were killed and fifty-eight were injured. Most of those who died were in their twenties. The youngest was six, a blond-haired, blue-eyed girl named

Veronica Moser-Sullivan. The oldest was fifty-one-year-old Texan businessman Gordon Cowden.

At his parents' home in Denver, Morgan tuned in to the Aurora police scanner and started posting updates under his username, Integ3r, on Reddit. At the time, the largest Internet message board in the world had thirty-five million monthly users, but it was still relatively unknown outside of tech-savvy circles. Morgan provided a meticulous and exhaustively detailed rundown of events that night, pulling in fragments of information from the police and online media and from messages and photos shared on social media by people at the cinema. His account ran to thousands of words, assaulting the reader with a vivid and at times upsetting timeline of the atrocity. "I stayed up all night, and I am exhausted now, but it feels like I'm helping out people who need to know this stuff," Morgan said the following day.

The way news of the Aurora shooting emerged that night is emblematic of how information travels in our digital world. The murders received wall-to-wall coverage that has become customary on twenty-four-hour cable news networks. Reporters and news anchors flocked to the town to report on the victims, talk to survivors and find out more about the alleged gunman. Together with the news coming from the media was another layer of information coming from people caught up in the shooting—eyewitnesses at the scene, and friends and relatives of the victims. Hundreds of people were in the movie theatre at the time. Some captured the confusion on their cell phones as people emptied out onto the streets, not quite knowing what had happened. Some took photos of their wounds and posted the pictures online. Some, like Morgan, tried to document what had just happened.

It has become commonplace for people to share their own experiences, photos, videos or opinions on Facebook, Twitter, YouTube and a multitude of other spaces, alongside reports from journalists. The result is that more information from more people with more perspectives is constantly flowing at a faster pace than ever before. But it also means more confusion, more mistakes and more noise.

In the hours and days following the Boston Marathon bombings on April 15, 2013, facts and falsehoods jostled for attention across broadcast, online and social media channels. The media made its fair share of mistakes, such as reporting an arrest when there was none. The *New York Post* was one of the worst offenders, mistakenly publishing a front-page photo of two men it said were wanted by law enforcement.

As tends to happen when big news breaks, a photograph of the scene, taken by college student Dan Lampariello, appeared first on Twitter. So, too, did a string of false reports. There was chatter of another explosion at the JFK Library and speculation that the bombing was the work of right-wing supremacists or of Muslim terrorists. Reddit, a site feted for its role at the time of the Aurora shootings, was widely condemned. The forum FindBostonBombers turned into a space where speculation ran riot, even as seasoned users cautioned about jumping to conclusions. No one seemed to notice the disclaimer on the page that Reddit was "a discussion forum, not a journalistic outlet" and that it did "not strive, nor pretend, to release journalist-quality content."

Despite rules banning the posting of personal information, names of innocent people were tossed around in the frenzy following the bombings. Reddit users were accused of being online vigilantes as they pored over photos and videos of the attack and speculated about the identity of the bombers. While the Aurora shooting demonstrated the wisdom of the crowd, the marathon bombings exposed the madness of the mob. Reddit shut down the discussion on its site and general manager Erik Martin apologized for what had happened. "However, though it started with noble intentions, some of the activity on Reddit fueled online witch hunts and dangerous speculation which spiraled into very negative consequences for innocent parties. The Reddit staff and the millions of people on Reddit around the world deeply regret that this happened."

The Aurora shootings and the Boston Marathon bombings illustrate the best and worst of how our need to know is being met at a time when the most trusted name in news may be either a veteran journalist at the scene or a kid playing video games in his bedroom. They are symptoms of what happens when two worlds collide—the world of traditional media that has developed over the past two centuries and the world of social media of the past few years. One is an old friend; the other is a young upstart that doesn't seem to follow the house rules, yet strikes a chord.

NEWS AS WE KNOW IT

After paying a visit to the United States, Charles Dickens described how the boys selling newspapers greeted the newcomers landing at New York Harbor. "Here's the *New York Sewer*!" shouted the newsboys, Dickens wrote in his 1844 book *Martin Chuzzlewit*. "Here's this morning's *New York Stabber*!

Here's the *New York Family Spy*! Here's the *New York Private Listener*! Here's the *New York Peeper*! Here's the *New York Plunderer*!" The fictional titles convey the salacious tone of these early newspapers that competed to grab the attention of the working folk of a bustling New York City.

Dickens was witnessing the creation of the American newspaper industry, when journalism became the business of packaging the day's events into a neat bundle that would appeal to the growing number of labourers, artisans and mechanics in New York "the city." Newspapers had been around in Europe since the seventeenth century, made possible by the development of the printing press, the availability of cheap paper and the rise of a merchant class hungry for information. But the printed word was still largely shared by hand, often passed on from friend to friend. In the U.K., the early newspapers of the eighteenth century had small circulations. London papers such as the *Daily Courant* sold less than a thousand copies. Provincial titles such as the *Norwich Mercury* had a weekly circulation of only two hundred.

This was a time of innovation and entrepreneurship in a fast-growing New York, much like the present day in Silicon Valley. One such entrepreneur was twenty-three-year-old printer Benjamin Day. On September 3, 1833, he launched a revolutionary product, the *New York Sun*. The newspaper broke the rules in several ways and created a business model for newspapers to come. It sold for just a penny when other newspapers were priced at six cents. Instead of having people pay for the news, advertising subsidized the costs of producing the paper.

Day bet that a cheap daily paper for the common man would prove popular with the rising working class and with businesses wanting to display their wares to reach them. "The object of this paper is to lay before the public, at a price within the means of everyone, all the news of the day, and at the same time offer an advantageous medium for advertisements," said Day in the first issue. He was also behind another innovation in how newspapers were distributed and sold, introducing the newsboys peddling *"the New York Sewer"* described in *Martin Chuzzlewit*.

The *New York Sun* not only changed the business of news, it changed the definition of news. In the past, newspapers would report and comment on politics or provide information useful for businesses, such as the shipping news. Day had a different idea of what New Yorkers would be interested in. He packed his paper with stories about people—human-interest stories of triumph and tragedy. The paper carried talk of crime, sin and immorality. It was accused of lowering the standards of journalism with its seemingly vulgar sensationalism. But it resonated with a newly literate working class and it was a thundering success.

The *New York Sun* was the first successful daily newspaper that put news within reach of a growing number of labourers, artisans and mechanics in the city. Within two years, the cheap, tabloid-style *Sun* was selling fifteen thousand copies a day. More penny papers followed, such as the *New York Herald* in 1853 and the *New-York Daily Times* in 1851, whose name was later changed to *The New York Times*. The new wave of newspapers found a ready audience in the growing middle and working classes in America. The penny papers laid the foundation for the model of news that persists to this day: paid employees sent out to witness events, interview citizens, police and officials, and then write it all up in a straightforward, realistic and accurate style.

The news provides order by compressing the world into a neat daily bundle of need-to-know information. The front page of the newspaper makes sense, as it has a well-established structure and hierarchy. The size of headlines, the use of photos and the location of stories bring order to a messy world. By comparison, "the front page of the Internet," as Reddit describes itself, seems gloriously messy and perplexing. Anyone can share anything, everyone decides everything and it changes all the time. On any given day, pop culture tidbits sit alongside stories about scientific discoveries, discussions about religion or online memes. It's news, but not as we know it. That's when things start to get confusing.

THE RULES OF THE MEDIA

The rules for different TV formats are so familiar that they require no thought on the part of the viewer. The differences between a TV sitcom and the local newscast are obvious. No one is going to mistake *How I Met Your Mother* for the evening news. Or, for that matter, *The Walking Dead* for a reality show. It seems silly even to mention it. Things get mixed up when the rules commonly used to make sense of one form of media no longer seem to apply.

Something like *The Daily Show* blurs the line between comedy and journalism. It satirizes the news, but it is also a source of information. When Pew Research studied the show in 2008, it found that the program covered much the same news as a cable talk show; it's just that the language was more blunt and direct. And when Americans were asked to name their most admired journalist, *Daily Show* host Jon Stewart came fourth, tied with news veterans Tom Brokaw, Dan Rather and Anderson Cooper. It demonstrates how the genre of "fake news" shows has become a familiar ingredient in people's information diet, even though they know in the back of their minds that it is a comedy show.

Every form of communication has a particular logic, a set of rules that affect how information is organized, presented, recognized and interpreted. What is new, different and unsettling becomes tried, tested and everyday as people come to learn and understand the rules. For more than two centuries, there has been a set of rules that mass media operated by. Social habits changed as new communication technologies were invented, but the flow of information, from institutions to the masses, was a constant.

During World War II, people experienced tragedy and triumph together as they gathered by their radio sets to hear the latest from the front lines. In the 1960s, families gathered to watch the evening newscasts on the new technology of the time, television. By the start of the twenty-first century, office workers were visiting websites to catch up with the latest news, sport and gossip. What all of these have in common is a one-way flow of information. Only the packaging was different.

For the past two hundred years or so, news has been shaped like an hourglass. Large amounts of information filtered through a narrow neck of paid professionals who packaged the material into familiar formats for an audience. News was a spectator sport. No more. From the Aurora shootings to the Boston Marathon bombings, news has become a shared experience. Virtually every time there is a major news event, from protests in Manhattan or Kiev to bombings in Boston to the death of a prominent figure like Margaret Thatcher or Nelson Mandela, the reporting by journalists sits alongside the accounts, experiences, opinions and hopes of millions of others.

Social media seems so new, but it heralds a return to the past. News existed before journalism, before it was processed and packaged into products for the masses. News fulfills a basic human need to know what is happening around us, in our neighbourhood, town, country and around the world. Being aware of what we cannot see for ourselves provides a sense of security and control. It is impossible to make good decisions about what actions to take without having information. News affects what we know of events and how we interpret them, influencing our decisions and actions. It can sway who we vote for, which route we take to work in the morning or whether we leave home with an umbrella.

Through social media, news is resurfacing as a social experience, shared by word of mouth between friends, relatives and strangers. Looking back, we see that the era of mass media seems more like an anomaly in the history of news than the natural order. Facebook, Twitter, YouTube and the myriad of other services resonate with the basic human urge to be social. The tools have changed, but human behaviour remains consistent. What have changed are the rules of the game, when a piece of news or comment can spread quickly through close and distant social circles like a infectious airborne virus.

CHALLENGING THE OFFICIAL STORY

On the morning of July 7, 2005, Justin Howard was travelling on the London Underground when the unthinkable happened. As the train was entering a tunnel heading towards Paddington Station, he heard a loud bang. In his blog, *Pfff: A Response to Anything Negative*, Howard recalled how the train left the tracks and started to hurtle through the tunnel. "When the train came to a standstill people were screaming, but mainly due to panic as the carriage was rapidly filling with smoke and the smell of burning motors was giving clear clues of fire," he wrote four hours later. "As little as five seconds later we were unable to see and had all hit the ground for the precious air that remained. We were all literally choking to death."

Howard was caught up in a coordinated terrorist attack on London's public transport system that killed fifty-six people, including the four bombers, and injured more than seven hundred. He was also one of hundreds of people who recorded and shared their experience of the tragedy. Grainy cell phone photos of Londoners stumbling through dark, smoke-filled tunnels documented the horror of commuters trapped underground. Together, they created a vivid tapestry of the day within hours of the attacks, as seen through the eyes of those who experienced it.

July 7 marked a turning point in how the news was made. That night, TV newscasts led with video taken by ordinary people rather than professional journalists, and the next day's newspapers were full of photos taken by the commuters themselves. It is now common to see jerky video shot on a cell phone by an eyewitness on the news. But in 2005, this was a novelty. On that day, hundreds of such images and video were sent directly to media outlets. The BBC alone received more than a thousand photographs, twenty video clips, four thousand text messages, and twenty thousand emails within six hours of the bombings, more than it ever had in the past.

Something else happened that day that pointed to the new realities of the media. Initially, transport authorities said the explosions on the subway had been caused by power surges. However, the official narrative was at odds with the stories and photos coming from the public. Something much bigger seemed to be going on. Within ninety minutes of the attacks, there were more than 1,300 online posts as London's blogging community shared what they knew and provided safety advice or travel tips.

At the BBC, an email from a viewer provided the first clue that this was much more than a power malfunction. The official story couldn't hold up against a steady stream of evidence from the public to the contrary, including photos of a blown-up double-decker bus. A little over two hours after the news first broke, the head of the police in London, Sir Ian Blair, formally announced that the capital had come under a coordinated terror attack.

The London bombings signalled how the flow of information is reshaped when hundreds of people can quickly spread the news as they see it. It is much harder for institutions to control public knowledge of an event when the official version doesn't match up with the story on social media. Since 2005, the pace has accelerated, with news now travelling at the speed of a tweet. Immediacy matters, because first impressions matter. The problem is that instant information encourages action rather than contemplation. In the confusion that follows a big news event, misinformation can just as quickly take hold, as it did with the misidentification of one of the Boston bombing suspects. Twitter may seem like a jumble of different views, but not for long. Scientists have found that public opinion tends to coalesce quickly as more and more people endorse a particular perspective. The majority ends up drowning out minority views. And once Twitter has made up its mind, it is difficult to change.

HOW CONTEXT WORKS IN SOCIAL MEDIA

Stephen Colbert has a reputation for skewering politicians, companies, celebrities and the media itself. Yet a tweet out of context thrust his show, *The Colbert Report,* into a Twitter tornado. The trigger was a message sent on Thursday, March 27, 2014, from the show's account that read: "I am willing to show #Asian community I care by introducing the Ching-Chong Ding-Dong Foundation for Sensitivity to Orientals or Whatever." The comment was taken from a segment on Wednesday night's show where Colbert poked fun at Dan Snyder, owner of the Washington Redskins football team, and his recently announced charitable foundation for Native Americans.

The joke wasn't funny for Suey Park, a twenty-three-year-old Korean-American writer and activist. She had previously made the news for her #NotYourAsianSidekick Twitter campaign. Park saw the tweet while she was having dinner and acted. That night, she tweeted to her thousands of followers: "The Ching-Chong Ding-Dong Foundation for Sensitivity to Orientals has decided to call for #CancelColbert. Trend it." A Twitter storm was born as thousands piled to berate Colbert, while some came to the show's defence.

Within twenty-four hours, there were more than 85,000 tweets bearing the hashtag, and most of them were negative. Just under half of the messages came from the U.S., but the hashtag ricocheted as far as Bahrain, Botswana and Bhutan. Comedy Central, the channel that airs *The Colbert Report,* clarified that the tweet, soon deleted, had come from the official corporate account for the show and not from the comedian himself, who goes by @StephenAtHome on Twitter. Colbert distanced himself from the fray, tweeting on his personal account: "#CancelColbert - I agree! Just saw @ColbertReport tweet. I share your rage. Who is that, though? I'm @StephenAtHome," with a link to a video of the segment. But the judgment of Twitter was that the comment was a crude racist joke, rather than a joke about racism. Media headlines followed that spoke of accusations of racism against Stephen Colbert and of a Twitter war on the comedian.

The uproar was understandable, given that the punchline was out of context. In the show on Wednesday night, Colbert assumed the part of a racist character to lampoon racism. Since many people who came across the tweet hadn't seen the segment, they took it at face value. There wasn't enough information in the 140 characters to correctly interpret the tweet. #CancelColbert turned out to be a storm in a tweet cup, as with so many Twitter tempests. By the Saturday, the number of hashtagged messages fell by 76 per cent to just under twenty-one thousand. But the flare-up was enough to skew the conversation away from why the Washington Redskins persisted in using an offensive term in its name. Colbert became the story, not Snyder.

Twitter makes it much harder to gain context. It breaks up information into atomic fragments that whiz past with little time for consideration. The fleeting shelf life of the medium works against any inclination to pause before retweeting. It is a medium that lives in the now. Immediacy privileges reaction rather than reflection. It fosters ardour rather than nuance. The paradox is that context exists on Twitter, just not in the usual way. Each message exists within a broader conversation, as people jump in and add a little bit of background or opinion. It's just very hard to see the bigger picture.

When it comes to Twitter, we are all like the French artist Georges Seurat. The nineteenth-century neo-impressionist developed the technique of pointillism. He created timeless works of art using small strokes or dots of contrasting colour that blend together when seen from a distance. Reading tweets is like standing next to one of his most famous works, *A Sunday Afternoon on the Island of La Grande Jatte*. Close up, it just looks like tiny, juxtaposed brushstrokes of random colour instead of people relaxing in a suburban park. Currently, it is hard to take a step back and see the overall context of each individual fragment of information on Twitter. Taken as a whole, there is background, context and meaning. It is a mistake to see any tweet as a lone fragment, isolated from wider context, as some prominent figures in the U.K. learnt to their cost over the McAlpine affair.

It started on a Friday, following a piece on the highly regarded BBC show *Newsnight* that wrongly suggested a senior Conservative from the Thatcher era was involved in child abuse. Ahead of the broadcast, there had been some speculation on Twitter on whether *Newsnight* would name the politician. "Are Newsnight still running their 'paedo politician' story? Also are Lord McAlpine's lawyers working overtime tonight? Just thinking aloud," said one message, since deleted.

In the end, the show didn't name the peer for fear of legal action. But it provided enough clues for viewers to figure out his identity for themselves. Anyone turning to Google for the name of a high-ranking Tory accused of being a pedophile would have found an article published in the early 1990s in *Scallywag* magazine. McAlpine didn't sue at the time, as the magazine went bankrupt and closed down soon after. But scans of the article have since been available online.

On Twitter, some openly mentioned the Tory politician, while others relied on innuendo. "Lord Mcalpine must not be happy with #newsnight then...," said journalist Asa Bennett in a tweet since deleted. High-profile figures such as Sally Bercow, the wife of the speaker of the House of Commons, tweeted, "Why is Lord McAlpine trending? *innocent face*." Author and *Guardian* columnist George Monbiot wrote: "I looked up Lord #McAlpine on t'internet. It says the strangest things." On Twitter, anyone searching for *Newsnight* at the time would have also received suggestions about related searches, including McAlpine.

The truth was that the *Newsnight* story was incorrect, based on a case of mistaken identity. Lord McAlpine was wrongly maligned, his character falsely assassinated. This time around, he took legal action against the more prominent of his tormentors, such as Sally Bercow. She said her tweet was meant to be "conversational and mischievous." Taken as a single message, out of context, Bercow might have had a point. But tweets always have context. Messages laden with innuendo were sent against the backdrop of the *Newsnight* allegations and speculation on Twitter. Anyone following the news would infer that such tweets were pointing to Lord McAlpine.

Social media interferes with fixed ideas of context. As *The Colbert Report* found, a few words taken from a satirical segment ended up disconnected from their original meaning. The McAlpine case showed how the meaning of individual comment is affected by the broader context. Author and researcher danah boyd calls the phenomenon "context collapse." In most situations, people know who they are addressing and tailor the message accordingly. They will behave differently depending on who they are talking to, in line with accepted norms and expectations. Politicians do this all the time. They will alter the tone, style and content of a speech to resonate with a particular audience. But social media flattens multiple audiences into one. The result is that a jokey aside, akin to what might be said between friends in a bar, can turn into a libellous remark when it is shared publicly on Twitter. Or worse.

THE PROBLEM OF INVISIBLE AUDIENCES

Paul Chambers never imagined that letting off steam on Twitter would result in the loss of his job and a lengthy legal battle. He was on his way to Belfast to see his girlfriend, Sarah Tonner. The U.K. was in the middle of an unusually harsh winter in 2010, with temperatures regularly dipping well below zero degrees centigrade and snow blanketing the British Isles. Chambers arrived at Robin Hood Airport in South Yorkshire to find that snow had closed the single runway. He vented his frustration by tweeting, "Crap! Robin Hood Airport is closed. You've got a week and a bit to get your shit together otherwise I am blowing the airport sky high!!" The wisecrack went out to the six hundred people following Chambers on Twitter. But his account was public, meaning that anyone could read his messages.

A week later, four officers from the South Yorkshire police turned up at Chambers's office in Doncaster, where he worked as a financial supervisor. He was arrested and accused of making a hoax bomb threat. Unbeknownst to him, an off-duty manager at Robin Hood Airport had stumbled across the tweet by chance. The airport didn't think the threat was credible, but by law was required to pass it on to South Yorkshire police. Chambers was later charged and initially found guilty of sending a menacing tweet in May 2010. He eventually won a high court challenge against his conviction two years later. Since then, the British authorities have drawn up new guidelines to distinguish between offensive or off-colour posts and those that credibly threaten violence.

What became known as the "Twitter joke trial" was one of the first high-profile examples of how off-colour banter intended for a few could backfire. Chambers never expected anyone to take his joke seriously, much less for it to be seen by the police. People might picture an intended audience for a comment or photo, but more often than not, they have to contend with invisible audiences. Invisible audiences are all those strangers who might stumble across a tweet that was not posted for them to read. But as a public message, it is there for all to see.

When a student at the University of California, Berkeley, was offered a job by Cisco, she turned to Twitter to tell her friends. "Cisco just offered me a job! Now I have to weigh the utility of a fatty paycheck against the daily commute to San Jose and hating the work," tweeted Connor Riley. A Cisco employee came across the public message and Riley rose to Internet infamy for tweeting her way out of a job. Similarly, Amanda Bonnen ended up being sued by her landlords for describing her Chicago apartment as mouldy. The case was eventually thrown out. In both cases, personal messages were sent out on a public network, though they were never intended to be seen by the public. The audience on social media is potentially both personal and public, full of familiar faces and an unknown mass.

Figures in the public eye, such as politicians and celebrities, have long had to contend with living life on the stage. It is little surprise when they get caught out for inappropriate behaviour on social media, as happened to U.S. congressman Anthony Weiner for sharing shots of his crotch and raunchy notes with women on Twitter. Stuart MacLennan, an aspiring British politician, torpedoed his chances during the 2010 general election with a series of ill-judged tweets, including one where he called elderly people "coffin-dodgers." No one is immune to the perils of inappropriate sharing—not even Olympic athletes. As public figures, they can expect interest in what they share. Voula Papachristou of Greece lost her chance to compete in the London 2012 games for an offensive message. On social media, everyone is potentially a public figure.

PRIVACY THROUGH OBSCURITY

Overnight, the life of Ashley Alexandra Dupré became public property. One day, she was an aspiring R&B singer, making ends meet by working as a call girl named Kristen; the next, she was identified as the woman at the centre of New York governor Eliot Spitzer's sex scandal in 2008. Within hours, photos of her in a bikini and details of her troubled childhood were all over the news. It was easy for journalists to cull the material from the web, as Dupré lived much of her life online on social networking sites. She might never have expected journalists and bloggers to pore over everything she had ever uploaded and then share it with such a broad audience. Since then, it has become routine for journalists to scour social media whenever someone falls within the media spotlight.

With millions sharing so much, so often, traditional ideas of privacy are being rewritten. Privacy used to mean being able to do things without being observed by others and being able to control what others know about us. In the world of traditional media, it was easy to separate the public from the private. Participants on a TV quiz show knew that everything they said was being broadcast. Even the contestants in the reality show *Big Brother* are aware of what they signed up for. Social media can be like being on *Big Brother,* except that most of the time, no one is watching.

To paraphrase Shakespeare, all of social media is a stage. The difference is that the only people regularly turning up for performances are friends or relatives. Privacy comes through obscurity, rather than control. It's like being at a loud party where everyone is chatting. Personal conversations are taking place in public, but they remain private as they are lost in the general chatter. That sense of obscurity vanishes if everyone else stops talking all of a sudden. On social media, everyone is one of many. There is no reason to assume that anyone aside from those in close social circles is paying attention to a quip about a delayed flight, a jibe about a job offer or grumbles about an apartment. Exchanges on social media are often of the here and now, seemingly ephemeral, like the spoken word. Yet the data persists beyond the moment. It is archived and searchable. Obscurity vanishes as soon as the media or others take an interest. In minutes, the personal becomes widely publicly visible.

SOCIAL MEDIA—IT'S COMPLICATED

The celebrated American sociologist Erving Goffman used the metaphor of the stage to talk about life as a continual performance. The "front stage" is where social interactions take place in public—for example, with office colleagues. The "back stage" is a more private space, reserved for time with one's spouse or close friends. What is shared, and with whom, depends on the stage. But social media can collapse the distinctions between front and back stages. It's like having tickets for one play and instead wandering into a different one.

One of the consequences is what tends to get labelled as oversharing—when people are seemingly divulging information online that makes others uncomfortable. The problem isn't that people are sharing too much information; rather, it is that an audience is seeing information not intended for them, and in the wrong context. As a result, they feel that social norms are being violated. The intended audience might feel differently. In the past, only the addressee would read a personal letter. Today, similar exchanges play out before a public eye on social media. Sharing is relational. What one person sees as a TMI (too much information) moment is an occasion to connect for another.

Facebook or Twitter may seem like nothing we've had before. But that would be oversimplifying things. People have always found ways to exchange facts, gossip and rumour, be it face to face in the office or over long distances by writing a letter. Social media technologies bring to the surface patterns of sharing that have always existed in society. The difference is that sharing used to happen in private exchanges, in conversations at work or in the home, invisible to most and largely lost to future generations. Today, such conversations take place in public on social networks, where they are recorded and archived, making them visible to all.

Social media taps into an innate human desire to connect with others. It is why it resonates with so many. It is familiar, yet at the same time works in a different way from the traditional mass media. There is some overlap, though. The word *journalism* has its origins in the French word for day—*jour*—and refers to the practice of keeping a daily journal or diary. The renowned communications scholar James Carey talks of journalism as transferring the private habit of recording one's life into a communal account of key events of the life of a community. We are using social media to take the private habit of chronicling our life and make it public, producing a collective and shared account of society. Every day, millions of people are openly recounting their life stories on digital spaces, telling everyone about their lives, experiences and views. We can't help it. We are made to be social.

#Why We Share
#Why We Share
#Why We Share
#Why We Share
#Why We Share
#Why We Share
#Why W
#Why W

CHAPTER TWO

#Why We Share

THE BMW VIDEO CAMPAIGN WAS A FEAT OF SOCIAL ENGINEERING to mirror the mechanical marvels of the machines themselves. Featuring a ruggedly handsome leading man, glamorous women and luxury vehicles, the ads were designed to be shared. Made by a range of A-list directors and crammed with top talent, the videos spread across the Internet at breakneck speed and were an early indicator of how far a message could reach online. This was in 2001, before the rise of YouTube, Facebook and Twitter. Today, millions of people regularly devote part of their day to a similar online ritual for seemingly no reward. They take it upon themselves to pass on a cute photo, a funny video or stimulating news story to friends and family.

There are some things we just cannot resist passing on. They tap into our innate urge to interact with others. Whether they are videos, photos or headlines, they are engineered to play on our emotions and impel us to take certain actions—to click the Like button, to tweet or email. By understanding the emotions that drive our desire to share, we will be better equipped to make informed decisions about what we tell others and what we keep to ourselves on the digital networks woven into the way we communicate. Emotions can lead us astray, and even the urge to do good by sharing what we know, or believe we know, can have consequences we never imagined.

The BMW videos remain a touchstone in understanding how to create material that people want to watch and share. The carmaker had commissioned a series of eight short films, averaging about ten minutes in length. *The Hire* featured actor Clive Owen as a driver who transports people or goods from place to place in a BMW vehicle. For the talent behind the camera, BMW recruited leading directors, from John Frankenheimer to Ang Lee to Guy Ritchie. On screen, Owen shared the limelight with Mickey Rourke, Gary Oldman, Forest Whitaker, Don Cheadle, Madonna and supermodel Adriana Lima.

A mix of charismatic male actors, glamorous women, seasoned directors and money does not always guarantee success. But *The Hire* proved extraordinarily popular when it debuted online in April 2001. Over the next four months, the videos were watched eleven million times. Two million people registered with BMW's website and 94 per cent of them emailed links to the film to others. The figures are astonishing for the early days of video sharing. More important for the carmaker, sales rose by 12 per cent. The films are seen as the first successful online video marketing campaign. But success came at a price. After eight films, more than 100 million views and DVD distribution in showrooms and accompanying issues of *Vanity Fair*, the high cost of the campaign led BMW to drop it in October 2005.

The success of the campaign provides clues to the psychology of sharing. The films provided compelling narratives, dripping with excitement and cool. They looked expensive because they *were* expensive. They were aimed at people who could discern quality, or at least thought they could. The hundreds of thousands who passed the videos on were doing more than entertaining their friends; they were signalling their sophisticated taste to their social circles. The media we share is an expression both of our personality and of our aspirations. BMW figured this out, basing its video campaign on knowledge of its audience. It knew that the age of its average customer was forty-six. Two-thirds of its customers were men in well-paid jobs, married with no children. They wanted to be Clive Owen, driving a plush car with Madonna in the back seat. As for the women, many of them probably wouldn't have minded being driven around by him.

LEARNING TO PLAY NICE

New technologies provide new channels for interactions that form the basis of society. The fact that we are social is old news. "Man is by nature a political animal," said Aristotle. "He who is unable to live in society, or who has no need because he is sufficient for himself, must be either a beast or a god." Social interaction sets humans apart from other animals. For social scientists, sharing food, experiences and knowledge is a fundamental aspect of these interactions. "Sharing has probably been the most basic form of economic distribution in hominid societies for several hundred thousand years," wrote the anthropologist John Price in 1975.

The study of human evolution charts how we are more inclined to cooperate with others than try to go it alone. Early humans needed to work together and share knowledge as they left Africa and spread out across the world. Humans increased their odds of survival by foraging and hunting in groups, and then sharing the spoils among the group. According to anthropologists Robert Boyd, Peter J. Richerson and Joseph Henrich, "humans may be smarter than other creatures, but none of us is nearly smart enough to acquire all of the information necessary to survive in any single habitat."

People are interested in news because news matters. News is driven by an innate need to be in the know and to know about things that might impact a way of life. Information is crucial to making informed decisions. Beyond the limits of our own knowledge, experience and awareness, we rely on others to fill in the gaps. Gathering and sharing news gave groups an inherent advantage, as an individual can only see and hear a fraction of the world. In early societies, telling fellow hunters to avoid a particular area because of the presence of a sabre-toothed tiger is a form of risk reduction and reciprocal exchange. What one hunter is communicating to another is effectively, "I tell you today about the dangerous animal in the hope that you will share similar news in the future, so we both live longer." The more such newsgathering and dissemination pays off, the more it becomes part of everyday behaviour.

Posting to Facebook, YouTube or any of the myriad social platforms isn't a matter of life or death; it is a way of gifting something in the expectation of gaining something in return. Digital sharing is the latest expression of the ritual exchange of goods and information that fosters social capital, serving as the glue that helps societies prosper and endure. These interactions form the basis of the connections, common values and shared understandings that bind communities and engender trust. The idea of social capital was popularized by Robert Putnam in his 2000 bestseller, *Bowling Alone: The Collapse and Revival of American Community*. Putnam distinguished two forms: bonding capital and bridging capital. Bonding takes place when we mix with people like us, such as family, close friends or people from similar backgrounds. Recommending a short film—say, one starring Clive Owen—is a way of exchanging bonding capital, cultivating a shared sense of identity. Bridging capital involves going beyond similar people and connecting with those with different backgrounds or views. Putnam argued that the two forms of social capital reinforce each other.

As children grow up, they become aware of the importance of social capital. Children who, as toddlers, throw tantrums when asked to share, learn to play nice when they reach age seven or eight. A team of researchers led by Ernst Fehr at the University of Zurich documented the process in children in the small medieval city of Rapperswil-Jona on the shores of Lake Zurich in Switzerland. The 229 children, aged from three to eight, participated in three experiments in sharing candy. Two children were partnered, with one of them in control of the sweets. In all three games, the child with the candy decided how to share it. In the first two, a child could choose to divide the sweets equally or to give their partner an extra piece.

The key experiment was the third one. For this one, the child with the candy could refuse to share and instead keep all the sweets. Given a choice, the overwhelming majority of toddlers—nine out of ten—chose not to give the other child a piece of candy. By age seven and eight, just under half chose to share one of the sweets. After taking into account all three experiments, the researchers concluded that, as children grew up, they are more likely to want to be fair and more consistently choose egalitarian outcomes.

Children learn to be more egalitarian as they progress from playgroups to kindergarten and on to formal schools. As they grow older, children will also become more aware of the opinions of others and start to care about what others think of them. By the time they are eight, they have learned that, as a society, we are expected to play nice. For children, sharing candy can be an important bonding ritual, just as sharing a meal is important for families and friends. These social interactions weave the fabric of community, as we give and receive non-financial social assets.

THE BONDS WE VALUE

Online networks build on the social capital that comes from relationships and systems of support and influence. The ability to reach beyond immediate circles helps to develop other forms of capital that confer status and power. The French sociologist Pierre Bourdieu extended the notion of capital beyond the economic and social to also include cultural and symbolic capital. Educational or intellectual knowledge brings with it cultural capital, while symbolic capital comes from prestige or recognition. Taking part in online discussions or posting links to informative articles is a trade in cultural and symbolic capital that benefits both sides. The person providing the information receives profile and recognition for their expertise, while the audience gains knowledge and understanding.

Such professional capital is the currency of business-oriented social networks such as LinkedIn. Professional capital is a hybrid of social, cultural and symbolic capital. It does not come solely from sharing what we know or the information we've found. It is dependent on others recognizing that a contribution was particularly valuable through clicking on a link or recommending it to their social circles themselves. By making these transactions in plain sight online, we leave a digital trail that others can observe, examine and interpret.

A retweet, for example, confers symbolic capital on the contributor, as well as indicating what is important to us. Often on Twitter, people add a line to their profile stating that a retweet is not an endorsement. Who are they trying to kid? In practice, they are endorsing the message, but not necessarily agreeing with a particular point of view. Rather, a retweet is a way of signalling to others that this piece of information matters. By paying attention, the people on the receiving end are recognizing the value of the message, as well as adding to their professional capital by enriching their knowledge. In social networks, the act of listening is as significant as the act of conversing.

EXPRESS YOURSELF

The desire to be heard is one of the five primary motivators for participating online. Everyone wants to be heard. The Internet provides an open mike, which one may use by engaging in conversations on forums or by posting a link on a social network. The Internet and social media platforms offer unparalleled opportunities as a soapbox for personal expression. Researchers who have studied online participation over the past decade have found that people value being able to express their opinions. In the early 2000s, a doctoral student called Jennifer Stromer-Galley interviewed people who contributed to online chat rooms on Usenet and Yahoo! The appeal of the chat rooms was the ability to reach a broad public at any time and any day of the week.

Stromer-Galley, now an associate professor at the University of Syracuse, also looked at why people liked to discuss politics online. Unsurprisingly, people liked being able to voice their views. At times, speaking out online is about letting off some steam. A quick glance at the comment section of a news website or at tweets about a controversial issue can give the impression that people are simply venting. This was one of the findings of a study of British and Israeli commenters. For some, comments were a way to rant about the news. But the value to most was having the space to express their point of view. Sharing our ideas with others is a way of showing what is important to us. We are sending out signals about ourselves as we highlight what we value and care about.

The role of sharing in defining ourselves emerged loudly in a study by *The New York Times*. The "Gray Lady" partnered with Latitude Research to dig into the psychology of sharing, combining in-person interviews in New York, Chicago and San Francisco, week-long panels and a survey of 2,500 online sharers. Two-thirds of the participants shared to give others a better sense of who they were and what they cared about. The spreading of news, information and commentary through social networks are symbolic declarations of the self. Social psychologists define such actions as identity claims that signal to others how we would like to be seen.

Clothing has long been a medium for symbolic declarations of identity. In Elizabethan England, laws were enacted to curb the sumptuousness of dress. Known as sumptuary laws, they dictated who could wear certain styles, fabrics and colours. In one proclamation, on August 13, 1597, Queen Elizabeth I ordered that only earls and knights could wear purple. There were more edicts on apparel during her reign than at any other time in English history. Before people starting dissecting the outfits of the rich and famous on social media, there was a real Elizabethan fashion police whose purpose was to control such symbols of the self.

The sumptuary laws served two purposes. One was to stop people spending money on frivolous displays of wealth. The other was to maintain class structures by making it simple to identify someone's social station by their dress. The material we share online serves as the digital clothing of identity. We aim for an idealized projection of ourselves through the selective choice of what we share, when, where and with whom. By publishing information on the Internet, we are trying to influence the impressions formed by others. Sharing becomes a means to shape how others see us. "I try to share only information that will reinforce the image I'd like to present: thoughtful, reasoned, kind, interested and passionate about certain things," said one of the men interviewed for *The New York Times* study.

ME, MYSELF AND I

Much of the information shared on social networks is "all about me." When Rutgers University researchers looked at the accounts of more than 350 Twitter users, they found most people talked about themselves or their views. The "meformers" accounted for 80 per cent of the Twitter users. These results may seem to suggest that social networks bring out the narcissist in us. But the thing is that we just love to talk about ourselves in everyday conversation. Between 30 and 40 per cent of everyday talk is devoted to telling others about our thoughts and experiences. The difference is how we react to the same comments on different media. Everyday conversation is a dynamic mix of experience, knowledge, opinion, fiction and fantasy. Mundane details about what we had for lunch or what happened to us on the way to work just seem more acceptable in passing chat that is ephemeral and transient than when the same information is recorded and distributed online.

Meformers may seem self-indulgent, but it looks like we are just programmed that way. Harvard scientists Diana Tamir and Jason Mitchell put this hypothesis to the test in a series of brain experiments. Using MRIs, they scanned the brains of test subjects to see if neural regions associated with reward lit up with they talked about their opinions and their proclivities. The results showed increased activity in parts of the brain that make up the mesolimbic dopamine system. This pathway carries dopamine, a neurotransmitter that helps control the brain's reward and pleasure centres. Talking about ourselves is intrinsically gratifying. The Harvard study found that test subjects would happily pass up monetary rewards to chat about their favourite subject: me, myself and I.

Talking about ourselves is good for society. It gives humans an adaptive advantage. Psychologists have looked at how sharing personal information kindles and strengthens social bonds, provides different perspectives and helps people learn more about themselves. Sociability is a core reason behind digital exchanges. The people in *The New York Times* study saw sharing as a way of maintaining and cultivating their relationships, helping them connect with others who have similar interests. Those who were cut off from their social circles online felt deprived. "I miss the companionship and conversations on Facebook," said one man. "I feel like I'm probably missing out on some things with the connection."

ALL ABOUT RELATIONSHIPS

The social rewards of conversation are a common thread in research on online participation. People who talk politics online like hearing the opinions of others and chatting with people from different backgrounds. The folks who populate comment sections are also motivated by social interaction. For some, it's about having a right old ding-dong, as this British commenter said: "I like to give opinions and read other opinions but most of all I love a good debate, whether in person or online any view is worth debating." People taking part in such comment threads are driven by a desire to nourish relationships with others. Commenters responding to each other drive the debate. An analysis of comments left on the websites of two local newspapers in the UK found that one-third of the comments consisted of exchanges between readers.

Online exchanges are often criticized for their robust tone. A cursory glance at comment threads or a stream of tweets can suggest the posters are more interested in shouting at each other than in engaging with substantive ideas. The success of French tennis player Marion Bartoli at Wimbledon in 2013 led to a stream of misogynistic remarks on Twitter about her appearance. For some, Bartoli was not blonde or skinny enough to be a "Wimbledon babe." Such misogyny was not restricted to social media, though. Veteran BBC sports commentator John Inverdale provoked outrage when he mused: "Do you think Bartoli's dad told her when she was little, 'You're never going to be a looker, you'll never be a Sharapova, so you have to be scrappy and fight?'" The crass comment came as Bartoli won her first Grand Slam title, beating Sabine Lisicki in straight sets. Never mind that it takes skill, strength and determination to become a Wimbledon champion.

The dynamics of how information travels online can foster a mob mentality. Social media doesn't cause someone to make derogatory comments, but it does make such attitudes far more visible than ever before. The circulation of abuse through social networks fuels the psychological phenomenon of social proof, when people take their cue from the behaviour of others. Seeing others make derogatory remarks publicly may make it seem more acceptable to be rude and offensive. Social media is a mirror to the rise of sexism and misogyny in popular culture. The higher visibility of such improper behaviour has sparked a wider debate on why some men consider it acceptable to write about or talk about women in a sexually offensive way online.

At the same time, the very publicness of these spiteful exchanges means such undercurrents in society rise to the fore where they are subject to scrutiny and condemnation. The statement by U.S. Justice Louis Dembitz Brandeis that "sunlight is said to be the best of disinfectants" applies as much today as it did when he wrote it in a 1913 *Harper's Weekly* article entitled "What Publicity Can Do." Malicious messages leave a digital trail that can make it easier to take action against the perpetrators. When the feminist campaigner Caroline Criado-Perez was bombarded with graphic threats of rape on Twitter in mid-2013, she took screengrabs of the tweets and passed them on to police. Criado-Perez had attracted the ire of Twitter trolls in July 2013 for her campaign get The Bank of England to agree to feature Jane Austen on the £10 note. After Criado-Perez appeared on TV welcoming the news, she received hundreds of abusive tweets. Six months later, two of the people who took part in the Twitter tirade against her were jailed in the U.K. for making extreme threats.

The reach and public nature of the Internet means ugly remarks are more wide-ranging and prominent than ever before. Examples such as the sexist tirades against Bartoli and Criado-Perez deservedly make headlines. Journalists themselves worry about abusive comments on their news websites from what one reporter described as "keyboard assassins." They tend to think that most contributions from readers are ill-informed, stupid or just plain puerile. But the attention paid to high-profile cases of abuse can also create a misleading impression about the tenor of online sharing. Offensive remarks tend to have more salience in our minds, even if they are relatively few in number when compared with the millions of messages shared every day.

Sending a message from a keyboard over the air to an undetermined audience provides a sense of freedom that can lead one to make comments that should remain private thoughts. By the same token, that sense of freedom can provide a sense of self-fulfillment. "I feel free to say what I really feel without any fear of criticism or reservation," said one of the respondents interviewed for a study on political talk online. "My feeling is it doesn't matter what they say about my opinion because 'they' are words that appear on the screen, although I do consider what is said."

SHOWING YOU CARE

Being able to say it out loud offers a sense of empowerment. When *The New York Times* asked people why they share, 69 per cent said it let them feel more involved in the world. For 84 per cent, sharing was a way to support causes or issues they cared about. Sharing online is a far cry from writing a letter to the editor which used to be the main way to get a viewpoint out to a mass audience. Regardless of the size of the audience, people value the ability to have a voice and spread their message online. Being able to show you care about an issue or cause is a powerful driver for sharing, as the spread of the *Kony 2012* video demonstrated in March of that year. The thirty-minute film aimed to raise awareness of and support for the arrest of war criminal Joseph Kony, the leader of the Lord's Resistance Army in Uganda.

The video, made by the U.S.–based advocacy group Invisible Children, quickly became an Internet phenomenon. Within four days of its release, it attracted more than fifty million views online and hundreds of thousands of dollars in donations to the group. Its critics said it oversimplified the situation in central Africa for Western audiences. But its simple message was one of the reasons it was highly contagious. Sending the video to friends was a symbolic action that signalled a political preference. *Kony 2012* illustrates how the political has insinuated itself into everyday social interactions. Messages about the video will have jostled their way alongside remarks about food, fashion or the famous. The millions who spread the link to *Kony 2012* were hoping to sway others and be part of something bigger.

GIVING IS ENRICHING

There is one major imperative that emerges from the research on why people take the time to tell others about something interesting they've come across. And it comes back to the notion of social capital. The exchange of information and knowledge is a way of increasing our value within our social relationships and networks. It might be by appearing to be "in the know," or because we want to give back to our community. The study by *The New York Times* underlined that people share to bring valuable and entertaining material to others. Asked why she was an avid sharer, one woman said it was "to enrich the lives of those around me." Telling others about what we know provides a sense of self-fulfillment. "I enjoy getting comments that I sent great information and that my friends will forward it to their friends because it's so helpful," said another of the women interviewed for the study.

It's not just people in the big cities of New York, Chicago and San Francisco, like those who featured in *The New York Times* study, who feel this way. The *Capital Times* newspaper has provided news, information and diversion for the people of the Midwestern city of Madison, Wisconsin, and its surrounding counties for almost a century. Faced with declining circulation, it was one of the first newspapers to abandon daily publication in 2008. Instead, it shifted its focus to the web, while still producing a twice-weekly, magazine-style print edition. University of Madison-Wisconsin researcher Sue Robinson watched the change unfold. As part of her study on the painful transformation from print to digital, she interviewed and surveyed one hundred Madison residents.

For these residents, concerned about what was happening in their city, commenting on a news story or sending it on to others was their civic duty. "It is more or less that we all have an obligation to leave the planet a little better than I found it, that there is a social responsibility that we have as humans," said one blogger in the study. Others talked about drawing on their expertise to "fix" incorrect information or challenge points of view, sharing their social, cultural or professional capital. For Robinson, "these citizens noted a transactional value for themselves—the satisfaction of 'knowing' and then contributing to the process of informing the citizenry." The Madison residents got a good feeling from knowing they had done good, boosting their social capital in the community. The same result came out of The New York Times study, where nine out of ten people said they carefully considered how the information they share would be useful to others.

The reason people are drawn to passing on information that others will value seems to lie in an area on the outer surface of the brain. Pioneering research by UCLA psychologists identified how the temporoparietal junction (TPJ) in the brain lights up when people find something interesting, helpful or amusing to pass on. "We wanted to explore what differentiates ideas that bomb from ideas that go viral," said lead author Emily Falk, who conducted the research as a UCLA doctoral student and went on to join the faculty at the University of Pennsylvania's Annenberg School for Communication.

For the experiment, the UCLA scientists asked students to decide what to share with others and mapped their brain activity using MRI. The students, who were either production interns or producers, had to choose which TV pilots to pitch or back. The results showed surprising action in the TPJ, a part of the brain involved in considering what other people think and feel. The scans revealed far more activity in the TPJ region in interns who were particularly good at persuading the producers. What they didn't find was similar activity in the parts of the brain associated with reasoning. "You might expect people to be most enthusiastic and opinionated about ideas that they themselves are excited about, but our research suggests that's not the whole story. Thinking about what appeals to others may be even more important," said Falk. "As I'm looking at an idea, I might be thinking about what other people are likely to value, and that might make me a better idea salesperson later."

The research suggests that when we see a piece of information, the brain is already reacting to the stimuli, processing the data and assessing its interest to others. It seems our brains are hardwired to filter what will be important, fascinating or amusing to others. The UCLA research provides clues into what sociologists have known for decades: how and why some individuals take on the role of information brokers and bask in the glow of being the source in the know. Virtually all the people taking part in *The New York Times* study into digital sharing said they reflected on the value of what they pass on. The survey found that 94 per cent said they carefully considered how the information they shared would be useful to others. Without noticing, our brain is helping us assess the social currency to be gained from sharing information.

Understanding the how and why of sharing is vital for news outlets such as *The New York Times* that trade in the currency of ideas. Today, the media encourages us to share, like or recommend a story on our myriad digital devices, tapping into an innate desire to be appreciated by others. Throughout history, people have used the communication tools and spaces available at the time to connect with others to sort, filter and manage information; form and nurture relationships; and signal what we care about.

The academies of scholars in sixteenth-century Italy were the Facebook of the day, commenting on and discussing the news in letters, speeches and yearbooks. In Stuart England in the 1600s, the place to share the news was the coffeehouse. In the early days of the republic in China, at the turn of the twentieth century, it was the teahouse. Eighteenth-century Parisians, poorly served by official channels at a time of revolutionary upheaval, turned to exclusive salons and public parks to learn of the news.

THE CONSTANT CURRENCY OF NEWS

In the salon of Madame Marie Anne Doublet, a select group of eighteenth-century Parisians would meet once a week to tell each other about the latest political machinations, fancies or follies coming from the court at Versailles. Madame Doublet's salon was more than a place for the exchange of salacious gossip. In the lounge were two journals prepared by one of her servants, who had gone around the neighbourhood and asked, "What's new?" One journal contained information that was considered to be truthful, while the other was made up of news of questionable origin.

Every Saturday, leading figures from the arts and sciences would come to the salon, read the journals, compare them with what they had heard, and add their own snippets. They realized that each of them might have heard only fragments of a story. By pooling their information, these Parisians would try to create as complete and accurate an account as they could. Once they had collectively vetted the material, the newsletters would be copied and sent to select friends. Some enterprising friends copied the reports by hand and sold copies to readers in the countryside. The newsletters told tales of prominent deaths and marriages, but also of military escapades and the tempestuous exchanges between king and parliament.

Madame Doublet's was one of the most prominent salons at the time, frequented by ambassadors, historians, mathematicians and poets. They were the bloggers of their time, commenting on each other's work over a glass of wine. The salon was the newsroom, where intellectuals discussed and shared news that the government press dared not print. The king ruled as an absolute monarch, and the officially sanctioned journals offered little more than court pronouncements. Yet it was a turbulent time in France, marked by expensive military adventures abroad, tensions over political reform and an extravagant court. Behind the splendour and glitter of eighteenth-century Versailles, the seeds were laid for the French Revolution, which would result in the overthrow of the monarchy in 1792 and the beheading of Louis XVI a year later.

The common people were not supposed to know about affairs of state at the royal court. Politics were *"le secret du roi."* However, the emerging Parisian bourgeoisie of merchants, shopkeepers and tradesmen wanted to be in the know about decisions that would affect their businesses and families. Among the places they would go to share and hear tales of bed-hopping or lavish parties by the royals was the Tree of Cracow. Facts and fiction flowed freely under the branches of this large, leafy chestnut tree in the gardens of the Palais-Royal in the heart of Paris. This shady spot was just one of the numerous parks, squares and boulevards where the common people gathered to hear from those who claimed to be in the know about what was happening in the corridors of power. The Tree of Cracow was the Twitter of its day, where news was contested, confirmed or contradicted. A Parisian turning up in the park would ask, "What's happening?" just as Twitter once used to prompt its users.

During this volatile time in French history, news was first spread by word of mouth. Sometimes, the news came out in the shape of a song or fable. Reports about the monarch's foibles, wasteful spending or infidelity were discussed and cross-checked with others. Some of the information was written down and sent to others. The palace took such talk seriously enough to spy on its own people, as the chatter undermined respect for the monarchy. Madame Doublet herself felt the ire of Louis XV in 1753, when he threatened to confine her to a convent unless she stopped spreading her "impertinent" news. In the words of historian Robert Darnton, "the media knit themselves together in a communication system so powerful that it proved to be decisive in the collapse of the regime."

Three centuries later, Facebook has become the salon where friends get together to catch up, compare notes and share the news. Twitter has taken the place of the Tree of Cracow. Every society comes up with a way to hunt for and gather information and then pass on what it has found. The way information is collected, cross-checked and circulated has changed since eighteenth-century France. The dynamics, though, have remained constant. Three centuries later, the people of Madison in Wisconsin are telling their community about an interesting or amusing news tidbit for the same reasons. They want to enhance their social capital by showing they are in the know. They want to express themselves and signal what is important to them. They want to enrich the lives of others by giving back to the community. News and information is a currency that shapes what we decide to share with our social circles.

#OMG! I Have to Tell You
#OMG! I Have to Tell You
#OMG! I Have to Tell You
#OMG! I Have to Tell You
#OMG! I Have to Tell You
#OMG! I Have to Tell You
#OMG! I Have to Tell You
#OMG! I

CHAPTER THREE

#OMG! I Have to Tell You

GAS ATTACKS ON CIVILIANS IN SYRIA, SECRET CIA FILES ON American backing for Saddam Hussein, Ben Affleck being cast as Batman and Miley Cyrus twerking were among the most shared stories in August 2013. Every day, a mix of the serious, the surprising, the shocking and the sexy spreads across social networks.

News about the situation unfolding in Syria was consistently among the more shared stories in August 2013. In the week after the August 21 chemical attack, more information emerged about the use of the nerve agent Sarin. Online images showed adults and children struggling to breathe, frothing at the mouth and convulsing on the ground. Outrage at the tragedy led more and more people to tell others about what had happened in Syria.

The reaction to the attack in Syria is an example of how emotions drive sharing. As more details surfaced about what had happened, so did the number of people spreading the news. Emotions play a vital part in the social transmission of news and information. Interest, happiness, disgust, surprise, sadness, anger, fear and contempt affect how some stories catch on and travel far wider than others. The news that Ben Affleck was to be the next Batman became a huge talking point as fans expressed surprise, shock and horror. "Holy smokes! Affleck?" summed up the reaction of many. *Variety*'s story on the casting was shared on Twitter by more than 14,000 users and attracted almost 100,000 comments on Facebook.

When we pass on a story, be it disturbing news from Syria or Affleck as Batman, we are replicating what we already do in everyday conversations. Most of our exchanges fall into what is called social talk. In conversation, we share details about our personal activities, indulge in gossip, highlight something in the news or relate far-fetched stories that make up urban legends. An exchange of information takes place. Our purpose is to let others know what we know, perhaps help them understand a complex situation or share useful practical advice. A story about traffic conditions could help drivers save time during the morning commute. We can appear well-informed and knowledgeable by telling colleagues about the latest trends in our industry. Or entertaining by passing on an amusing song we found online. Behind our actions are emotional drivers that underpin the social transmission of news and information. We may think we are making rational choices, but underlying our actions is an emotional response to the news.

NEWS THAT'S FIT TO SHARE

News editors have long understood how to use emotions to capture the attention of a busy audience. In journalism, the true skill lies not in knowing what to write about but in deciding which of the millions of events taking place every day across the planet to ignore. Only the "news that's fit to print" makes it to the page. New Yorkers caught their first glimpse of this famous phrase in American journalism in October 1896. The red sign in Madison Square that read ALL THE NEWS THAT'S FIT TO PRINT was the advertising slogan for an ailing New York newspaper. It was the brainchild of Adolph S. Ochs, a thirty-eight-year-old publisher who had started his newspaper career as an office boy and printing apprentice in Knoxville, Tennessee. He had made a name for himself by taking a bankrupt small-town newspaper in 1878 and turning it into one of the most influential dailies in the South. Almost twenty years later, he did the same for another ailing newspaper, *The New York Times*.

When Ochs acquired that paper on August 18, 1896, for $75,000, the phrase was part of a strategy to reverse the fortunes of a paper that was selling only 9,000 of the 19,000 copies printed each day, was losing $1,000 a day and carried debts total-ling $300,000. Ochs hoped the slogan would help to set the *Times* apart from the more popular and sensational papers in the city by signalling that it was going to be far more selective in what it covered. What started as an advertising slogan became a leitmotif for the *Times,* encapsulating its commitment to journal-istic integrity. The front page of the newspaper still carries the seven words, which first appeared in print in 1897.

The emotional impact of a story is one of the values that shapes news coverage. News values are the not-so-secret sauce that journalists use to evaluate the elements that come together to make a good story. As well as emotion, editors assess impact, weight, controversy, the unusual, prominence, proximity, timeliness, currency, usefulness and educational value. Journalists use news values as a framework to estimate the level of interest in a potential story. During the four years I edited the front page of the BBC News website, I would aim for a balance of the most important developments in the U.K. and abroad, with reports from the world of health and science, together with a dash of entertainment and things that were just plain weird.

If Ochs were alive today, he might have fashioned the slogan as "All the news that's fit to share." In 2010, readers were sending out a link to a *New York Times* story on Twitter every four seconds. It is hard to visit a news website without stumbling across calls to tweet this article or recommend that video. Media organizations are aware that one of the best ways of getting their stories out there is by word of mouth, as social media becomes an extension of the office water cooler. Personal recommendation is an increasingly important source of readers for news websites. By 2010, almost half of all people online in the U.S. were passing along links to news stories or videos.

The trend for social recommendation has been gathering pace as platforms such as Facebook have evolved into marketplaces for the spread of news, information and ideas. Facebook alone accounted for about one in every ten readers visiting a news website such as HuffingtonPost.com in 2011. For *The New York Times*, about 6 per cent of its readers found their way to the site through links posted by friends on Facebook. By January 2014, the official *Times* page on the social network had been "liked" by almost 5.2 million people, up from 2.5 million in November 2012. Digital sharing is part of the fabric of news in modern society. Publications such as *The Times* offer a myriad of ways for readers to tell their friends about a story they saw online. But what the audience decides are the important stories of the day does not necessarily mesh with the decisions of experienced news editors who select all the news that is fit to print.

On news websites, there is usually some overlap between the top news items of the day and the list of most shared stories. But the most read items aren't always the most shared. The news that's fit to print isn't always the news that's fit to share. It points to the divergence between the stories we consume and those we share. Readers tend to spread the most distinctive and unusual stories, as well as the big news of the day. How a story makes us feel plays a vital role in triggering our desire to tell others about it. When Wharton business professors Jonah Berger and Katherine Milkman studied the most emailed stories from *The New York Times*, they found that news and information that provoked an emotional reaction was 20 per cent more likely to be widely shared than more neutral stories. Similarly, a British study found that news about disasters and death, quirky stories or provocative columns were among the most shared types of stories at five big U.K. news organizations. The most shared items tended to evoke emotions of shock, amusement or surprise. Interest alone was not enough to explain why the stories were spread by the public. The stories that pop up on social networks are about "mood and the way a story makes you feel," concluded the former editor of *The Guardian* website, Janine Gibson.

MAKING SENSE OF EMOTIONS

People are far more likely to share details of everyday personal things that provoke a strong emotional response. Sentiment also comes into play when talking about other aspects of life. We are more likely to tell a friend after seeing a particularly moving film or after hearing shocking news, such as the death of Diana, Princess of Wales. As social animals, we are engineered to share news. By studying the stories that people choose to pass on to others by email or Facebook, researchers are discovering how fear, sadness, happiness, anger and disgust affect how news spreads. Making an emotional connection serves as a catalyst for sharing. The key is in understanding the reactions that spark social transmission. The difference between emotions that increase or decrease sharing is physiological arousal. The emotions that trigger a response lend themselves to being shared more than others.

SPREAD THE JOY

On the night of November 6, 2012, millions of Americans were on the edge of their seats. One of the most closely fought elections for the White House was coming to an end, as polling stations closed and votes were counted. America's first black president, Barack Hussein Obama, was hoping for a second term. Mitt Romney, the former Republican governor of Massachusetts, was the man trying to unseat him. After months of arduous campaigning, millions of dollars spent on political messages and three robust televised debates, the election seemed too close to call.

For Obama supporters, relief came shortly, at 11:15 P.M. Eastern. It came in the form of a post on Obama's official Facebook and Twitter accounts, some two hours before he gave his formal victory speech. The message carried a photograph of the president hugging his wife, his sleeves rolled up and eyes closed, framed against grey clouds in the background, with the caption FOUR MORE YEARS. The photo dated to a campaign stop at Dubuque, Iowa, on August 15. It quickly set a new record for the most shared post in the history of social media. In less than twenty-four hours, almost four million people clicked to "like" the photo and more than 500,000 people shared it on their own Facebook pages. On Twitter, it was passed on more than 750,000 times.

The photo of the hug struck a chord with supporters, both in the U.S. and abroad. By sharing the message, they were stating their political views and associating their online identity with the Obamas'. As explored in Chapter 2, people tend to manage their presence online and express a particular persona through the material shared with others. The Obama tweet was the trigger for emotions of joy—and, to some degree, relief—among supporters hoping for four more years. After a seemingly never-ending presidential campaign, they were primed to share positive news signalling the end.

The impact of the message went beyond the words about the result of the election. The accompanying photo conveyed the ideal image of the president as a man who, to supporters, symbolized hope, loyalty and family. The photo captured a key emotion that drives communication: happiness. By forwarding the photo, individuals were sharing the joy of the Obamas with their loved ones, friends and colleagues. Social networks allowed individuals to feel part of something bigger than themselves and participate in a collective expression of delight at Obama's victory. Four years earlier, the Obama camp had scored a similar viral victory with its *Yes We Can* video. The message of hope and change became the most popular online video of the 2008 campaign, with more than twenty million views.

Happiness is one of the most influential drivers of sharing. It is a positive emotion that we want to share with the world. It explains the popularity of funny videos like the famous *Charlie Bit My Finger* from 2007, one of the most watched videos on YouTube. In six years, the video of a one-year-old biting the finger of his three-year-old brother had racked up more than 500 million views. The most widely shared videos are not simply amusing. They are exhilarating, hilarious, astonishing or uplifting. The secret to their success is their ability to trigger a positive physiological response, making us laugh or squeal with joy. Such videos are shared 30 per cent more on average than others.

The power of emotion to override a more rational assessment became clear in the early days of the Internet. In the late 1990s, an email supposedly from Microsoft founder Bill Gates was one of the things many felt compelled to pass on. The message explained that Gates was trying out a new email tracing program. It asked people to forward the message to everyone they knew, promising $1,000 if the email reached a thousand people. The message was started as a joke by software programmer Bryan Mack in 1997. It was widely shared, spawned numerous versions over the years and remains one of the top ten Internet hoaxes.

A letter from Bill Gates offering $1,000 for clicking on the Forward button sounds too good to be true. Many thought that, but still felt compelled to share their apparent good fortune. "I have ab-so-smurfly no clue as to if this is a farce or not, but believe in it or not, the prospect of an extra grand is enticing," wrote one person. The Gates hoax highlights the power of happiness as a driver for social transmission, even if we have doubts about the authenticity of the message.

The structure of social networking sites works to reinforce upbeat feelings. Ever wonder why there is no Dislike button on Facebook? It is structured to encourage a positive emotional environment. And the plan works. Most people feel good about themselves when they spend time on such social networks. We tend to be connected to people we know, rather than strangers. It means we are more likely to forward feel-good, amusing or awe-inspiring stories, because we want our friends to experience the same vicarious delight we did.

A doctoral student at Michigan State University, Sonya Song, dug further into the phenomenon of Facebook sharing when she was a Knight-Mozilla Fellow at *The Boston Globe* in 2013. She analyzed 215 stories posted on the *Globe*'s Facebook page over a two-week period. Among the pieces that spurred the most conversation was a photo gallery marking the return of two swans that take up residence at the Boston Public Garden during the summer and a "miracle" win by the Bruins against the Toronto Maple Leafs. Both are feel-good stories. In contrast, factual stories devoid of emotion failed to get much traction on Facebook.

While traditional media gives space to bad news, social transmission favours positive news. Even for discerning readers of *The New York Times*, the more positive a story, the more likely readers are to email it to a friend. It means we are less likely to stumble across a story that is potentially important but lacking emotion on social networks. Television is still the leading source of news for most, but it is on the decline as people are increasingly turning to the Internet and social networks. By

2012, 20 per cent of Americans were regularly getting some of their news from a social networking site, up from just 2 per cent in 2008. For young people, the number is up to a third. The prognosis could be a news diet of beautiful sunset photos or cute cats. But it's not quite that banal. News that stirs negative emotions does spread. It just has to be the right kind of negative emotion in the appropriate context.

DON'T BE SAD

Say a friend mentioned that she had raised enough money from running a marathon to sponsor expensive eye surgery for an Indian child. Another friend then said he had just been told he had a congenital eye disorder and would probably be blind in five years. Chances are, you would share both anecdotes with others. Both examples provoke strong emotions—happiness in the case of the marathon runner and sadness for the friend with the eye condition. But one of the stories would be passed on more than the other. According to psychology researchers from the U.K., Australia and the Netherlands, it would be the anecdote of the marathon runner. It is a feel-good story. The eye story is a heartbreaking, tragic story without a happy ending. Nobody wants to be like *Saturday Night Live*'s Debbie Downer. ("You're enjoying your day. Everything's going your way. Then along comes Debbie Downer.")

Professors Berger and Milkman at the Wharton School found that sadness affected which stories readers of *The New York Times* shared. They analyzed thousands of articles that made the "most emailed" list on the *Times*'s website over three months, taking into account factors that would influence a story's popularity, such as its prominence on the website, the gender of the writer, or the story's length. Sad stories, such as President Obama mourning the passing of his grandmother or the suicide of a Korean actress, were far less popular than an upbeat account of a play telling the story of newcomers to New York City who fall in love.

The more depressing the story, the less likely we are to want to tell others about it. With happiness, intensity fuels sharing; sadness triggers the opposite response. The Penn professors tested the idea by exposing their students to two different news articles about people recovering from injuries. One was the heartbreaking story of a person maimed in the 9/11 attacks. The other was about a person recovering after a fall down the stairs. The students were reluctant to pass on the story about the 9/11 victim, even though it had a much greater emotional impact.

Yet sad stories can go viral if they are presented in the appropriate context. In January 2014, the British newspaper the *Daily Mail* reported on a thirty-three-year-old mother dying of cancer who would never get to see her toddler grow up. At first glance, it seems to be a depressing tale of loss. But visitors to the *Daily Mail*'s website shared the story almost four thousand times. The key difference was the framing of the story: the article focused on how the mother, Rowena, was leaving a legacy for her son by writing cards to celebrate his birthdays up to age twenty-one, as well as cards for his first day at school, his graduation and his wedding. The article framed Rowena's story as one about the perseverance of the human spirit in the face of adversity. It was designed to leave readers feeling inspired, rather than dejected.

Media outlets are getting smart about framing stories that involve a problem but also have some kind of positive outcome. Sonya Song spotted the trend in the most conversational stories posted to Facebook by *The Boston Globe*. People shared stories about runners who, having failed to finish the Boston Marathon after the bombings in 2013, had been invited back to complete the race. Or about a child saved after a natural disaster. We seem to be suckers for a happy ending. Websites that make a virtue of generating buzz around their stories, such as Upworthy and Viral Nova, have become skilled in coming up with headlines that turn a sad tale on its head. On Viral Nova, Rowena's story was headlined: "Her Little Boy Has No Idea His Mother Is About to Die. What She's Doing About That Is Amazing." As well as piquing curiosity, it primes a reader to tell a friend about such a moving story. Shifting the focus away from sadness changes a story's emotional footprint, helping it travel further on social networks.

BE WARY OF FEAR

The old adage in news is that if it bleeds, it leads. On any evening newscast, there never seems to be a shortage of murders, shootings or traffic accidents. Crime appears to be everywhere, and the more unusual and violent the crime, the more coverage it gets. Crime reporting has long been a media staple: bad news sells, while good news is no news. The coverage seeks to grab our attention by tapping into the emotion of fear. A newspaper headline warning of "stranger danger" is designed to lure more people to buy the paper. TV anchors going on about a gangland shooting are trying to stop viewers from switching channels.

Fear is visceral, instinctual. It is a reaction to danger that serves as a survival mechanism. In a socially hostile situation— say, someone being aggressive at a bar—most people will try to extricate and protect themselves. They see a threat, assess it and react to it. But we are lousy at accurately evaluating risk, because fear works on an emotional, rather than rational, level. Take the public perception of crime. Most Americans believe violent crime has been increasing over the past decade. The truth, though, is that violent crime has been on a downward trend since 1994.

While fear has long been used to sell newspapers and boost TV ratings, it is not an emotion we share readily with others. Fear can be a powerful motivator for action, but for not sharing. Researchers Kim Peters, Yoshima Kashima and Anna Clark tested the idea with Australian university students to see how they would deal with frightful anecdotes about college life. They found that the students were unlikely to pass on a story about a random beating of a fellow student. While bad news is a mainstay of the media, people tend to avoid passing on information that makes others feel badly or fearful.

As a general rule, fear tends to diminish the desire to share. But there are situations when we deliberately take on the role of Debbie Downer. When Stanford University professor Chip Heath was at the University of Chicago in the 1990s, he was curious about whether people had a preference for good or bad news. He put the idea to the test by seeing how willing undergraduate students were to tell others about muggings in the Hyde Park neighbourhood the university occupies. The results

contradicted the general belief that people shy away from passing on bad news. The students consistently chose to share bad
news about muggings, even though it might trigger emotions
of fear among friends.

The difference here is the context for these conversations.
At the time, muggings were a common topic of conversation
for the residents of Hyde Park. Since the topic was already commonplace, students would have felt less inhibited about sharing
their fear. In such situations, there is a social good at play.
Telling others about the level of muggings is a way of warning
them of the dangers of crime in the area. It shows that there
are times when spreading fear is helping the community, if
the context is right. But as a general rule, fear is not a negative
emotion we want to provoke in others, in much the same way
we don't want to share sadness. However, there is one negative
emotion that inspires action—and that is anger.

GET ANGRY

The tale of Dave Carroll, his broken guitar and United Airlines
has become legend as to what can happen to a company's reputation in the age of social media. The Canadian musician
became an Internet sensation in 2009 along with his song,
"United Breaks Guitars." Carroll wrote the song to vent his
frustration with customer service at United Airlines after his
$3,500 Taylor acoustic guitar was broken on a flight with the
airline. The music video poking fun at United went viral on
YouTube (at the time of this writing, it has been viewed almost
fourteen million times).

The song struck a chord with people who passed it on to their friends. Carroll went from being an obscure country-and-western singer from Timmins, Ontario, to a YouTube celebrity. It was a public relations nightmare for United, one that affected the company's share price. United finally paid attention to Carroll, offering him the cost of repairs to his guitar and flight vouchers for his trouble.

One of the reasons the story of Carroll and his broken guitar resonated with the public is that we all have our story of a flight from hell. There is even a website called FlightsfromHell.com, where travellers are encouraged to share the trials and tribulations of air travel.

Such tales trigger emotional arousal. They make us seethe with frustration. We are all prone to react to anger. In their study of *The New York Times*, Berger and Milkman discovered that readers were drawn to pass on stories that stirred an angry response. Among the stories that left readers fuming were reports on big bonuses paid to Wall Street executives at a time of financial crisis and about an adviser to Senator John McCain receiving nearly $2 million from a major loans firm. Anger made a news piece more viral. And the more it incited a passionate reaction, the better. The Wharton professors calculated that the odds of a story being shared would increase by 34 per cent if it were written in such a way as to incense readers.

Harnessed in the right way, a negative emotion like anger can fuel social transmission. The way a story is presented can make all the difference. The Wharton researchers tested two versions of the Carroll story to see which one resonated the most with readers. One story, headlined "United Dents Guitars," said the airline was willing to pay for the damage caused by baggage handlers dropping the guitar. The other version, headlined "United Smashes Guitars," said baggage handlers were indifferent in handling the guitars and that the airline was loath to pay damages. The second version was designed to provoke a strong emotional reaction—and, unsurprisingly, it made people more likely to tell others.

Anger is a negative emotion, yet it can be used effectively to incite action if it spurs an emotional response. Part of the success of the *Kony 2012* video produced by Invisible Children was due to the sense of moral outrage it provoked in viewers. As well as making people angry, it directed those feelings at the villain of the piece, Joseph Kony. Research shows people are far more likely to share such material if it doesn't involve their own social circle. Instead, they forward it to like-minded friends who would have a similar reaction. The effect is to strengthen social bonds in a group through a communal expression of aversion to the acts of another. When anger tips over into disgust, the urge to share becomes even more powerful.

OMG! THAT'S DISGUSTING

Most people will have heard a version of the story about the rat served instead of chicken. In one of the most popular accounts, a woman is eating Kentucky Fried Chicken as she watches TV at home when she notices it tastes odd. Turning up the lights, she sees it isn't chicken, but a rat with extra-crispy coating. A kid working at KFC had fried it as a prank. Or so the story goes. The Kentucky Fried Rat yarn has become one of the more widely known and persistent urban legends. By 1980, more than a hundred versions of the tale were in circulation in the U.S. alone.

The combination of eating something inappropriate and unsuitable contact with animals is irresistible. The yuckiness of a story contributes to its appeal. The persistence of the Kentucky Fried Rat story helps to explain why some material spreads rapidly online. At the core is the emotion of disgust. It may seem odd that such a negative emotion would be one that people want to share. But disgust is a surprisingly powerful motivation for sharing.

Researchers Chip Heath, Chris Bell and Emily Sternberg decided to test how far people would go in passing on disgusting anecdotes, no matter how far-fetched. They chose twelve disgusting urban legends and altered them to be either more or less revolting. In one example, the story of a man finding a dead rat at the bottom of his glass of soda was made more nauseating by having him ingest bits of the animal. The less repulsive version had the man notice a bad smell and spot the rat before drinking the soda. The results showed that people were far more likely to share the most disgusting account of a story, even if the tale was truly repulsive. The researchers found similar results when they looked at the most popular stories on websites that specialized in urban legends. The more disgusting a story, the more likely it was to be distributed online.

There is a science to grossness. Psychologists who have studied why some things, actions and people elicit feelings of repulsion point to several key elements. They come together to provoke a reaction of disgust. There is the inappropriate use of food, such as the Subway employee who shared a picture of himself with his penis on the restaurant's sandwich bread on Instagram.

Sometimes bodily products are involved. Or animals. Poor hygiene, sex and death can also elicit disgust. Finally there is deviant behaviour that goes beyond societal morals and practices. Disgust is an emotion that started off as a way to avoid harm to the body and has expanded to become a way to avoid harm to the soul. It explains the gut reaction to moral violations, such as when the NRA sent a pro-gun tweet at the time of the Aurora massacre or when Home Depot posted a photo of two African Americans and a man in a monkey suit with the caption, "which drummer is not like the others?"

Disgust provokes both an intense moral and physiological reaction. Watching a video of a young woman eating a live preying mantis may leave a viewer feeling like throwing up. Yet it was also one of the videos that students taking part in a psychology experiment were most likely to forward to others. It may seem odd that people would react by turning to friends and saying, "OMG! You have to see this." But according to researchers in Belgium and the Netherlands, the more intense an experience, the more we want to share it.

The team found that students talked the most about a clip from the notorious cult film *Faces of Death*. It was deliberately chosen because it usually prompts a visceral response from viewers. The excerpt showed people at a restaurant smashing a monkey's skull and eating the brain. The scene looks real enough, but it was faked using Styrofoam hammers and cauliflower for the brains. After watching the clip, students were eager to talk about it with others and compare their feelings. Sharing disgust provides an emotional release. It also is a way of confirming with others the boundaries of what is socially acceptable.

THE TALE OF ROSE THE GOAT

I remember the first time I realized just how much emotions could affect how news travels online. I had been the daily news editor at the BBC News website, deciding on the mix of stories on the front page. It is the most coveted real estate of the site, as millions visit the front page every day. As the daily news editor, my job was to make sure visitors to the site saw the main news of the day, as well as the amusing or entertaining. One day in September a few years back, my colleagues noticed something odd happening on the site.

A story published seven months earlier was suddenly the most read article. It continued to be popular for days, even though it was buried within the site in the Africa section. Adam Curtis, then the World editor at the BBC News website, started investigating why a 185-word story that was months old had unexpectedly become a hit with readers. "It had not been re-published, re-written or revised," he wrote on the BBC's editors' blog. "So how is it that upwards of 100,000 people a day were passing it on to their friends and acquaintances?"

The clue lay in the headline: SUDAN MAN FORCED TO 'MARRY' GOAT. The article told the story of a Sudanese man who had been caught having "improper relations with the beast." He was ordered to pay a marriage dowry of $50 to the goat's owner. "We have given him the goat, and as far as we know they are still together," the owner of the goat was quoted as saying. The tale of one man and his goat "wife" attracted some attention at the time of publication in February 2006, but soon disappeared into the archive. When it resurfaced in September, Curtis wasn't sure whether people were really reading the story "some crazed animal lover has been repeatedly hitting the site with fake requests."

This was no scam. During that morning in September, readers from across the world had stumbled across the story and emailed the link to their friends. The more people read it, the more they told others about it. People in the U.S., Australia, France, India and elsewhere—even in the tiny Grand Duchy of Luxembourg—could not get enough of the story. Other news outlets reported on the travails of Rose the goat.

Rose came to an unfortunate end in May 2007. Eating scraps on the streets of Juba in southern Sudan, she died after choking on a plastic bag. The BBC carried a mock obituary, noting how, during her short marriage, "friends would joke about how she had reached the end of her tether, about whether the couple would have any kids, and if they did, whether they would employ a nanny."

By the time of her death, Rose had become an Internet phenomenon. Even a year after publication, the original article continued to be among the BBC's most emailed stories. It became one of the most popular stories published since the site's launch in 1997. The goat's tale was one of the first major examples of the impact that sharing can have on the news, taking an obscure story from a remote part of the world and propelling it to international notoriety. The short news item was surprising and unusual, but it also had several of the elements that elicit disgust: animals, sex and moral violations. No wonder it was so widely read.

The story of Rose highlights how, in the marketplace of ideas online, some stories spread due to a gut reaction, not on the basis of whether it is true, useful or entertaining. It was an early sign of the power of emotions to determine the sort of news that was fit to share online. When we email a story from *The New York Times*, we are not just judging it on whether it is well written or whether we believe everything it says. We react to the amusing, the inspiring, the positive. More surprising is the desire to share stories, photos or videos that arouse negative emotions of anger and disgust.

Emotions have always played a role in how information spreads. Consider the endurance of urban legends that are just too far-fetched to be true. But emotional engagement becomes even more significant in an online world. Social networks make it much easier not only to reach out to a large group of friends, but also to see how they react. When we see others doing something, we tend to ape the same choices. The result is a feedback loop that validates how we feel about a particular story and reinforces our sense of belonging. There are consequences when our social circles become our editorial filters, privileging the sensational over the important and the amusing over the earnest.

#The Daily We
#The Daily We
#The Daily We
#The Daily We
#The Daily We
#The Daily We
#The Dai
#The Da

CHAPTER FOUR

#The Daily We

THE AMERICAN BOBSLEDDER JOHNNY QUINN WAS ONE OF THE MEDAL hopefuls for Team USA at the 2014 Winter Olympics. But the thirty-year-old Texan made headlines well before he even went for gold. What caught the public's imagination was not his prowess in navigating the twists of the narrow bobsled track; it was his skill at getting out of tricky situations in Sochi. Trapped in a bathroom in the Olympic Village, Quinn smashed his way out, and then snapped a photo and tweeted about his experience. Alongside a photo of a door with a gaping hole in the middle, he wrote: ". . . With no phone to call for help, I used my bobsled push training to break out. #SochiJailBreak." His mishap propelled him into a social media Olympic phenomenon.

His message received 29,000 retweets and counting, with Quinn gaining more than 15,000 followers on Twitter in just three days. The tweet was also widely reported by the media, embedded in thirty-three news articles and counting. When Quinn and two teammates got stuck in an elevator, he naturally took a photo and shared it. That, too, was picked up by the media. Quinn's tribulations were widely shared because they offered funny glimpses into the everyday life of a Team USA athlete. But they were also topical, tapping into a growing discussion about problems with the Olympic Village at Sochi, as people talked about their experiences, ranging from unfinished rooms without curtains or furniture to a lack of heating and yellow-tinged water. The hashtag #SochiProblems was used more 331,000 times after the world's attention turned to the Black Sea resort town.

The Russian Olympic Organizing Committee had already contended with stories in the Western media about exorbitant costs, unfinished venues and even stray dogs, never mind on-going criticisms of Russia's anti-gay legislation. Big events tend to be plagued with teething troubles, but #SochiProblems highlighted how social sharing, powered by digital technologies, influences and reinforces public perception of the news. Instead of stories celebrating the herculean achievement of athletes, Sochi became a stream of funny, embarrassing, "only in Russia" anecdotes.

The story of Sochi's problems illustrates how mainstream and social media intertwine to influence what makes the news and how the news is presented. The media has traditionally been one of the elite groups interpreting events around us, presenting them in a certain way. For the past two hundred years, the news industry has been the main gatekeeper of information, deciding what was important enough to report and transmit to the rest of us. Our use of social networking technologies to filter the news means we have taken back some of the power of the media. It has given rise to a complex system in which the way people make sense of the news is shaped by the choices of thousands of ordinary people, prominent figures such as Olympic athletes and traditional elites such as journalists.

Remember Mitt Romney's "binders full of women" comment on October 16, 2012? The Republican candidate used the phrase in the second presidential debate as the election campaign neared its climax. He was replying to a question about the hiring of women for top jobs during his tenure as governor of Massachusetts in 2002. The phrase could have been interpreted in a positive light, as Romney was saying he had many talented women to draw on. But it wasn't. Instead, the awkward phrasing became an Internet meme. Within minutes, it became a running joke on Twitter, spawning its own hashtag and thousands of parody photos poking fun at the idea of "women in binders."

The mainstream media picked up the story, and "binders full of women" became the news, overshadowing the substance of the debate. The interplay between the social media reaction to the debate and a press primed for an electoral gaffe set the terms for the news coverage. Out of the thousands of words spoken by Romney, those four are the ones that many will remember. It is just another example of how social sharing is changing not just who decides what is important, but the way news is presented, interpreted and understood. The social filtering of news and information is transforming how we learn about the world and is having an impact on what we think and do.

Much of the change is being experienced first in the U.S. By 2013, a third of Americans were finding news via social media, almost as many as do using Internet searches. The proportion is even greater in Spain and Italy. What these countries have in common is weakened legacy media. In countries with strong online news brands—Denmark, Germany, Japan and the U.K.—social media is far less important as a source for news.

There is a risk of overstating the importance of sharing and failing to recognize national differences. In most Western liberal democracies, television remains the main source of news for most people. It is vital to understand how this mix of mainstream media, our social circles and technologies hidden from sight shape the what and how of the information that commands public attention.

WHERE WERE YOU WHEN . . . ?

For every generation, there are dates in history that become part of our collective memory. From the assassination of John F. Kennedy to the death of Princess Diana to the attacks of 9/11, some points in time become indelibly inscribed as "where were you when" moments. In the 1960s, when television was the new technology whose importance was growing, one such occasion was the landing of the first man on the moon. On the night of July 20, 1969, some 125 million Americans gathered around their television sets to watch the Apollo 11 landing. Over the course of that night and the early hours of the next morning, they watched astronauts Neil Armstrong and Buzz Aldrin bounce weightlessly across the grainy, grey landscape and collect rock samples.

The moon landing was broadcast live on the three U.S. networks that ruled the airwaves at the time. But there was one network anchor to whom Americans turned above all others: Walter Cronkite of CBS. That night, 45 per cent of the TV audience tuned in to hear Cronkite exclaim, "Oh boy! Phew!" as the *Eagle* module touched down on the lunar surface. More than fifty million Americans turned to Uncle Walter to experience one of the historic highlights of the twentieth century.

During the 1960s and 1970s, Walter Cronkite was a reassuring nightly presence in America, anchoring the *CBS Evening News* and helping to establish television as the dominant news medium of its time. An estimated twenty million Americans tuned in nightly to the avuncular anchor who became known as the most trusted man in the U.S. On the passing of Cronkite on July 17, 2009, President Barack Obama described him as "someone we could trust to guide us through the most important issues of the day; a voice of certainty in an uncertain world."

The late 1950s and the early 1960s are known as the golden age of American television. During this period, TV grew to be the dominant form of home entertainment. By 1960, nine out of ten American homes had a TV set and television had become a staple of the news diet of Americans. When President Dwight Eisenhower decided to run for a second term in 1956, most Americans heard the news on television. When "Ike" suffered a stroke in November 1957, television was again the main source of news. By the late 1950s, TV played a pivotal role in spreading important news, even though it was considered at the time primarily as an entertainment medium. For decades thereafter, most people first heard about a major news story from television, radio and newspapers, rather than word of mouth.

Cronkite ended his broadcasts with his trademark sign-off, "And that's the way it is." The phrase sums up the place of television in telling audiences how to view the world. Fifty years later, a more appropriate catchphrase might be, "And that's the way it *was.*" TV news anchors persist, but they do not command the same authority and audience in a multiplex of cable channels. Word of mouth is enjoying resurgence, amplified by social media. How Americans heard of one of the defining moments in America's ten-year "War on Terror" provides some insights into the way information spreads today.

On the night of May 1, 2011, the White House surprised the media and the nation by releasing a terse message that President Obama was going to make a televised address later that evening. He then took to the air to announce the killing in Pakistan by U.S. Navy Seals of America's most wanted man, Osama bin Laden. By then, the president had already been scooped by Keith Urbahn, chief of staff for former defence secretary Donald Rumsfeld, who broke the news on Twitter. "So I'm told by a reputable person they have killed Osama bin Laden. Hot damn," he tweeted. The information spread swiftly when it was retweeted by then–*New York Times* reporter Brian Stelter, who had more than fifty thousand followers and a credible news outlet to his name.

For some, then, the answer to "Where were you when you learned bin Laden had been killed?" is "On Twitter." While President Obama was still working on his speech, Twitter was abuzz with talk of bin Laden. Most of the tech-savvy readers of technology news website Mashable said they found out through Twitter or Facebook. However, the notion that social media has become the default channel for the news is too simplistic.

Researchers Barbara Kaye from the University of Tennessee-Knoxville and Thomas Johnson from the University of Texas surveyed Americans interested in politics to discover how they had learned of bin Laden's death. Twitter might have been first, but the news reached a tiny fraction of the public. Only 5.6 per cent got the news on Twitter, and even fewer—4.6 per cent—on a social network. Since the study involved people interested in politics, just over a third had heard the news from political websites or blogs. And don't write off television, as 12 per cent cited broadcast TV as the source for the news. A similar number heard it on the Fox News Channel on cable.

Others, like Lauren Mary Gotimer, were told by family or friends, either in person or by email and text messages. As the twenty-something Bentley University graduate recorded in a blog, she was asleep in bed after an exhausting day. When she woke up in the middle of the night, she checked her phone. To her surprise, there were forty-two text messages. One was from her sister, and the rest were from people she followed on Twitter. Gotimer read her sister's text first. "Osama dead go amurrca—I hope you caught the address," read the message. Gotimer was confused. At first, she thought her sister meant Barack Obama, but she soon realized it was Osama bin Laden. "I slept through a huge event in life," wrote Gotimer on her blog, "but fortunately it didn't take long for me to hear it all thanks to social media. Now all that's left is for me to turn on my computer tonight to watch Obama's address online."

The Internet and social media have given rise to a hybrid media system. TV anchors still broadcast the news to the masses. Alongside them, people use social media services and technologies to create, share and comment on the news. Twitter CEO Dick Costolo summed it up in a marketeering yet shrewd observation when he described the platform as "this indispensable companion to life in the moment." The idea of a commanding presence such as Walter Cronkite today seems an anachronism; social filtering is becoming increasingly significant in the circulation of information. The idea of friends and family select-ing and recommending news to others isn't new; social filtering has always been a part of how we run our lives. With blogs, email, text messages, Facebook and Twitter, social filtering not only has become much easier and more prevalent, but it is also changing our behaviour. Instead of seeking out the news, a gen-eration is growing up expecting the news to come to them.

THE NEWS WILL FIND ME

When Barack Obama first sought the American presidency in 2008, he ran on a promise of change, a break from what was labelled as the failed policies of the Bush administration. It was a message that resonated with the young. Two-thirds of voters under the age of thirty backed Obama, leading the Pew Research Center to conclude, "a significant generational shift in political allegiance is occurring." At the same time, there were signs that a similar shift was taking place in the way these young voters were finding out about politics.

Surveys and interviews by market research companies found that younger voters were passing on the news to their friends via email and social networks. Conversely, they then expected their online connections to alert them to what they needed to know. "If the news is that important, it will find me," a college student was quoted as saying in a May 2008 *New York Times* article. A year later, the editor of tech bible *Wired*, Chris Anderson, noted the trend towards information that "comes to me" even if we're scorning the morning newspaper or evening TV newscast. "It's news that matters. I figure by the time something gets to me it's been vetted by those I trust. So the stupid stuff that doesn't matter is not going to get to me," he told the German magazine *Der Spiegel.*

What started out as anecdotal evidence of a paradigm shift in news habits has since been backed up by further studies. Social networks make it much easier to be alerted to news that "comes to me." The Pew Internet and American Life Project found that, by 2010, half of Americans on social networks said they were getting some of their news from people they followed on sites like Facebook. Our relationship to the news has changed. By 2010, a third of Americans online were turning to Facebook to filter information, swap stories and react to them. This is not simply a U.S. phenomenon; an online survey of 1,682 Canadians in August 2010 revealed a similar trend. The study found that two out of five social media users said they received news and information on a daily basis from family, friends and acquaintances via social networks.

The young are the bellwether of upheaval. The trend among young adults is far more pronounced in the U.S. than in other similar developed democracies. A 2013 survey showed that almost twice as many eighteen- to twenty-four-year-old Americans cite social media as a source of news than print newspapers— 45 per cent to 25 per cent. Denmark is close behind, with half of young adults getting news from social media compared with a third from print. In other countries, such as Germany, Italy, Spain and the U.K., the numbers are close to parity.

The young have never lived in a world where news only came at certain times of the day from an elite group of people who told you the ways things were. "Why have to turn on the television for some entertainment, go get the newspaper for current events or pick up the phone to make a phone call when you can get all of that through one simple visit to Facebook or Twitter?" student Louis Medina told *The Observer*, the college newspaper of the University of Notre Dame in Indiana in 2011. "I get news from Facebook and Twitter all the time, especially because of the trending topics," said another student, Paul Anthony, quoted in the same article. "I don't check news sites daily."

What was novel back then has since become everyday—if not for everyone, then certainly for a significant number of people. It is no longer just a young person's game. It is no longer surprising to hear "I saw it on Facebook." When Pew Research talked to Americans on Facebook in 2013, half said they got some of their news via the social network. "If it wasn't for Facebook news, I'd probably never really know what's going on in the world because I don't have time to keep up with the news on a bunch of different locations," wrote one person.

The expectation that the news will come to us has unexpected consequences for the definition of news. News is usually thought of as something current and topical—of interest to a large number of people. When the media report on an event, it becomes news. Expecting the news to come to us turns this idea on its head. Something becomes news when it is widely shared and starts appearing on our networks, not when it was published. New Yorkers learned this lesson in February 2014, when they started coming across warnings that a severe blizzard was about to hit the city. The story on Gawker warned of up to thirty inches of snow for New York City. With hundreds sharing the story, it became a trending item on Gawker, drawing even more attention to it.

In the end, New York was not buried in snow that weekend, even though the story was true. People sharing it had failed to notice the date of the story in small print above the headline. It had been published in February 2013, and readers had been passing it on without checking the date of publication. This happens all too often, but it is easy to blame people for failing to note when a story was published.

Much of what is reported in the media has a short shelf life. But stories can gain new life online, well after their sell-by date. Old news frequently becomes news again when it appears in the daily stream of stories that flow across social networks. It is news because it is new to us. Sharing transfers the power to decide the news of the day to the audience. Equally, it transfers the responsibility to assess the timeliness and currency of the material flowing across our timelines.

THE ACCIDENTAL NEWS CONSUMER

The rise of social networks as sources for news adds a further twist to the way we learn about the world. What is novel is that people get the news on Facebook even when they are not deliberately trying to find out what's happening. Most stumble across news items on Facebook by accident. They see the news while they are doing other things—chatting with friends, looking at family photos or updating their status. As one person told the Pew researchers, "News on Facebook is just something that happens." The good news is that some people are being exposed to the news who might otherwise not be. But as Chapter 3 illustrated, not all types of news are deemed worthy of sharing, and that affects the range of information that people stumble across.

One of the selling points of the daily newspaper was that it contained a wide selection of news and information designed to be of interest to a broad audience. The serious and important shared inches of column space with the amusing and frivolous, even if a reader ignored the dry stuff. On Facebook, the editors who decide what matters are members of our social circles, and they want to amuse. The most common type of news on Facebook is about entertainment.

We shouldn't be too dismissive about the editorial choices of our connections. There is substance alongside the inconsequential. Pew found that two-thirds of Americans regularly come across news on Facebook about people and events in their community. Just over half stumble on national news and just under half encounter stories about local government and politics. Our friends, it seems, are not completely obsessed with the fluff.

More people than ever before are taking on the job of editors, filtering and selecting what is important, interesting or diverting. Traditionally, the role of gatekeeper fell to professional journalists who decided what was worthy of being reported on and published and what should be dismissed and ignored. Thousands of journalists continue to do this on a daily basis. The Internet was supposed to do away with the idea of gatekeepers who guided the flow of news and information. It was a revolutionary technology that would let citizens bypass these established editorial gates. Instead, we have all become gatekeepers for our social circles, adding an extra layer of control in deciding whether something in the paper merits attention.

The mainstream media itself has been complicit in sharing

editorial control. It is hard to encounter an online news story that doesn't urge us to give an item a thumbs-up, to recommend it or send it on by email. A study of 138 daily newspapers in the U.S., from big national papers to small local ones, showed that virtually all offered a way for readers to exercise editorial sway by sharing stories online. Readers have been recruited as digital paperboys to deliver the news to their friends, helping to increase the reach of a publication. We do this as the news industry has made it easier for us to do what we have always done: tell others about that thought-provoking, remarkable or quirky story in the news. Clicking a Like button requires much less work than clipping an item from the paper and sticking it in the mail, so we do it much more often.

Facebook makes it a virtue to share, but that doesn't mean we always see what our friends are recommending. The social network uses algorithms to judge what might be of most interest. The lines of computer code decide the prominence of items on the news feed, meaning that some of your friends see more of your posts than others. They work as behind-the-scenes editors, which the company argues identify the most relevant material for each individual. But Facebook's use of filtering algorithms is contentious. As with other tech giants who use algorithms, how they work is a commercial secret. The everyday user has little idea how Facebook acts as an intermediary, making editorial choices on his or her behalf. Journalists and researchers are increasingly scrutinizing the values embedded in the code of algorithms.

The question is how the new gatekeepers are affecting the mix in our daily news diet. The most active sharers tend to watch more local, national and cable news. Research in the

U.S. suggests that people regularly see news on six or more different topics when they while away the hours on Facebook. In Canada, too, people who are active on social media tend to draw from a wide range of news sources. Yet the persistent concern is that one gets a narrower view of the world when it is filtered by friends and acquaintances. Social networks tend to bring people together around shared values and interests, connecting us to others like us. Such tendencies, though, are not due to technology. They are down to human behaviour.

BEYOND THE ECHO CHAMBER

Ever wondered where the expression "sour grapes" comes from? It's from an Aesop's fable that sheds light on how we make certain judgments, even when things point in a different direction. The fable features a hungry fox that cannot get what it wants. It sees some grapes hanging high on a vine, but no matter what it does, the fruit remains out of range. In frustration, the fox concludes they must be sour grapes and not worth eating. The fox falls victim to cognitive dissonance, a concept American sociologist Leon Festinger put forward in his influential book published in 1975, *A Theory of Cognitive Dissonance*.

Cognitive dissonance means rationalizing a choice in the face of the contrary evidence. The fox tries to rationalize its inability to reach the grapes by deciding they are sour. Humans are subject to the same limitation. We tend to seek information that supports our beliefs and assumptions, that fits with our view of the world. Conversely, we try to avoid details that increase our mental discomfort. Through selective exposure, we favour information that reinforces pre-existing beliefs and avoid information that would challenge our beliefs and attitudes.

Selective exposure is why a Republican voter in the U.S. would be more likely to read a right-leaning newspaper, listen to conservative talk radio or watch the Fox News Channel. Selective exposure is an instinctive human activity. For early humans, knowing what to pay attention to and what to ignore was a matter of life and death. In modern society, selective exposure comes into play in what the researchers call a "low-energy armchair behaviour"—entertainment activities such as watching TV. Viewers tend to choose media that meet and reinforce their preconceptions and prejudices and avoid ideas that challenge them. But does that mean that the Internet and social media are making us more insular, paying attention only to news from people like us?

Even before Facebook, YouTube and Twitter, prominent thinkers were sounding the alarm. In his 2007 book *Republic.com 2.0*, Harvard law professor Cass Sunstein described a future where we could filter media with perfect accuracy. We would only receive the information we wanted, connect with people like us and avoid what we disliked. For him, "the imagined world of innumerable, diverse editions of the Daily Me is not a utopian dream, and it would create serious problems from the democratic point of view." The consequences of the "Daily Me," in Sunstein's view, would be a more fragmented, polarized and intolerant society.

It may never have been easier to craft a news diet to fit a particular view of the world and avoid opposing viewpoints or ignore important but dull news, such as local council decisions. Newspapers, television and radio have traditionally been viewed as providing shared experiences for communities as everyone reads the same news. "A good newspaper, I suppose, is a nation talking to itself," said playwright Arthur Miller in 1961, summing up the ideal view of the press as a unifying force for good in society. For some, social media is the antithesis of the newspaper, allowing people to live in filter bubbles and echo chambers online. The prominent *New York Times* columnist Nicholas Kristof was one of the many voices sounding the alarm. Taking as his starting point the demise of the print edition of a West Coast newspaper, the *Seattle Post-Intelligencer,* in March 2009, he wrote that, online, "we may believe intellectually in the clash of opinions, but in practice we like to embed ourselves in the reassuring womb of an echo chamber."

Figuring out whether people are retreating into their own filter bubbles is a complicated business. Social media does reinforce homophily—our tendency to associate with others with similar characteristics and interests—as it makes it simpler for like individuals to find each other. Homophily plays out at school and at work, as we seek out and connect with others with whom we share similar characteristics and interests. Individuals who interact frequently are alike and are increasingly likely to share similar information from similar sources, effectively narrowing their diet of news. Social networks can foster our inclination to share and receive from like-minded connections. Researchers have found that homophily is common on Twitter, above all when it comes to controversial and divisive issues. Whenever the conversation turns to politics, two polarized crowds tend to emerge on Twitter, frequently divided along liberal and conservative lines. Each group shares its own distinct set of links and comments. But the people who talk politics on Twitter are not representative of the millions of daily users. They are a concentrated number of politically active citizens.

Twitter helps to reinforce group identity, but different types of conversations bring together a varied mix of groups. Professionals or hobbyists connect with each other over a common topic to form tightly knit clusters. At other times, individuals come together because of a shared interest in a brand or celebrity to form a fragmented crowd that has little else in common. In contrast, tighter circles form around people and topics in the news, just like people cluster around different stalls at a market. Social networks are predicated on common interests, but to dismiss them as echo chambers is to deny that we all have diverse interests. Moreover, there are also signs that the way information travels on digital social networks may counter our predilection for selective exposure and instead nurture a diversity of information.

THE IMPORTANCE OF WEAK TIES

The way information travels on digital networks mirrors how it spreads by word of mouth. A recommendation from a trusted friend carries more weight than that of a casual contact. Thanks to homophily, people close to each other tend to have similar interests, so a piece of information may be more relevant. The same dynamics are at play on social media. Researchers at the School of Information at the University of Michigan worked with Facebook to study the sharing patterns of more than 250 million users from 236 countries over two months in 2010. The results showed that people were more likely to share a post, photo or link from a close contact than one from a casual acquaintance.

On the face of it, this would lend weight to arguments that social networks serve as echo chambers. However, digging deeper into the numbers revealed that the vast majority of material shared on Facebook came from loose ties—people we vaguely know, or whom we knew at school or met in passing years back. It turns out they play a fundamental function as social filters. The reason for this lies in math.

Individuals have strong ties with a small number of close friends, but weak ties with a much larger number of more distant connections. Even though we will share less from weak ties, there are more of them than there are of close friends. The much larger number of these distant contacts means that weak ties account for the majority of information spread on Facebook. The sheer abundance of weak ties means most information comes not from our closest friends but from distant connections.

Here's the math: Mary has 100 friends who are weak ties and ten who are strong ties. The likelihood that Mary will share a link from a close friend is high—around 50 per cent. But the chance she will share something from a casual friend is much lower—around 15 per cent. If 10 close friends share a link, Mary will share five links, or half of them. If 100 friends share something, the chances of it being passed on are lower, at 15 per cent. But 15 per cent of 100 is fifteen, so Mary ends up sharing more from these loose connections.

"Since these distant contacts tend to be different from us, the bulk of information we consume and share comes from people with different perspectives," explained Eytan Bakshy, one of the Michigan researchers who went on to join Facebook.

Other computer scientists have come up with similar conclusions. A team at Beihang University in Beijing analyzed sharing on YouTube and Facebook. Loose connections turned out to be crucial to the widespread circulation of information. Take them out of the equation, as the scientists did, and the spread falls dramatically. The weak ties serve as bridges between different communities, helping information jump from one social circle to another.

Online social networks are built around weak ties, mirroring the way social networks behave in the physical world. The importance of weak ties was first noted in 1973 by the American sociologist Mark Granovetter. In the influential paper *The Strength of Weak Ties*, he showed how an individual was far more likely to hear about a job from people he or she saw only occasionally or rarely than from close friends. In tight-knit groups, everyone tends to share and know the same stuff. But a casual acquaintance moves in different social circles and is likely to know different stuff. As a result, casual acquaintances, rather than close friends, are the leading source for new ideas and information.

The same dynamics are amplified online. It is easier to maintain loose connections, keeping up with past school friends, work colleagues or old acquaintances. The ease of online sharing creates a situation where the time and effort required to keep some kind of connection with weak ties alive is much lower than in an analogue world—a simple click will suffice. Out of the 229 "friends" the average American has on Facebook, a third are people whom they vaguely know or knew in the past. Having distant connections introduces a degree of serendipity. "The findings suggest that there is little validity to concerns that people who use social networking sites experience smaller social networks, less closeness, or are exposed to less diversity," concluded a 2011 Pew report.

THE AUDIENCE AS EDITOR

In the stacks at the library of the British Museum in London are copies of the *Evening Post*, the first evening newspaper in England, published in 1706. These early newspapers regularly left space at the end of the third page for people to add personal observations before sending it on to relatives in the country. The fourth page was blank so that the paper might be folded and addressed like an ordinary letter. (One newspaper referenced this in its full and rather cumbersome title: the *London Post, with the best Account of the whole Week's News, Foreign and Domestick; with Room left to write into the Country without the Charge of Double Postage*.) The *Evening Post* of August 10, 1710, bears a handwritten message from Thomas Walter to his brother William, who was at the family's estate in Chatham on the outskirts of London. Thomas brings to his brother's attention a report in the newspaper about price fluctuations in bank stock.

Thomas also added more personal messages. He describes his trip to London as "my worst passage" and writes that he has sent their mother "those things she desired." Other editions of the newspapers have messages to their father, Gabriel Walter.

Three centuries later, the descendants of the Walter family are probably adding their own observations to the news. Once again, they have the power to make editorial judgments for others on material that merits attention. But here's the paradox: we pick, choose and share more news and information than ever before, yet at the same time we expect to be told about what matters. Our behaviour challenges the notion of an informed citizenry that keeps abreast of events around them and is able to make educated choices based on accurate and reliable information.

The amount of news available at any time in any place on any piece of gear is overwhelming. There are so many news outlets filling airtime 24/7 to keep audiences watching, listening and clicking by squeezing just a little bit more from the day's events. Some of it is meaningful, but too much is PR masquerading as news. The important stuff is lost in the noise.

In his 1998 book, *The Good Citizen*, American journalism scholar Michael Schudson argued that the world had become too complex for citizens to be well informed about everything all the time, especially when it comes to public affairs. Schudson put forward the idea of the monitorial citizen. Instead of expecting citizens to be following everything, Schudson recommends that they should scan events around them and respond when required, similar to how parents act when watching over their children at a swimming pool.

When we select what to send on to friends, we are acting as monitorial citizens. There is a difference between deliberately taking on such a role and assuming it as a result of everyday actions. A minority of people go to the trouble of recommending stories on Facebook, ranging from a third in Italy and Spain to a fifth in the U.S. and less than a tenth in Germany and Japan. Many more, though, get their news from websites. Clicking to read a news story online is a way of voting for that item, and those decisions are often unwittingly shared with others.

Gatekeeping decisions are made visible to all by tools that aggregate editorial picks, such as the lists of most read or most emailed stories on news websites. Personal choices gain greater authority when they are seen collectively and reach beyond social circles to a much wider audience. As with the Sochi Olympics of 2014 and presidential debates of 2012, individual voices and actions, made visible and amassed through social networks, can shape how news is presented and understood.

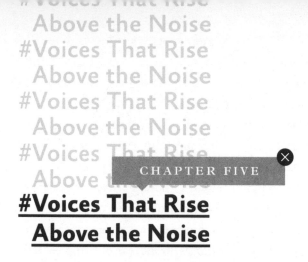

#Voices That Rise
Above the Noise
#Voices That Rise
Above the Noise
#Voices That Rise
Above the Noise
#Voices That Rise
Above the Noise

CHAPTER FIVE ✕

#Voices That Rise Above the Noise

THOUSANDS ANSWERED THE CALL FOR A NATIONWIDE DAY OF anger, crowding into Cairo's Tahrir Square to protest thirty years of corrupt, authoritarian rule. Eighteen days later, on February 11, 2011, President Hosni Mubarak stepped down.

Among those Egyptians facing the riot police with their tear gas and water cannon on that first day of the Arab Spring was twenty-four-year-old Gihan Ibrahim, who goes by Gigi. At the time, she was much like any other young adult. On her Facebook profile, she described herself as "a crazy-funny person, who enjoys company of cool people." Her musical tastes included Lady Gaga, Justin Timberlake, Coldplay and the trance tunes of Armin Van Buuren. Among her favourite TV shows were *CSI*, *Grey's Anatomy* and *The Daily Show*. How this young woman became one of the faces of the revolution reveals how some voices rise above the noise and make themselves heard, in both mainstream and social media, while others go unheeded.

In the 1960s, Andy Warhol declared that in the future everyone would be world-famous for fifteen minutes. Now everyone can be famous in 140 characters. Never has it been easier, cheaper or faster to broadcast to millions. The idea of the Internet as a place where anyone can be heard is woven into the lore of the web. Back in 1996, retired Wyoming cattle rancher and former Grateful Dead lyricist John Perry Barlow issued "A Declaration of the Independence of Cyberspace." It imagines a world where "all may enter without privilege or prejudice accorded by race, economic power, military force, or station of birth." In this utopian space, anyone "may express his or her beliefs, no matter how singular, without fear of being coerced into silence or conformity."

Barlow was overly optimistic. The problem isn't having a voice; it is getting attention. Being noticed requires the right mix of timing and topicality, as well as of network and audience. During the Egyptian uprising, bloggers, activists and intellectuals tried to grab the attention of the world with their experiences, opinions, photos and videos. Often, they delivered raw emotional testimonies about violence by pro-Mubarak thugs. Thousands of people expressed their desire for a better life using smartphones, Facebook, Twitter and YouTube after decades of state censorship and repression. Gigi threw herself into the protests in Tahrir Square, charting the hopes and fears of the demonstrators on social media. She sent a steady stream of 140-character messages on Twitter, posted photos to Flickr and shared videos on YouTube capturing the struggles and aspirations of a nation demanding change. In an interview with *The New York Times*, Gigi explained that she was "trying to spread accurate information and paint a picture at the ground for people who aren't here, via Twitter and Facebook."

Gigi's Facebook profile pointed to the activist within. She listed as her key interests politics, news and human rights, as well as watching soccer and being happy. One of her favourite quotes is from Karl Marx: "Every struggle is a class struggle." She declared her passion for politics and talked about "planning to have a career in it somehow (not a politician) but more as a revolutionary professional (go figure out that)." During those tumultuous weeks in Egypt, Gigi became a "revolutionary professional." Her voice was heard across the world, rising above the cacophony of dissent during a period that saw the most dramatic increase in freedom of expression in the region.

Her accounts of the struggle for the soul of Egypt reached far and wide. She was one of the group of bloggers, activists and intellectuals who became influential on social media. During this time, people turned to Facebook, Twitter and YouTube for the latest from Tahrir, alongside the reports from journalists from major media outlets such as CNN and Al Jazeera. Gigi was one of these unlikely sources, known on Twitter as Gsquare86. When the Western media reflected on the fall of Mubarak, Gigi was among those featured prominently as representing the protesters. By then, she had gone from being an unknown Egyptian student to being an influencer.

THE INFLUENTIALS

The notion that some people act as filters in the flow of information is one of the most prevailing theories of communication. Sociologists Paul Lazarsfeld, Bernard Berelson and Hazel Gaudet first introduced the idea of key opinion leaders in their 1944 book, *The People's Choice*. They came up with a surprising result when they interviewed 2,400 U.S. citizens to find out how they decided to vote in a presidential election. The newspapers and radio weren't nearly as powerful in shaping political views as they imagined. Most people got their information second-hand, through a two-step flow of communication. A select few within the community acted as a filter between the media and the mass public. They were the opinion leaders to whom others turned for news and information

In the world of marketing, these are the key audiences that can generate buzz for a brand among their social circles. It is why Red Bull recently sent free samples of three new flavours to 17,500 British university students identified as trendsetters. The presumption is that, if the students can be persuaded to adopt the new flavours, then others will follow, regardless of whether the new line is any better or worse than other products. Marketing experts Ed Keller and Jon Berry popularized the idea of Influentials in their 2003 book of the same name. Influentials are the 10 per cent of Americans who are engaged with their communities, have a voracious appetite for news and information, and know lots of people. Keller and Berry identified their Influentials as people in their forties with a college education, married with children, who tend to own their own homes. Reach them, and your message will spread to others. Malcolm Gladwell picked up on the idea in *The Tipping Point,* with stories of how a few plugged-in individuals could make or break a product or idea.

Social media hasn't done away with Influentials. It has just made it much harder to predict in advance who will be influential, about what and when. Most things don't just go viral. One of the most contagious viral videos of 2012 was *Kony 2012,* produced by the nonprofit campaign group Invisible Children. The video told a compelling story that touched a nerve with audiences. But it didn't just catch on by accident. By the time of its release, Invisible Children had been around for eight years, building up a robust network of supporters, particularly among college students. The organization targeted its 180,000 supporters on Twitter to amplify its message and urge others to spread the video. Actors and musicians soon took up the rallying call, many at the beck and call of their fans. The hashtags #kony2012 and #stopkony became a worldwide phenomenon on Twitter.

But who would have bet on a Norwegian comedy duo having the top viral video of 2013? Bård Ylvisåker and Vegard Ylvisåker, known as Ylvis, captured the Internet's attention with the bizarre "What Does the Fox Say?" It was part of a promotional campaign for their talk show on Norwegian TV. The video caught the eye of web comic Jeff Wysaski, who shared it on his popular Tumblr blog, *Pleated Jeans*. It then appeared on Gawker, was featured on YouTube's Twitter account and was tweeted by actress and self-confessed new media geek Felicia Day. And suddenly, everyone seemed to be asking, "What *does* the fox say?" And then wondering how to get the infernal tune out of their head.

HOW INFLUENCE PLAYS OUT ON SOCIAL MEDIA

The secret to becoming an Influential on social media is that there isn't one. The alchemy of influence is erratic and elusive. Scientists who study how information spreads through social networks have found that it is difficult to predict with any certainty whose content will be most shared. One of them is Duncan Watts, a network theory scientist who joined Microsoft

Research in 2012, after five years at Yahoo! Research. Watts has made a name for himself by questioning the whole idea of Influentials. "A rare bunch of cool people just don't have that power. And when you test the way marketers say the world works, it falls apart," he argues.

During his time at Yahoo! Research, Watts worked with fellow scientists Sharad Goel and Daniel Goldstein to test how information spread on different online services. One experiment involved leaving comments about acts of kindness on a website and sharing those with friends. Another looked at videos shared by instant messaging. One involved the circulation of news stories and video on Twitter. Information tended to travel only from an individual to close friends and no further. Regardless of the different experiments, the comments, videos or tweets didn't spread like an epidemic across the Internet. "Our findings," they concluded, "indicate that strategies based on triggering 'social epidemics' are likely unrealistic." It explains why your friend's cute cat doesn't become an overnight sensation when he or she posts yet another amusing video to YouTube.

Standing out among the millions of messages flowing on Twitter is even harder. For another study, Watts and other scientists at Yahoo! Research tried to identify opinion leaders on Twitter by analyzing how information spread on the network. They examined 1.6 million users who shared an average of forty-six links each. They came to two seemingly contradictory conclusions. Some influencers are easy to identify; they are those who have been influential in the past and amassed a substantial following, so they are more likely to be influential in the future. They tend to be personalities who enjoy a high profile in the world of politics, business or culture, such as Felicia Day.

The actress has built up a core and loyal fan base through her appearance on the TV show *Eureka* and her work with Joss Whedon. When she urged her more than two million followers on Twitter to find out what the fox said, they listened.

Once we look beyond celebrities, politicians or TV personalities, it becomes much harder to predict who will be the loudest voice on Twitter at any particular time. The research casts doubt on the strategies of companies who attempt to target specific individuals on social media to help promote their brand. Posting on Twitter is like dropping a pebble in the ocean; most tweets barely cause a ripple, let alone amount to anything like a wave. Information tends to go no further than a close circle of friends and acquaintances, regardless of the importance of the message.

That's what happened to Aja Dior. On Saturday, February 11, 2012, the American teenager heard from her aunt that Whitney Houston had died. She forwarded the news immediately, tweeting: "omgg , my aunt tiffany who work for whitney houston just found whitney houston dead in the tub . such ashame & sad :-(." Dior was the first person to break the news. Given the forty-eight-year-old Houston's fame—based first on her career as a singer and actress and latterly on her drug problem and abusive marriage—Dior's scoop should have caught on. It appeared to cite a credible source, and the poor grammar and typos gave the tweet an authentic feel. Yet the message faded into Twitter's archive.

It wasn't until forty-two minutes later that the world learnt of the passing of Whitney Houston, when the Associated Press agency sent out a news alert on Twitter. "Breaking: Publicist Kristen Foster says singer Whitney Houston has died at age 48." The AP message spread far and wide, with at least ten thousand people retweeting it. Celebrities like Justin Bieber, Lil Wayne and Katy Perry immediately brought hundreds of thousands of fans into the loop. In the first hour after the news broke, there were almost two and a half million tweets as people expressed their sorrow and paid tribute.

Aja Dior's message languished in obscurity until researchers went back to analyze how news of Whitney Houston's death spread on social media. One of these researchers was Gilad Lotan, who wondered why no one had picked up on Dior's tweet. At the time, he was vice-president of research and development at the social media marketing company Social Flow, earning a living by making sense of the flows of information through social networks. When he looked at the data, he found that Aja Dior's news only reached fifteen people. The teenager was part of a tight-knit set of friends. None of them was well connected or prominent enough for the news to travel beyond the group. Aja Dior had three of the ingredients for success: a topical piece of information at the right time for a receptive audience. But she didn't have the connections to make it go beyond her immediate social network. Her tweet was lost in the sheer volume of experiences, opinions, photos and videos shared on Twitter, Facebook and YouTube.

Infinite information competes for finite attention. To paraphrase Thomas Hobbes, the life of an idea on social media is brutish and short. Indiana University researchers created a virtual Twitterverse to examine the lifespan of an idea, based on 120 million retweets from 12.5 million users and 1.3 million hashtags. Rather than look at the sharing of one piece of information, they tested what happens when multiple ideas are trying to catch on simultaneously. It was as if they were constantly releasing a bunch of diseases in a city to see which ones infected the most people.

The results embody a marketer's worst nightmare. It turns out that an idea can sometimes go viral just by chance. It doesn't need an influential figure to be promoting it, and it doesn't need to be particularly clever or quirky. In the survival of the fittest on social media, the personal power of any one personality can be negated by the choices of hundreds of thousands of others. The researchers don't discount the fact that some messages are more interesting than others, or that some people have greater impact than others. But they caution against overestimating the importance of Influencers. When something goes viral, "you don't have to assume it's because some people are influential. You can still get some random thing that gets 50 million views on YouTube," said Filippo Menczer, one of the co-authors of the study.

It is a problem of demand and supply. More and more is being shared, but the supply of attention is fixed. Social media can only support a limited number of ideas at any one time. As new ideas rise, others become extinct. While some things become extremely popular, the vast majority die off quickly. Rising above the noise is not just about being a well-connected Influential plugged into the right networks. Equally important is saying something that resonates with what people are talking about. For Gigi Ibrahim, the topicality and timing of her work helped her connect with the others who could help to amplify her voice, through a process that involved both traditional mass media and social media.

HOW RESONANCE AFFECTS INFLUENCE

At the start of January 2011, Gigi attended a candlelit vigil in downtown Cairo for the twenty-one people killed in a suicide bombing of a Coptic Christian church a week earlier. She documented her experience at the vigil on Twitter, Facebook and YouTube, and she came to the attention of Robert Mackey at *The New York Times*. He writes a blog called *The Lede*, which reflects on the news and draws on the information from the web and social media. (His blog is named after the term traditionally used to describe the first paragraph of a news story. It dates back to the days of hot metal typesetting, where the alternative spelling was used to distinguish it from the lead using in printing.)

Mackey wrote a blog post about the vigil, based largely on Gigi's material. When the uprising started on January 25, Mackey included her in his post for *The Lede* featuring YouTube videos of the protests. Her voice was further amplified when she was featured in a 1,500-word story on the first day of protests by the Associated Press. The AP sends out its news stories to around 1,400 U.S. daily newspapers and thousands of television and radio stations. The article described the clashes between Egyptian police and demonstrators in Tahrir Square, citing Gigi as an eyewitness. Her testimony was picked up by U.S. news outlets like *USA Today*, *The Boston Globe* and Fox News, as well as by the BBC. In the coming days, she was frequently interviewed by BBC domestic programs, as well as by the BBC World Service.

Within a month, Gigi Ibrahim became the face of the revolution for much of the Western media. In February, the flagship current-affairs show on PBS, *Frontline,* aired a short documentary called *Gigi's Revolution*. When it was broadcast on *NewsHour*, host Judy Woodruff touted Ibrahim as "a symbol of the uprising." Around the same time, she was featured on the BBC's equivalent news and current affairs show, *Newsnight*, where she was introduced as one of the unofficial leaders of the protests. She even made the front cover of *Time* magazine at the end of February as a member of "The Generation Changing the World."

A woman who describes herself as a revolutionary socialist came to be feted in the U.S., where the term "socialist" is used to smear and discredit politicians. The media chose to ignore her politics and focus instead on aspects of her identity that resonated with audiences in the U.S. For a start, Gigi Ibrahim was no ordinary Egyptian. She came from one of Egypt's elite families. Though she was born in the southern California coastal city of Long Beach, she was raised from the age of two in Egypt. When she turned fourteen, she returned to California to go to high school and college. But the lure of Egypt drew her back in 2008. "I consider myself as a person with a bipolar identity of part free-spirit American and part just simply angry Egyptian," she shared on Facebook. In Cairo, she attended the American University in Cairo, becoming a student activist and graduating with a degree in political science in 2010.

As an American-Egyptian woman often described as attractive, Gigi was an ideal bridge between Egypt and the West. She offered journalists a model eyewitness. Finding a good interviewee is golden in journalism. Reporters turn to eyewitnesses to lend authenticity to their reporting, as such accounts have the feel of truth. They are the voices of "real people," rather than officials in suits.

Given a choice, anglophone journalists will gravitate towards sources who speak English, especially if they work in TV or radio. Gigi was a gift for English-language news outlets. Her English was flawless, as she had grown up in the U.S. and had attended the English-language American University. She made for an eloquent eyewitness who could express the frustrations of a generation in a way that resonated with audiences back in the West.

Like many of the activists in Egypt, Gigi realized the power of speaking in English. Her updates on social media tended to be in English. Others were posting in English to attract international attention and reach people outside the country. Almost three-quarters of the tweets sent from Egypt between January 25 and the fall of Mubarak on February 11 were in English. As has become the norm during major news events, journalists scoured social media for reports, photos and videos of the latest from Egypt. Activists who shared information in English were far more likely to be picked up by the media.

One of the leading media professionals who turned to social media to report on Egypt was Andy Carvin. A former social media strategist for U.S. public radio broadcaster NPR, Carvin became a one-man clearinghouse for news on the Arab Spring. From Washington, D.C., he selected bits and pieces from social media to share, spitting out thousands of messages seven days a week for up to sixteen hours a day on Twitter. He amassed tens of thousands of followers for his personal newswire of minute-by-minute accounts of the Arab Spring. Activists tweeting in English heavily influenced his reporting. During the Egyptian uprising, his most retweeted sources were activists, among them Gigi Ibrahim. Accounts from activists made up just under half of his messages, meaning Carvin gave a higher priority to the messages from citizens who were expressing their demands for social change, recording and sharing their experiences on Twitter.

Language is only part of the story. Activists such as Gigi Ibrahim had a message that the West wanted to hear. She stood as a symbol of a nation struggling to shake off the yoke of three decades of Mubarak's rule. In many ways, she represented what many in the West want to see in the Middle East: well-educated liberals who aspire to life, liberty and the pursuit of happiness. The media in the West reflected this aspiration in their coverage. The press is presumed to report events accurately and without bias, but media coverage tends to mirror prevailing attitudes in society. News editors strive to be in step with the views and values of their readers, reflecting and reinforcing their view of the world. Media coverage of a topic shifts as attitudes change, such as on the issue of gay marriage.

In Western liberal democracies, the protests in Egypt and across the Middle East were seen as uprisings against unjust and corrupt regimes, and the media echoed this viewpoint. *The Guardian* and the *International Herald Tribune* favoured the protesters in their coverage and gave far more space to opposition voices than to pro-government representatives. The state media in China reflected the political agenda of the regime there; the English edition of the *People's China Daily* devoted more inches to pro-government voices and avoided writing about corrupt officials or human rights abuses. In contrast, much of the U.S. media was dismissive of the Occupy Wall Street movement rather than portraying it as an uprising against the excesses of an unjust and unbridled economic system.

At the time of the Egyptian uprising, the idea of a technologically savvy youth armed with camera phones and Facebook pages overthrowing a corrupt regime was a seductive one. Individuals like Gigi did play a role, but so did thousands more in their forties and fifties, fed up with years of oppression, economic stagnation and high unemployment. Yet the media tended to highlight youth, such as another young female activist, Mona Seif.

A twentysomething university graduate, Mona grew up in a family of activists. Like Gigi, she took it upon herself to document the fight for freedom. She, too, was cited as an eyewitness by the BBC, *The New York Times* and MSNBC. The U.K. newspaper *The Independent* profiled her in a story headlined QUIET HEROINES WHOSE COURAGE HAS HELPED KEEP UPRISING GOING, which also mentioned Gigi Ibrahim. Al Jazeera English featured both graduates as "women of the revolution."

Gigi, Mona and others like them were the acceptable face of the uprising, rather than the bearded sheikhs associated with Egypt's banned Islamic movement, the Muslim Brotherhood. Yet when Egyptians voted for a parliament after the fall of Mubarak, they overwhelmingly chose the Muslim Brotherhood's Freedom and Justice Party. The hardline Salafist Nour Party came second. Liberal and secular parties were trailing in the wake of the Islamic parties. A year later came a military coup.

The public in the West didn't want to hear the story of Islamic parties coming to power. They wanted to hear about brave young demonstrators who were sharing their experiences on social media. For a message to catch on, it has to resonate with a significant number of people who are receptive to it. An idea has to be timely, topical and reach an audience primed to share it.

Network scientist Duncan Watts likens this to the conditions for a forest fire. A single match is unlikely to start a blaze in damp weather. But it could spark an inferno in a parched forest where brushwood litters the ground. "When this critical mass existed, even an average individual was capable of triggering a large cascade," he argues, "just as any spark will suffice to trigger a large forest fire when the conditions are primed for it."

Individuals like Gigi Ibrahim and Mona Seif found fertile ground in journalists hungry for eyewitnesses who could embody the values of democracy. But they also found a willing audience on social media. The newspapers, TV and radio played a part in highlighting their voices, but so did the tens of thousands of people on Twitter. The dynamics of how information flows through social media means ordinary people can collectively affect whose voices rises to the top.

HOW THE CROWD ASSIGNS INFLUENCE

During the winter of 2012, politics in Canada was dominated by demonstrations by the Idle No More movement. The protests were triggered by concerns over the impact of a federal omnibus bill on land, water and aboriginal rights. What started out as an indigenous movement grew to encompass environmentalists and opponents of the Conservative government of Stephen Harper. As with the Arab Spring and Occupy, the movement turned to social media to mobilize supporters and amplify their message under the umbrella of the #Idlenomore hashtag on Twitter. The voices that rose to prominence on the network were in stark contrast to those in the mass media.

Press reports quoted government ministers, MPs, indigenous leaders and experts discussing the significance of the protests. It's the way the news works. Journalists tend to turn to people in positions of power as sources of information, be they politicians, business leaders or police. They derive their authority and credibility from their institutional status. People in positions of power gain more influence through the media because they are considered influential to start with. On the other hand, the media will tend to marginalize voices considered deviant, for example, members of the Occupy Movement.

Who gets to speak through the media fundamentally affects the way events are interpreted. A police spokesperson commenting on an Idle No More protest will highlight the need for law and order. The demonstrators will have a different perspective, often arguing that police curbed their right to be heard. But the media tend to rely on the police perspective to report on what happened. How the protests are reported and interpreted will be shaped by the police, rather than the activist, perspective.

A different story can emerge from social media coming from different sources chosen by the crowd, rather than by journalists. The act of sharing is a way of assigning influence to particular messages and specific people. Multiply this by thousands of retweets, and collectively, the crowd is casting votes on who should be heard. At the height of the Idle No More protests in December 2011 and January 2012, the most retweeted messages came from activists. People engaged with the cause through #Idlenomore decided who mattered, leading to the rise of some unlikely Influentials such as Patricia Stein, a Lakota from North Dakota.

At the time, Stein's Twitter handle was @pygmysioux. She later changed it to @SiouxweetNSauer. She had been living in Egypt since 2010, teaching English and art to young children. When she heard of the protests in Canada, she decided to hold her own demonstration outside the Canadian embassy in Cairo. On December 21, 2011, she stood outside the building with two signs. One had the name of the movement over a painting of an indigenous dancer. The other said HARPER WILL NOT SILENCE ME. The Aboriginal Peoples Television Network (APTN) reported on Stein's protest. The story was posted on the Idle No More Facebook page, further raising her profile among the supporters. Stein went on to become one of the most retweeted voices on #Idlenomore.

Her story illustrates how ordinary individuals can become Influentials through the collective decisions of thousands on Twitter. Sociologist Zeynep Tufekci describes them as networked microcelebrity activists. They are politically motivated individuals who use social media to build support for a cause. Their brand of activism mixes journalism and advocacy. They take part in protests and share their accounts, often using sympathetic and emotional language that resonates with like-minded individuals. At first, they get attention from other people on Twitter, but their microcelebrity breaks out of social media when they are featured in the traditional media.

It's what happened to Gigi Ibrahim. On the first day of the uprising on January 25, Gigi was one of the people who provided a steady stream of practical tips for the protesters. "People going to Shubra please tell us how you got there. Massara station is not close it is just surrounded with heavy security #Jan25," she tweeted. Throughout the day, she warned about blocked streets, the closures of metro stations and the location of police, and shared photos of the situation on the ground. She provided details that others considered important and passed on to their circle of contacts. Gigi had timely and topical information for an audience hungry for it.

Her reporting on the day brought her to the attention of prominent Egyptian activists. Within Egypt, respected dissidents circulated her updates to their networks. They included political activists and bloggers Wael Khalil and Alaa Abd El-Fattah. Outside of the country, the Egyptian-American journalist Mona Eltahawy, a prominent speaker on Arab issues based in New York, recommended that others follow Gigi. It meant that her account of the unfolding protest on January 25 was expeditiously exchanged and transmitted to tens of thousands of people inside and outside of Egypt. Gigi became a networked microcelebrity whose status was further enhanced when she was featured in the mass media.

She was part of a group of activists, bloggers and intellectuals that emerged as opinion leaders as their messages were retweeted by thousands. Other influential voices were Wael Ghonim, the senior Google executive who set up the Facebook page that contributed to sparking the uprising, and Mona Seif. People were voting for their alternative sources for news from Egypt. Individual acts across the network were collectively deciding whom to trust for the latest from Tahrir Square.

Influence is complicated when it comes to social media. Some of the old rules still apply, but the dynamics of who decides who is important are far more complex. Some people rise to prominence to become opinion leaders on social media through a layered process that combines old and new media. Once they have reached a certain standing, they benefit from the "rich get richer" feedback loop.

It is just much harder to figure out from the start who will be noticed and become an Influential. Ordinary people can emerge as thought leaders through a bottom-up process. A mass of others on the network can chose whom to listen to. The attention of the media and of prominent figures matters. But the timing and nature of the message is crucial. To survive and thrive in a fast-moving marketplace of ideas, the message needs to find a receptive audience excited to share the news with others.

for the Planet
#A Nervous System
for the Planet
#A Nervous System
for the Planet
#A Nervous System
for the

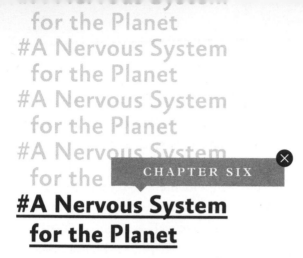

CHAPTER SIX

#A Nervous System
for the Planet

Shinya Takatori was at home in Yamagata when he felt the first rumblings of the biggest earthquake to ever hit Japan. At first, on that Friday afternoon of March 11, 2011, Shinya wasn't sure what was going on. At 2:46 P.M. local time, there had been an 8.9-magnitude tremor some seventy kilometres off the coast of northern Japan. Though he felt the tremors, Shinya emerged unscathed, as Yamagata is far inland. The massive quake caused widespread power outages and fires and a tsunami that laid waste to everything in its path. Thousands were killed, and more than half a million displaced. At the nearby Fukushima power plant, there was a nuclear meltdown.

For Shinya, his immediate concern was for his friends in the port of Sendai. A ten-metre wall of water had struck the city, sweeping away buildings, cars and even planes on the airport's runway. Shinya, a dance DJ and electronic musician, knew the city well. He would regularly make the one-hour commute to Sendai to earn a little bit of extra money by working in a music store. Having been born and raised in the northern province of Tohoku, which had been hit by the tsunami, he was worried about the fate of friends and family. With fires raging across the region, power lines down and a patchy phone network, Shinya turned to Twitter. "Yamagata is pretty much OK. I can't get through to Sendai. Twitter is basically the only way," said one of his tweets.

In the hours following the earthquake and tsunami, the volume of messages on Twitter hit more than 5,000 per second at five separate times. By the end of the day of the quake and tsunami, some 177 million tweets had been sent, compared to an average of fifty million one year earlier. The number of tweets from Japan increased by 500 per cent as survivors reached out to friends, relatives and colleagues in North America, Europe and Asia. They were all, like Shinya, fulfilling a basic human need to connect and communicate. Tales of survival and of loss unfolded at lightning speed in 140-character bites across the web, weaving a patchwork of human fragility in the face of the fearsome power of nature.

Technology has changed the nature of crisis communications in the twenty-first century. The availability of instant information is reshaping how society learns and responds to crises in the hours and days that follow. The ubiquitous cell phone, near-universal connectivity, and free and easy sharing services create an infrastructure that enables words, images and video to spread almost instantly.

During a crisis, timely information can be a matter of life and death. Such information coming from the people in the midst of disaster can help to inform, speed up and improve the emergency response. At the best of times, it can overcome the gulf between the reality on the ground and assumptions about what is needed. The way word of mouth fills the news vacuum following a natural disaster has much in common with how it used to do in the past.

FAST NEWS IN OLD TIMES

All Saints' Day on November 1, 1755, was a beautiful Sunday morning, with clear skies and a dazzling sun. Across Lisbon, the faithful were crammed into the city's great majestic cathedrals and smaller churches to mark one of the holiest days of the Roman Catholic calendar. At the time, Lisbon was a thriving port and one of the most beautiful cities in Europe, legendary for its commercial prosperity and cultural sophistication. In a matter of hours, a natural disaster on the scale of the Japanese quake and tsunami of 2011 reduced to rubble the city's sumptuous palaces, imposing cathedrals and grand mansions.

As priests led the pious in prayers, an earthquake off the coast in the Atlantic Ocean sent shockwaves through Portugal and western Europe. Over ten minutes, three seismic shocks struck Lisbon, destroying buildings and enveloping the city in a thick blanket of dust that blocked out the sun. One of the few contemporary accounts of the cataclysmic event is found in a letter by a visiting Anglican pastor, Richard Goddard. "No words can express the horror of my situation at that instant, involved in almost total darkness, surrounded with a city falling into ruins, and crowds of people screaming, and calling out for mercy," he wrote about the first few minutes of the quake.

The worst was far from over, as a series of gigantic waves pounded the waterfront. The water swallowed up warships and merchant vessels in the port and flattened the warehouses that lined the harbour. Fires broke out across Lisbon, many sparked by candles lit in devotion to mark All Saints' Day. The fires quickly engulfed the city as flames spread through the narrow streets and enveloped the timber houses of the city's medieval centre. There was barely a building untouched by the combination of tremors, water and fire.

News of the catastrophe spread across the continent the same way it does now: through first-person observations, secondhand reports, rumours and speculation. First accounts of the earthquake were shared by word of mouth, and travelled as fast as a horse could gallop. It took about a week to ten days for the news to circulate in Spain and about a fortnight for it to reach London and Paris. The first official account reached England on November 10, in a despatch sent by the influential British ambassador to Spain, Sir Benjamin Keene.

The news spread quickly for the time, but it was met with incredulity. The notion that one of the most celebrated cities in Europe could be wiped off the face of the earth was too shocking for many. It was simply unbelievable that Lisbon, one of the most devout cities on the continent, would be singled out by what many saw as the wrath of God. It didn't help that the initial reports were often embellished and contradictory, much as happens now on social media. In the absence of timely and reliable information, Europeans exchanged stories, opinions, rumours and theories for months following the disaster.

It was weeks and months before the full extent of the 1755 disaster in Portugal became apparent. Even three weeks after the tragedy, the left-wing *London Magazine*, subtitled *The Gentleman's Monthly Intelligencer*, expressed doubts about the veracity of some of the accounts, saying "we must wait for more exact accounts." By the turn of 1756, the earthquake was "still on people's lips," reported the German *Gazette de Cologne*.

The speed at which people heard of the tragedy that befell Lisbon in the eighteenth century was extremely slow compared to the pace of news in the twenty-first. But there is much similarity between the events in Portugal and in Japan. In both cases, tales of shaking buildings, massive waves and human loss were spread by word of mouth through conversations or letters. In 1755, these stories were amplified by the media of the time: cheap pamphlets and early newspapers. They were then passed on in family letters, pamphlets, engravings and poems that mixed fact and fiction and sensationalized the tragedy. Today, the same process takes place at a much more accelerated pace, where days become minutes and weeks are hours.

No one is sure how many people died in what became known as the Great Lisbon Earthquake, but historians estimate that between thirty and forty thousand perished in the city alone. By the end of the disaster, only three thousand homes were left standing out of an estimated twenty thousand. The Japanese quake and resulting tsunami of 2011 killed 15,853 people and injured 6,023. A year after the disaster, 3,282 people were still missing and more than 330,000 were living in temporary accommodation. Whole communities were swept away by the crushing tidal wave. The scale of the destruction is hard to capture in numbers. Almost 300,000 buildings were levelled, and a million more were damaged. At times of a natural disaster like the Japan quake and tsunami, minutes matter.

A NETWORK OF PEOPLE SENSORS

Early warning of a quake could give someone in the affected area just enough time to turn off the gas or dive for cover under a table. But it can take several minutes before monitoring stations detect seismic activity, and several more minutes before an official announcement is broadcast to the nation. People are much better sensors of immediate danger. Thanks to the Internet, smartphones and Twitter, they not only get the news out faster than official sources but also with surprising reliability. And people are very good at telling everyone when the ground shakes.

One of the first studies to show the value of monitoring Twitter for quake information came out of Japan, a country prone to tremors. A team of researchers at the University of Tokyo developed a computer program to monitor Twitter for news about quakes. They ran it during August and September 2009. Over that period, there were ten earthquakes in Japan. Their system detected all the quakes that were powerful enough to be felt by people in a building. The scientists found that the first reports of shaking or swaying came within a minute of an earthquake. By watching for tweets mentioning shaking buildings, the researchers were able to send alerts at least five minutes sooner than a broadcast announcement by the Japan Meteorological Agency.

Today, one of the ways the U.S. Geological Survey (USGS) keeps tabs on earthquakes is by monitoring Twitter. People can either follow alerts on quakes picked up by its seismic equipment or its Tweet Earthquake Dispatch. TED has proved to be remarkably good at detecting the first signs of an earthquake on Twitter. In one of its first experiments run over five months in 2009, TED was able to spot forty-eight earthquakes across the world just by analyzing Twitter. In 75 per cent of cases, it was able to detect the tremors within two minutes. At the time, a scientifically verified alert by the USGS could take anywhere from two to twenty minutes. In the case of the 2011 Japan earthquake, the USGS first detected the disaster 3.8 minutes after the first tremor and sent out its first official warning of a tsunami in just under ten minutes.

Quake detection by tweets works because it is such an "OMG" experience that most people feel compelled to share it with others. It is the one of the most interesting examples of how strangers are brought together by social media technologies into an instant, ad hoc network of sensors. But relying on people as sensors has its limits. Thousands of quakes are either too small to produce noticeable shaking or they take place in remote regions. No tweets means no quake is reported. Tremors in urban centres, where everyone has a smartphone, are more readily reported. When there was an earthquake in Marina Del Rey, California, in July 2012, TED noticed it within twenty-four seconds as an average of two thousand tweets per minute was sent. It took TED two minutes and thirty seconds to discern a similar tremor in Indonesia, where there was only an average of 127 tweets per minute. Once the world is alerted to a crisis, the emergency response kicks in.

COLLECTIVE INTELLIGENCE

At 5 P.M. local time, photographer Frederic Dupoux sent out what was possibly the first recorded tweet of an event that would reshape Haiti forever. "On shiet [sic] heavy earthquake right now! In Haiti," he wrote on January 12, 2010. Within minutes, dozens of people rushed to report on what was happening. "Earthquake 7 Richter scale just happening #Haiti," said FutureHaiti. In those first few hours, social media was one of the few ways to get any sense of the impact of the earthquake. In forty seconds, 70 per cent of the capital, Port-au-Prince, lay in ruins, as did other towns and cities. An estimated 220,000 died and 1.5 million became homeless.

As the international community geared up to help, Haitians sent hundreds of thousands of text messages, tweets, videos and images, composing a vivid immediate picture of the devastation. Despite being one of the poorest countries in the world, most Haitian households had access to a cell phone. Only a third of cell towers in Port-au-Prince survived the quake, but the network was quickly repaired. Among the tales of survival was the story of a Canadian woman trapped under rubble. She managed to send a text message to the Foreign Affairs office in Ottawa, some three thousand kilometres away. She told them she was safe and gave her location. The message was relayed to Canadian diplomats in Haiti, who quickly arranged her rescue.

With reports from citizens gathered from text messages, Twitter and Facebook, relief workers were able to map needs as they arose. When the relief teams got to Haiti, some then used social media to help coordinate where to send doctors, patients and medical supplies. "Without information sharing, there can be no coordination. If we are not talking to each other and sharing information, then we go back thirty years," reflected Ramiro Galvez, who was in charge of operations for the UN Disaster Assessment and Coordination mission during the Haiti disaster.

Thirty years ago, they would depend on reaching affected areas, making notes on clipboards and using radios to send the information back to base, where someone added pins on a paper map to document the crisis. In 2010, the wealth of

information from people caught in the disaster helped to mitigate the impact and speed up recovery. "On the timeline of the
Internet's evolution, the 2010 Haiti earthquake response will
be remembered as the moment when the level of access to
mobile and online communication enabled a kind of collective
intelligence to emerge," concluded the Harvard Humanitarian
Initiative in a report for the United Nations Foundation.

The Haiti earthquake wasn't the first time when people in
the midst of a natural disaster turned to new communication
technologies. A handful of residents used Twitter at the time of
the 2007 southern California wildfires that destroyed nearly
1,500 homes. Far more were tweeting a year later, as Hurricanes
Gustav and Ike struck the coasts of Louisiana and Texas in
September. With Haiti, the world sat up and took note of how a
real-time communications network can literally save lives, but
also challenge agencies unaccustomed to coping with so much
instant information. A huge amount of data needs to be collected
and analyzed in a timely manner. It then needs to be added to
the array of information sources already used by relief agencies
to direct the appropriate resources to where they are needed.

The speed and volume of messages in the immediate aftermath of a disaster can help or hinder. Vital updates and appeals
for help are mixed in with irrelevant information and spam
messages, making it hard to separate the important from the
trivial from the redundant in a constantly updating stream of
data. During the crisis in Haiti, one of the challenges for the
rescuers was the number of false leads about people who were
still alive but trapped in the rubble. Many came from family
members who wanted help in recovering the body of a dead
relative. The problem shifts from not having enough

information to collating and analyzing a flash flood of data. But there are patterns that can help to extract knowledge from raw, real-time data.

THE RHYTHMS OF INSTANT NEWS

On the evening of October 29, 2012, as Superstorm Sandy hit the eastern seaboard of the U.S., a Con Edison substation exploded in Manhattan's East Village. It plunged much of lower Manhattan into darkness. Around the same time, use of Twitter in New York went through the roof. Millions were without power, but they could still connect to the Internet on their cell phones and tablets. Over the night and the coming days, Twitter once again emerged as a main channel to spread information and updates from the authorities, media and ordinary citizens. There were more than twenty million tweets about the storm between October 27 and November 1, double the number from earlier in the week. The torrent of constant updates on Twitter looks like chaos itself. But there is a rhythm to the messages. Understanding the pulse of tweets during a crisis helps to identify and focus on potentially lifesaving information.

The first wave in a crisis is made up of eyewitness accounts from those in the eye of the storm. People living through the disaster are driven to share their shock, warn others or appeal for help. Tweets from Miyagi, the area worst affected by the 2011 Japanese quake, captured the horror of the day. "We've been having frequent aftershocks. A tsunami alarm has been announced. Escape immediately," urged one message. Another read: "Buildings are burning and this is like a battlefield."

Among the real-time reports were dramatic appeals for help. "We're on the 7th floor of Inawashiro Hospital, but because of the risen sea level, we're stuck. Help us!!"

These firsthand accounts tend to account for only a minority of the overall volume. Such messages are soon overtaken by others providing information about a crisis. Tweets sharing news and information tend to make up the largest number of messages. During Superstorm Sandy, such messages accounted for a third of all tweets. Some are updates about the latest developments, while others give background and context. Official reports are complemented, rather than usurped, by first-person observations. Mixed in with updates from news outlets and the authorities are tidbits from citizens providing detailed local information, from fallen trees to downed power lines. When storms battered Memphis in April 2011, residents shared updates on the latest weather conditions in their neighbourhood using the #memstorm hashtag. They filled a gap left by news outlets and officials by taking a microscopic look at the areas affected by the storms.

It has also become common for people to shoot photos and videos of a disaster to share with the world. Just about every cell phone has a camera, making it easy to take a snapshot and post it online. During Sandy, the second-largest number of tweets involved people sharing photos or videos. There were photos of flooded streets and of local landmarks submerged by water as people documented the disaster. The images create a vivid, visual record of a crisis as it happens. But it also gives rise to faked images, though others then heavily contest these on Twitter.

The volume of messages on Twitter during a crisis is deceptive. Not only are a small minority from people actually on the ground, but many others are not original messages. Instead, they are retweets as people pass on the messages of others. At the time of the floods in Queensland, Australia, in January 2011, 50 to 60 per cent of messages with the #qldfloods hashtag were retweets. The retweet works as an informal recommendation system used to make some information more visible. People come together as a transient news crowd on Twitter to make sense of an event, filter relevant information and spread it via their networks. Concerned citizens take it upon themselves to focus almost exclusively on amplifying emergency information, usually by posting statements from the media and emergency service providers. Time-sensitive information can get a boost and reach a much wider audience than if it were just sent by a journalist or official.

As news of a disaster sinks in, there are messages of support and condolences. But some also turn to humour, which is known to be one of the ways of coping at times of adversity. In Australia, one of the hashtags used to talk about the Queensland floods was #thebigwet. In the U.S., people poked fun at Superstorm Sandy. Some 14 per cent of tweets at the time involved jokes, such as wondering if the hit song "Gangnam Style" was just a giant rain dance that had caused the hurricane. While humour can defuse a stressful situation, the joking is tempered by the severity of a crisis.

Taken together, the rhythms of real time show how Twitter becomes a place to come together when everyday societal bonds are strained. It serves as a fleeting town square for people to share their sorrow, fear and hopes. In the immediate aftermath of a disaster, there is an urgent need not just to receive information but also to share stories of survival and hope, as well as messages of sympathy and support. People turn to social media to restore the fabric of community shattered during a natural disaster. "We have something in common, and it allows us to feel connected," said a Memphis resident after the 2011 storms. "We share stories, photos, happenings at the moment. I think it brings a continuity to the city we haven't had before."

The experiences shared by those caught up in a disaster tell a story of citizens coming together, of everyday acts of kindness and courage as neighbours seek to help those in need. Knowing how people act at such times is crucial in dealing with the aftermath of a crisis. Through the lens of social media, the story of how people behave in the face of adversity is a far cry from the archetypal disaster movie. Fictional tales of disaster are filled with terrified mobs and helpless victims. The way these stories have been told over the ages in Elizabethan plays, newspapers and B-movies presents a picture that is often out of sync with what really happens in times of crisis.

COUNTERING THE DISASTER MYTH

The narrative of a typical disaster movie is all too familiar, be it a volcanic eruption, an asteroid hurtling towards Earth, a gigantic Godzilla thundering through Manhattan or lurching zombies advancing on survivors who are too scared to move. On screen will be people fleeing, pushing others out of the way, while others take advantage of the chaos to loot shops and grab whatever they can. A disaster provides the setting for stirring stories of valour and woe against a backdrop of panic, with the requisite cast of heroes and villains.

The fictional tales on screen are reinforced by media coverage of real-life crises. Disasters make for good stories for journalists, just as they do for Hollywood producers. A crisis provides strong visuals of destroyed homes and dazed victims, in a state of shock, unable to look after themselves. Reporters often speak of the dangers of looting and efforts by law enforcement to restore order. It is an irresistible narrative that makes for human-interest stories that resonate with the audience. Except that the narrative is usually far from accurate. Media reports and fictional accounts present a distorted picture of what happens by focusing on the most dramatic and exciting elements of a crisis. Much more attention is paid to scenes of destruction than to areas that have made it through unscathed.

The upshot is disaster myths that people believe are true and that are perpetuated in the media and popular culture. The myths are so prevalent in society that people believe certain things happen during a disaster. A seminal study in the 1970s showed how far the media influenced people's beliefs. Sociologists from the University of Delaware and Ohio State carried out a survey of 354 residents of New Castle County in Delaware. Most of them had no direct experience of a disaster. Instead, they relied on television and newspapers for their information about disasters. The sociologists found that eight out of ten people thought panic was a major problem. Many expected survivors to be in a state of shock and dependent on local officials and relief agencies. The study is just one in a raft of work that shows that preconceived notions about disasters are essentially wrong.

Yet these myths keep resurfacing because they make for compelling stories for both the movie and the news industries. Since most have never been through an earthquake or hurricane, their views come from what they see in films and in the media. When there is a lack of information, people will tend to fear the worst. The result is a disconnect between how we think people behave in times of crisis and what they actually do. One widely held belief is that people always behave irrationally. Somehow, disaster seems synonymous with the notion of hordes frantically running for their lives, every person for themselves, without thinking about others.

People do flee in the face of imminent danger. When the twin towers of the World Trade Center collapsed following the 9/11 terrorist attacks, New Yorkers in downtown Manhattan ran for their lives. It is a natural and rational response to get out of harm's way. This type of behaviour tends to be portrayed as panic. The reality is that people do not resort to the type of mindless flight of hysterical crowds often seen in movies. More often than not, residents tend to ignore warnings of an impending calamity and disregard calls to evacuate the area. The people hit by a disaster are far from helpless victims. The opposite tends to be true, with survivors of a tragedy being the first to take care of the injured and search for survivors.

One of the earliest examples of how social media challenges the media narrative was during the Virginia Tech shootings in 2007. In the early hours of Monday, April 16, the deadliest school massacre in U.S. history by a single gunman shattered the stillness of the campus in Blacksburg, Virginia. In two separate attacks, undergraduate student Seung Hui Cho killed thirty-two students and faculty and wounded seventeen more before turning his gun on himself. An official report into the tragedy found that Cho, a South Korean national with U.S. permanent residency, had a history of mental health problems.

Early on that Monday morning, Cho fatally wounded his first victim, Emily Hilscher, in her room in a residence. A residential assistant, Ryan Christopher Clark, was also killed. Cho then went back to his room to change out of his bloody clothes and pick up a backpack with two semiautomatic handguns, almost four hundred rounds of ammunition and several chains and locks. He proceeded to Norris Hall, where he chained the main entrances and went from classroom to classroom, firing at students and professors.

The scale and nature of the tragedy shocked the nation. Disbelief, outrage, grief and recriminations followed as people tried to make sense of what had happened. One student, Jamal Albarghouti, captured part of the drama on video using his cell phone camera. The grainy video, broadcast on CNN, showed police outside campus buildings, with the sounds of gunfire in the distance. "This place is in a state of panic," said a student featured on CNN, Shaver Deyerle. "Nobody knew what was going on at first."

Behind the scenes, though, students turned to the Internet to figure out what was happening on campus. Facebook was still in its early days, but was becoming increasingly popular among college kids. Rather than panicking or being paralyzed by fear, students holed up in dorms or in classrooms turned to Facebook to counter the anxiety that comes from a lack of information during a crisis. Some set up Facebook groups to create a virtual meeting place to connect, get to know each other and discuss common concerns. The group I'm OK at VT served as a place for students to tell others that they were safe. Another popular group was Prayers for VT, where people could share their grief and condolences.

One of the focal points for the students became a discussion thread in the latter group entitled "You know a student is confirmed dead?" "My roommate just found out that he lost a very dear friend MR pray for her family and her soul tonight . . . thank you," read one message. Another described how the sender heard about one of the victims from the victim's girlfriend: "I just finished speaking with his girlfriend, and it appears JH is a fatality as well. God rest his soul." Some students monitored other Facebook groups and served as information brokers, gathering information and reporting back to the Prayers for VT group. "RS has reported to another Facebook group," read one update.

During the tense and traumatic morning of April 16, students turned to Facebook to try to find answers to a pressing question: Are my friends safe? The list of victims compiled by the students in various Facebook groups was never incorrect. Far from spreading rumours and speculation, the students worked together in a concentrated, well-intentioned and serious manner to provide timely and accurate information. The use of social media in the hours following the Virginia Tech shootings made visible what researchers who study disasters have always known. Under pressure, people are remarkably resilient and will rise to the occasion to help others.

DISTANT WITNESSES OF THE NEWS

In the hours after the Japanese earthquake and tsunami, Shinya Takatori sent out a steady stream of messages and chatted with others in Japanese. He used Twitter to check on the condition of friends, offer comfort and share information about relief efforts. By the evening, Shinya was reflecting on how social media had affected his experience of the disaster. Twitter turned out to be an invaluable tool that helped him make it through a nerve-racking day. "Thanks to Twitter, I found out things like my friend in Ishinomaki is on the roof of his house and is waiting for help because of a flooded first floor, and that friends in Natori are safe. We who are removed from the situation might have more info. Keep us posted! If someone from Sendai is safe, too, let us know. Keep the information coming!"

The information has kept on coming. When a crisis shakes the world, there is an instant flare-up in activity on Twitter. Social media swings into action as a nervous system for the planet. When the world hiccups, Twitter twitches. The upsurge in messages serves as an early warning system that can help emergency services act quickly. At times of crisis, accurate and reliable information about the location and needs of victims is at a premium. Facts have a short shelf life. In the hours and days after a disaster, needs change as people are found, requiring medical attention, clean water and food. For the emergency services, monitoring social networks offers a real-time feed of data that can help inform rescue efforts and the allocation of scarce resources.

When a crisis stretches the normal bonds of a community, people caught up in the event turn to whatever technologies are available to connect and communicate. The cell phone and a sporadic Internet connection tend to be the only forms of communication still functioning after a disaster. When no voice calls can make it through, sometimes the only thing that still works is a 140-character text sent to Twitter. The volume and mix of messages depends on the type of disaster and its location. There will be far more tweets from cities with good cell phone service than from more remote areas.

But some patchy information is better than none in the news vacuum immediately after a disaster. Taken in aggregate, the instant snapshots shared on Twitter, Facebook or YouTube generate a living representation of the concerns, priorities and anxieties of everyday citizens in the aftermath of a catastrophe. They are visible for all to see on social media, contradicting stereotypical portrayals of panicked and helpless victims. Social media changes the experience of a disaster for those most affected by it. But it also affects everyone else at a distance from the event.

Many of the people active on Twitter during a crisis are nowhere near its geographical location or have any direct experience of it. Instead, they are taking on the role of distant witnesses, brought together by a shared interest or fascination by a major news event. From the safety of their home or office, they get involved in the crisis by monitoring social media and choosing relevant bits of information to bring to the attention of others. The mechanics of Twitter enables anyone to be part of a community drawn together by common interest.

When Malaysian Airlines flight MH370 went missing in March 2014, the story made headlines across the world and galvanized an international search-and-rescue effort. There was nothing to suggest anything out of the ordinary when the Boeing 777 took off from Kuala Lumpur for Beijing just after noon on March 8. There were 239 people on board, including the twelve crew members. The final words from the cockpit as it left Malaysian airspace were a standard and routine sign-off: "Good night, Malaysian three seven zero."

The disappearance of MH370 captured the imagination of the public. It seemed like something out of the plot of the TV series *Lost*. In today's wired world, how could an airliner with 239 people simply vanish? Twitter became a public square for the circulation of news updates and speculation about what might have happened. In the three weeks following its disappearance, there were more than five million tweets with the #mh370 hashtag. But only a million were original messages, many of them from media organizations sharing the latest news. The remaining 80 per cent were retweets.

During the MH370 mystery, Twitter users were acting as distant witnesses, picking out relevant announcements and links to pass on to their social networks as events happened. Real time turns a crisis into a drama where anyone can play a role in the spread of information. In the past, the public's experience of a crisis came largely through newspapers, television and radio. Social media enables people to interact with the news as every twist and turn is shared on Twitter. A crisis situation can seem more real and more immersive when concerned individuals can be part of the urgency and drama as it plays out in real time. Every twist and turn is described, discussed and dissected on an instant news network that is open to everyone, for better or worse.

#When Consumers Strike Back
#When Consumers Strike Back
#When Consumers Strike Back
#When Consumers Strike Back
#When Consumers Strike Back
#When Consumers Strike Back
#When Consumers Strike Back

CHAPTER SEVEN

#When Consumers Strike Back

IT HAS BECOME SOMETHING EVERY COMPANY DREADS: CUSTOMERS or employees going on social media and trash-talking the brand. The world of business is littered with examples. There was the Starbucks barista in California singing on YouTube about annoying patrons. In Australia, a Vodafone employee ranted on Facebook and Twitter about idiot customers. In the U.K., an HMV employee used the chain's corporate account to fire back at the company for firing staff. And these are examples of businesses coming under fire from their staff, let alone when they are on the receiving end of a twitstorm of fuming customers.

Social media is an arena that offers unrivalled opportunities to reach consumers and get them excited about a brand, with potentially tremendous rewards. McKinsey consultants estimate there is an untapped pot of gold in social media of between $900 billion and $1.3 trillion (both figures U.S.) in value for businesses. But while the rewards are lucrative, the risks are high if business executives don't have a deep understanding of how social media works.

Applebee's is one business that learned the hard way. The trouble started when Pastor Alois Bell went to the restaurant for dinner with members of the congregation of her St. Louis church in February 2013. Since it was a party of more than six people, Applebee's added an automatic 18 per cent tip. Pastor Bell crossed out the tip and wrote zero instead. "I give God 10% why do you get 18," she added above her signature. The waitress showed the receipt to a co-worker, Chelsea Welch, who then did what many do when they see something surprising, amusing or annoying. She took a photo and shared it on the online forum Reddit.

The receipt became an Internet phenomenon. It sparked a social media backlash against the pastor and resulted in Applebee's sacking Welch for what she had thought was just "a lighthearted joke." That should have been the end of the affair. Instead, it was the point when things started to spiral out of control. Welch's firing prompted thousands of messages of support for her on the restaurant's Facebook page. Applebee's justified the firing on grounds of the privacy of its customers, prompting a further deluge of angry retorts. The to-and-fro between Applebee's and commenters continued into the early hours of the morning. The restaurant was accused of deleting negative messages while it stuck to the corporate line.

The mainstream media picked up on the bun fight with headlines of Applebee's "social media suicide" or "social media meltdown." Somehow, an incident at one of its two thousand franchises turned into an online sensation, an international news story and a public relations fiasco that serves as an example of how not to handle a social media crisis. Applebee's failed to recognize it no longer controls the message about its brand when employees and customers have to tools to hold companies accountable in a very public way.

LESSONS FROM A SOCIAL MEDIA CRISIS

Applebee's should have known better than to try to silence its critics rather than addressing their concerns. It could have learnt about damage control from the experience of Domino's Pizza in 2009. All it took was a couple of pranksters with a video camera and an Internet connection to plunge a pizza giant into a public relations debacle that has since become a cautionary tale for brands.

Two Domino's Pizza employees, Kristy Hammonds and Michael Setzer, decided it would be fun to film themselves messing around with the food and share the videos on YouTube on Monday, April 13, 2009. In the kitchen of a Domino's franchise in the town of Conover, North Carolina, Kristy filmed Michael sticking bits of cheese up his nose and brandishing slices of salami around his behind before putting them on a sandwich. She provided the narration.

"In about five minutes these will be sent out on delivery and somebody will be eating these—yes, eating these," says Kristy. "And little do they know that the cheese was in his nose and that there was some lethal gas that ended up on their salami. Now that's how we roll at Domino's." In another video, Kristy laughs as Michael sneezes on a cheesesteak sandwich before adding that it is destined for "some unlucky customer who is in need of some snot—yes, I said snot."

When Domino's Pizza found out about the YouTube videos, its communications team thought they were a hoax. But they also realized they could damage the reputation of a company with 125,000 employees in the U.S. and in sixty countries across the world. "Any idiot with a camera and an Internet link can do stuff like this—and ruin the reputation of a brand that's nearly fifty years old," reflected Tim McIntyre, vice-president of corporate communications. The next day, the owner of the franchise in Conover fired Kristy and Michael. A health inspector visited the premises and all open food was thrown out. Kristy emailed McIntyre to apologize and insist it was all a prank. "It was fake and I wish that everyone knew that!!!! Michael never would do that to any customer, EVER!! I AM SOO SORRY!" When the company later checked the phone logs at the North Carolina franchise, it found that no orders had been taken when the videos were shot.

Within twenty-four hours, Domino's seemed to have quashed a potential PR disaster. The communications team had adopted a tried-and-tested strategy to deal with bad news: identify the problem, take action to fix it and try to avoid drawing more attention to it. But it had failed to take into account how social media makes it easy for a video to reach beyond a town in North Carolina. News of the stomach-turning videos spread as people posted links to the videos and expressed their disgust and shock.

By Wednesday, less than two days into the crisis, one of the videos had amassed a million views. To get an idea of the scale of the story, for the first time ever, more people were searching the web for information about Domino's than about the latest shenanigans of socialite Paris Hilton. The pizza giant had not anticipated the "OMG, you have to see this" appeal of the videos.

It had underestimated the power of disgust to fuel social sharing. Worse still, Domino's was caught unawares by how the online chatter had shifted in the space of a few hours to people questioning what the company was doing to sort out the crisis.

A study of how the videos were passed on on Twitter reveals just how quickly bad news can spread. Computer scientists in South Korea found that the number of people talking about Domino's spiked in the forty-eight hours after the videos were posted to YouTube. There were almost seven thousand Twitter messages in just two days—compared with the daily average of several hundred—reaching a potential audience of 16.5 million. Much to the pizza giant's dismay, far more people forwarded links to the videos than to the company's apology. The spread of the videos slowed down after the first couple of days, as did negative sentiment; but while there were fewer critics, the scientists found that positive sentiment about Domino's barely increased.

Domino's traditional response to the crisis was out of step with the way news spreads in a networked world. It didn't realize that the news was out, and then it lost control of the story as it shifted from being about tainted food to people questioning how the company had handled the prank. "What we missed was the perpetual mushroom effect of viral sensations," admitted McIntyre. A survey just after the scandal erupted found that 65 per cent who would previously visit or order from Domino's were less likely to do so after seeing the videos. In the end, Domino's took to the same channels that had damaged its brand to reply. It posted a video to YouTube of its president, Patrick Doyle, directly apologizing to customers. It also created a Twitter account with the username @dpzinfo to talk to consumers about the crisis and share the link to its apology.

The case of the Domino's Pizza prank videos has become a staple of any discussion about how to handle a reputation crisis. The company was oblivious for too long to how its brand was being trashed in conversations on Twitter and beyond by messages such as "and I don't think I will be eating Domino's again . . . *throw up in my mouth*." Before sharing tools became widespread and easy to use, companies would respond to bad news by issuing a dry, staid press release to the traditional media—days or even weeks after an event. Such methods are out of step when millions share photos of lunch, comment on their latest purchases or trash a poor-quality product, all in near-real time.

Since then, it has become routine for brands to listen to the social web, whether they are selling fast food like Burger King or high-end fashions like Burberry. Social media monitoring is considered a way to identify potential customers or respond to fans and critics. Listening is meaningless unless it leads to action. Social media is a two-way street rather than simply another marketing channel. Part of the success of the Old Spice campaign "The Man Your Man Could Smell Like" in 2010 was down to its response on social media. The daft video, starring a shirtless former NFL athlete named Isaiah Mustafa, was an instant online hit, with 5.9 million views on the first day. Rather than leave it there, Old Spice engaged with the online conversation. A team in Portland, Oregon, filmed Isaiah Mustafa making 186 personal video responses over the next two and a half days. A viral video entered social media lore. And Old Spice saw a big jump in sales of body wash.

At times of crisis, it's even more important to listen and act, as Domino's learned to its cost. Consumers expect some kind of response and more than just a "we hear you and we are looking into this." When the U.K. mobile company O2 suffered a major network failure for two days in July 2011, thousands of peeved customers vented their frustration on Twitter. By the end of day one, negative tweets had reached an estimated 1.7 million people. How O2 handled the crisis is a master class in the management of social media outrage. Instead of taking shelter from the barrage of anger behind a faceless corporate message, O2's social media team crafted personal replies. They ranged from the obvious apology to more witty responses. Even abusive messages were acknowledged, but rather than arguing, O2 sought to rise above it all. Through a mix of honesty, humanity and humour, the company turned around the tone of the conversation.

The immediate nature of social media can be a friend to businesses, if used smartly. Twitter is a constantly updating window into what is top of mind at any particular moment for millions across the world. One of the most celebrated examples of real-time social media marketing came during the 2013 Super Bowl blackout. The makers of Oreo cookies had a fifteen-person social media team in place during the Super Bowl, ready to act when something happened—be it an amazing play or the lights going out. During the thirty-four-minute power outage, Oreo tweeted, "Power out? No problem." The accompanying photo showed a cookie against a dark background with the caption YOU CAN STILL DUNK IN THE DARK. It was retweeted thousands of times, tapping into the huge interest in the Super Bowl with wit and creativity. The message combined speed and relevance, and it cost much less than the product's actual Super Bowl TV ad. Marketers have always sought to tap in to public interests to promote a brand. In 2012, Procter and Gamble noticed a jump in the number of people talking about Tide on social media. Workers at the Daytona 500 using the detergent to clean a track crash had been featured on television. Within days, the company created a TV commercial referencing Daytona and talking about a new use for laundry detergent.

But real-time marketing campaigns on social media can go spectacularly wrong. A search for "social media marketing fails" brings up tens of thousands of results, ranging from the clueless to the insensitive to the offensive. The fashion designer Kenneth Cole managed to be all of these, not once, but twice. During the Egyptian uprising in 2011, Cole quipped on his personal Twitter account that the millions in uproar in Cairo must have heard of the new spring collection. The joke backfired, with Cole deleting the offensive tweet and apologizing. Two years later, Cole managed to make a similar off-colour joke, shilling his "sandals, pumps and loafers" in a comment about "boots on the ground" in Syria. What may seem like an off-the-cuff attempt at humour can mushroom online into a PR fail.

By digging into the conversations on Twitter, Facebook and online forums, companies hope to gain insights into the reactions, attitudes and opinions of consumers. Businesses have realized how a message shared and amplified by the crowd can be far more powerful than a multimillion-dollar traditional marketing campaign. The entertainment industry, in particular, has had to learn the lesson fast, tapping into the power of sharing to pre-empt bad publicity.

FORECASTING ENTERTAINMENT GOLD

Not many people saw the movie *Transylmania* when it hit the cinemas in time for Christmas 2009. The spoof horror flick told the story of a group of teens who end up at a university in Romania, where vampires have an annoying habit of getting in the way of the partying. It is a cross between *American Pie* and *Scary Movie*, trying to tap in to the vogue for vampires triggered by *Twilight*. *Transylmania* was universally panned by critics, with a rating of 0 per cent on the review aggregation site Rotten Tomatoes. On its release in December, it earned the dubious honour of having the lowest-grossing opening for a movie playing in more than a thousand cinemas, taking in just $263,941.

The producers of the movie should have talked to researchers Sitaram Asur and Bernardo Huberman of HP Labs in California. The computer scientists noticed something that is now part of most marketing campaigns. They realized they could predict whether a film will be a hit or miss, based on the social chatter ahead of its release. Using movie titles, they tracked 2.89 million tweets from 1.2 million people who mentioned twenty-four motion pictures over three months from November 2009 to February 2010. The films ranged from the science-fiction epic *Avatar*, to the *Twilight* sequel *New Moon*, to the coming-of-age teen comedy *Youth in Revolt*.

The scientists discovered that the volume of social media chatter was directly related to box office success. They knew *Transylmania* would bomb. The comedy didn't generate much excitement ahead of its release, with an average of just 2.75 messages per hour. The movie simply failed to grab the attention of the public and was pulled from theatres at the end of the second week. If executives had known about the low level of buzz around *Transylmania*, they could have decided to reduce the number of cinemas and downsize the capacity of auditoriums, and instead devote more screens and seats to a more lucrative film.

Listening in to what people share on their social networks is a better way to predict celluloid gold than the Hollywood Stock Exchange. The exchange is a popular online market where people trade shares in their favourite movies and actors in an imaginary currency of Hollywood Dollars. The prices for movie stocks can accurately forecast whether it will be a hit or miss. What Sitaram and Huberman discovered was that tracking the volume of online chatter alone outperformed the artificial stock market.

Marketing executives have long known that audience buzz can affect a film's success or failure, alongside factors such as star power, the production budget and the marketing spend. The opinion of a friend or colleague is usually considered more credible and trustworthy than anything else. Word of mouth helps to increase awareness among potential moviegoers, especially when it is backed up by heavy spending on television and newspaper advertising.

Around the summer of 2009, the entertainment industry started to notice that conversations about their products were taking place on Facebook and Twitter. The exchanges were a trove of information on whether audiences loved or hated a movie. Among the movies that played big on social media was *New Moon,* the second instalment in the *Twilight* series. Its fans took to Twitter to share their expectations, hopes and fears of the sequel, posting an average of 1,300 tweets per hour over the week before release. Such social media buzz by a pre-existing audience for a movie is a gift to Hollywood, as it adds to the hype. In its opening weekend, *New Moon* made $142 millon as fans flocked to the theatres to see the unfolding story of the love triangle of Edward, Bella and Jacob.

Figuring out how social chatter can get people to the multiplex has become part of the playbook of movie studios. It has turned into a complex analytic game as studios deconstruct tweets, likes and shares to guide marketing decisions. Studios now monitor chatter on Twitter because of the close connection between the number of people tweeting about how much they want to see a movie and its performance at the box office. Hollywood takes social media so seriously that *Variety* now includes a section on its website that charts the likes, tweets and views of new movies ahead of release. The unanswered question, though, is whether social media is creating buzz or responding to a multimillion-dollar marketing campaign.

Getting people talking about a new release is particularly important for entertainment products such as movies, TV shows or video games. Since consumers are unable to try something out first, these discussions are based on hopes and expectations rather than actual experience. In the week before its release in mid-March 2014, the movie spinoff from the *Need for Speed* video game franchise was playing big on social media. Video games don't always make for movie magic. But *Need for Speed* could count on a solid launch pad as it hit movie theatres, with 16.7 million likes on Facebook, 28.4 million trailer views and 326,000 tweets. Numbers are only the start; as social media monitoring has become more sophisticated, the next step is to analyze sentiment in a bid to understand the opinions being shared, as well as the speed at which these sentiments can spread and influence decisions.

THE RISE AND FALL OF THE HOLLYWOOD BLOCKBUSTER MODEL

During the long, hot summer months of 1975, people were afraid to go into the water. Maybe not everyone, but certainly those who had cooled off in an air-conditioned cinema and watched *Jaws*, the story of a great white shark terrorizing the beachgoers at the fictional resort of Amity Island. Steven Spielberg's gripping account of a police chief's struggle to protect beachgoers from the killer shark went on to become one of the most influential movies of all time, spawning three sequels, a theme park ride and a raft of merchandise.

Jaws set the template for the summer blockbuster business model that has become a familiar fixture. It was the first film to open in hundreds of cinemas across the U.S., backed by a nationwide promotional campaign on television to ensure maximum exposure. The strategy to go big paid off: *Jaws* recouped its production costs within two weeks of its release and went on to dominate the box office all through the summer. Hollywood found a winning formula that continues to this day.

But the formula hasn't been working quite so well lately. Blockbusters no longer have the staying power of *Jaws*. Instead, studios rely on making a big splash on the opening weekend. By 2002, the average movie took in 46 per cent of its revenue in the first week, compared with 34 per cent in 1998. "With *Jaws*, we didn't obsess about being No. 1 for one weekend," recalled producer Richard D. Zanuck. "We wanted to own the entire summer. And we did." In 1975, Zanuck didn't have to worry about what the ability of people to tell friends instantly what they thought of a film would do to the box office. Today, the speed of word of mouth is a headache for studios counting on a big opening weekend.

It started at the turn of the century, when moviegoers would text friends as they left the theatre with a "must-see" or "avoid at all costs" piece of advice. The spread of messages was limited to immediate connections. Fifteen years later, the same tidbit on Twitter or Facebook can reach total strangers. But that's not the problem; the real worry is that thousands of these instant reviews can be aggregated through social media to create a tsunami of bad publicity within hours of a movie's opening. It is a nightmare scenario for any executive who works in an industry that relies on asymmetries in information between the producer and the consumer.

In a situation where there is such an asymmetry in information, the producer has far more information available to them than the consumer, who makes a purchasing decision based on limited data. There is no "try before you buy" option for seeing a movie. In the past, moviegoers made decisions based on the slick promotional trailers, the allure of big stars, flashy special effects and maybe a handful of reviews by newspaper critics. It was the same in the music industry. It was pretty much impossible to sample a music album before purchase. Instead, a hit single on constant rotation on the radio would sway consumers to take a gamble that the album would be full of similar delights.

Movies and music are products that are experienced. It is hard to figure out whether you like a film or album until you've seen or heard it. Experiential media industries tend to rely on instant success before consumers have a sense of the real quality of the product. In the travel industry, tourists will only know if they like a resort once they've travelled there and experienced what it has to offer. But the problem is most acute in the entertainment industry. A strong opening weekend can make or break a big-budget movie. Similarly, approximately 50 per cent of sales of hit albums and 40 per cent of video game revenues come in the first week of release. When word of mouth is digital and instant, consumers have extraordinary power to decide the fate of a movie, album or game within hours.

THE COST OF INSTANT FEEDBACK

It's been called the "Brüno Effect" after the Sacha Baron Cohen comedy about a flamboyantly gay Austrian TV personality. The film was the first to suffer from instant negative feedback on social media on its opening night. It was expected to make $50 million in its opening weekend, backed by a strong marketing campaign. It took in $14.4 million on the Friday night. Box office takings tumbled down nearly 40 per cent on the Saturday, to $8.8 million. Twitter didn't cause *Brüno* to bomb; the movie stank. What Twitter did was to provide a quick and easy way for people lured into theatres by the marketing to trash the movie with tweets such as "Bruno is the worst film I have ever seen."

The Brüno Effect was no fluke. It was a sign of the growing importance of instant critiques on social media, as researchers from London's Cass Business School and the University of

Münster in Germany discovered. The team analyzed the opening-weekend performance of 105 movies between October 2009 and October 2010, each shown in more than 800 U.S. theatres on release. The sample ranged from sci-fi extravaganzas such as *Avatar* and *Inception* to chick flicks such as *She's Out of My League* and *The Back-Up Plan* and animated adventures such as *How to Train Your Dragon* and *Toy Story 3*. Out of four million tweets, they found 829,576 were people passing judgment on a film they had seen.

The results make for uneasy reading for an industry that wants a big weekend opening at the box office. Most moviegoers typically shared their impressions of a film at 10 P.M. on a Friday night as they left the cinema. Some did it while still sitting in the cinema.

Two-thirds of the one-line movie reviews were circulated on Twitter from Friday until Saturday noon. "We found that sentiment spread via Twitter immediately after a new movie's release systematically influences other consumers' decisions about whether to attend a screening of the movie during the remainder of its opening weekend," explained researcher Caroline Wiertz. Just to make sure they were onto something, the team looked at other elements that affect a movie's success, such as the production budget, marketing spending, pre-release buzz, star power and professional critics' ratings. The Brüno Effect held.

Since *Brüno,* entertainment companies have become increasingly sensitive to social media sentiment. Almost three-quarters of social media users share their take on a movie after seeing it. And 8 per cent do it while the film is still playing, despite the pre-movie notices to put away cell phones. The reviews help to shape opinion about a movie. A third of social media users decide whether to go to a movie based on what they read on Facebook or Twitter. A similar number were persuaded by comments on social media to watch a TV show.

Movie moguls can take some consolation in the fact that loud or slick trailers in rotation on TV, at cinemas and online remain the biggest factor in persuading someone to go to the movies. But studios know that social media can help move the needle in their favour, particularly when it comes to reaching the elusive audience of young adults. Rotten reviews on Twitter don't have much of an impact on movies aimed at families. Often, going to the cinema is less about the actual movie and more about having a family excursion, with popcorn for the kids and a couple of hours of peace and quiet for Mom and Dad. But teenagers are swayed by what their peers might say, whether it be in person or on Facebook.

With days to go before the opening of the sci-fi thriller *Super 8*, Paramount Pictures realized it had a problem. The studio was hoping for a big summer blockbuster, especially with J.J. Abrams in the director's chair and Steven Spielberg producing. But its research suggested that younger audiences were lukewarm about the movie, even though the lead actors were young. At the last minute, Paramount turned to Twitter to announce secret screenings a day ahead of release, with free popcorn thrown in. Fortunately for Paramount, the reaction on Twitter from those early moviegoers was largely positive. *Super 8* went on to make a better-than-expected $35 million on its opening weekend in the U.S., with total domestic box office sales of $127 million.

Business models that have worked well in the past are challenged by the scale and pace of sharing. The entertainment industry has been on the front line of dealing with word of mouth that could spread so quickly and widely. But it is hard to think of an industry immune to social media. The unique combination of immediacy, social connection and reach of communication technologies such as Twitter means that consumers can sink a product within hours. But it also means that consumers can be the most powerful marketing weapon in spreading positive messages and defending the brand.

FANS AS BRAND AMBASSADORS

High school senior Timothy Oldham may be the only teen to have earned a detention by shouting out a movie catchphrase in the classroom. A few days after the March 2012 release of the big-screen adaptation of the young-adult novel *The Hunger Games*, the teen was at his school in Texas when another student dropped a book on the desk. "That is mahogany!" yelled Timothy. He was imitating one of the characters of *The Hunger Games*, Effie Trinket. In the movie, the exquisitely coiffured Effie utters the phrase, aghast after the heroine, Katniss Everdeen, angrily plunges a knife into an expensive mahogany table. The phrase was not in the original book, but it went on to become one of the most quoted lines from the film.

Timothy published a photo of his detention slip on the social sharing service Tumblr. It mentioned his outburst of "That is mahogany" as the reason for his detention. More than a thousand people liked it or reposted it to their Tumblrs. It went viral when the team running the movie's official Facebook page saw the detention slip and shared it with the page's six million fans. Almost two thousand fans commented on it, more than five thousand shared it on Facebook and some sixty thousand liked the post. *The Hunger Games* team wrote on Facebook, "Effie would have been proud." At the time, Timothy changed his Twitter bio to "Effie is indeed proud of me."

And the studio behind the movie, Lionsgate, would indeed be proud of how Effie and the cast of characters performed at the box office. Given the popularity of the books, a film version of *The Hunger Games* looked like a winner. The movie went on to exceed expectations, taking in $155 million in its opening weekend in March 2012 in the U.S. It set a new record for a film opening outside the traditional summer blockbuster season. *The Hunger Games* accomplished the rare feat of topping the U.S. box office for four weekends in a row. It was the first motion picture to do this since James Cameron's sci-fi epic, *Avatar,* in December 2009.

Behind the commercial success of *The Hunger Games* and its longevity at the box office is the story of a sophisticated marketing campaign that made the most of the audience's urge to share in a pop-culture phenomenon. It empowered fans to become brand ambassadors. Having real people acting as the face of a company or brand is nothing new. Subway has its Subway Guy, Jared Fogle. In 1999, the university student became a spokesperson for Subway after attributing his weight loss of 245 pounds in one year to the sandwich brand. Since then, he has starred in dozens of commercials and visited stores across America. Walmart has its Walmart Moms, an online community of "mom bloggers" to share advice on parenting, healthy living and politics.

Social media makes it possible to more easily identify and recruit loyal fans by monitoring who's sharing what and with whom. Such brand ambassadors tend to have greater credibility because they are not paid spokespeople. Instead, the reward comes in the form of kudos and recognition from their social circles. Lionsgate's campaign to mobilize fans of the book ahead of the film's release is a textbook example of social media done right. It offered a myriad of ways for fans to experience the dystopian world of *The Hunger Games*.

The aim was to make fans live the film, instead of just seeing it, hoping they would then share their passion with friends and family. Lionsgate sought to connect and mobilize the book's ardent young readers through Facebook, where fans got the latest details and connected with others. The official Facebook page was mirrored by a website designated as an "official citizen information terminal" that imitated the world of *The Hunger Games*. Online, Lionsgate encouraged enthusiasts to create a physical district ID card, run for positions such as mayor or recruiter or explore outlandish fashions of the ruling city, the Capitol. "We felt that this was something that we would start with the core fans and then we could see how much we could broaden it out from there," explained Lionsgate's senior vice-president for digital marketing, Danielle DePalma.

SHARING THE BRAND

What singled this campaign out is the different approach to the work created by fans. Often, a media company will come down hard on copyright infringement by enthusiasts who take characters or scenes and create their own stories, artwork or videos. Lionsgate decided to celebrate the work of those who were expressing their devotion creatively. Every Friday, the official Facebook page chose a fan of the week to highlight the imagination of its followers, from three friends who designed their own costumes to a young woman who created a *Hunger Games* Monopoly game. Universal Studios adopted a similar approach for its musical comedy *Pitch Perfect*. It invited fans to send in videos of themselves singing the hit song "Starships" by Nicki Minaj.

Such an approach involves co-opting consumers to become part of the experience. When it is done successfully, the fans become the message. But that means relinquishing a degree of control to fans for them to remake and reinterpret a product or brand—and recognizing that while fans may be the toughest critics, they are also the most loyal defenders. When the Cleveland Indians were in a slump in 2011, the team turned to fans to help it out. Attendance for its games had dropped significantly after a couple of poor seasons. The management of the major league baseball team had already made some efforts to engage with local bloggers and leading social media figures a year earlier by providing them with seats in the outfield bleachers.

For the coming season, it upped its game, creating a luxury suite indoors where select fans received all the amenities usually afforded to accredited journalists, from pregame media notes to TVs with game broadcasts and access to team staff. The move was unusual, as the professional sports world has been hesitant to open up to fans who want to share their experiences and opinions through social media. The lucky fans handpicked by the Cleveland Indians ranged from social media-savvy twentysomethings to mommy bloggers to hardcore Indians bloggers. Imagine watching your favourite sports

team for free in a luxury suite at the stadium, with all the crea-
ture comforts. The fans didn't report on the game as a journalist would but shared the ups and downs they went through as
they followed the team. They saw themselves as cheerleaders
for the Indians on social media.

Following the club's new strategy, more people started
coming to the stadium in 2011. But then the side won twelve
more games than in the previous year. Team officials thought
the initiative had successfully raised the profile of the team,
adding to its traditional promotional campaign. The Cleveland
Indians had converted supporters with a vested interest in the
team into ardent evangelists. Just as Lionsgate developed online
spaces where fans could chat about Katniss Everdeen, the Indians
had created a space in the stadium to bring supporters together
to share their excitement and spread it across the online world.

In both instances, the businesses benefited from creative
and innovative ways for consumers to represent the brand,
albeit unofficially and perhaps unwittingly. They both had a
product that fans could get behind. No amount of marketing
buzz or courting of fans will work if the product or service is
bad. Instead, social media will amplify a minor incident into a
corporate crisis in a matter of hours—just ask Applebee's.
Businesses have always known that consumers tend to heed
information from peers far more than corporate messages. The
ability of people to share their delight or disgust on a colossal
scale with massive reach through social media can harm or
help. What businesses cannot afford to do is ignore it.

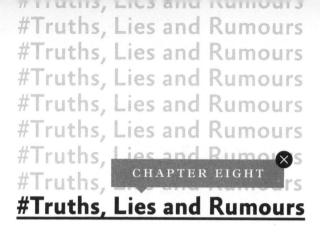
#Truths, Lies and Rumours
#Truths, Lies and Rumours
#Truths, Lies and Rumours
#Truths, Lies and Rumours
#Truths, Lies and Rumours
#Truths, Lies and Rumours
#Truths, Lies and Rumours
#Truths,
#Truths,

CHAPTER EIGHT

#Truths, Lies and Rumours

SOMETIMES ALL IT TAKES TO SWAY PUBLIC OPINION IS ONE photograph. During the Vietnam War, a picture of a naked nine-year-old girl fleeing a napalm attack captured the horror of the conflict in a way that words could not. In the midst of the Syrian civil conflict, a picture circulating on social media seemed to show the ruthlessness of the regime of President Bashar al-Assad. It showed neat rows of dozens of bodies shrouded in white as a child skipped over one of the rows. The BBC was alerted to the photograph and decided to publish it on its online report about the massacre of more than a hundred people, most of them women and children, in the Syrian region of Houla in May 2012.

It was the kind of image that could have galvanized public outrage and increased pressure on politicians to act over the ongoing violence in Syria. It didn't. The photo was bogus. A photographer for Getty Images had taken the shot almost a decade earlier in Iraq. "I went home at 3 A.M. and I opened the BBC page which had a front page story about what happened in Syria and I almost fell off from my chair," photographer Marco di Lauro told the U.K. newspaper *The Daily Telegraph.* "Someone is using someone else's picture for propaganda on purpose."

The photograph was only on the BBC News website for ninety minutes, but the damage had been done. A news organization that prides itself on its accurate and impartial reporting had been duped into taking sides in the Syrian conflict. "Efforts were made to track down the original source and, having obtained some information pointing to its veracity, the picture was published, with a disclaimer saying it could not be independently verified," explained the BBC's social media editor, Chris Hamilton. "However, on this occasion, the extent of the checks and the consideration of whether to publish should have been better."

Hoaxes such as the Houla case have been a feature of the news for almost as long as newspapers have existed. In 1835, the *New York Sun* was tricked into running six articles reporting the existence of fantastical creatures on the moon, including bat-like people. It is the sort of story that many people would share with each other, if only to express incredulity that there could be bat-people on the moon. On social media, such hoaxes are quickly contested but also quickly spread. A rumour can easily take hold and circulate widely as people jump into the news and became part of the process of making the news. Misinformation can spread at lightning speed on the digital grapevine, giving greater urgency to the need to develop skills to sort fact from fiction.

Traditionally, the journalist has been the professional who filters raw information, checking it for accuracy and veracity before making it available to the public. Journalists have always

struggled with the tension between being fast and being accurate. Missteps by the media are more common and have greater
impact during breaking news, when details are confused, contradictory and changeable. Public figures are prematurely declared
dead, as happened with Representative Gabrielle Giffords and
former Penn State football coach Joe Paterno. Or terror suspects
are misidentified, as happened in the hunt for the Boston
Marathon bombers. When anyone can publish freely, "verify
then publish" becomes "publish then verify" as people share eyewitness accounts, comment on the news or evaluate information
posted by others. The skills that were once the domain of professional journalists are something we all need in order to assess
sources of accurate and reliable information.

The challenge is particularly acute at times of crisis, when
access to reliable information in a timely manner is crucial, yet
traditional sources are stretched or nonexistent. For most, these
situations are the exception, often in times of a natural disaster.
But not for parts of Mexico, where drug violence, an ineffective
state and a muzzled press have left citizens finding their own
ways to navigate information coming from the many voices on
social networks. What is happening in cities like Veracruz
highlights the challenges over issues such as misinformation,
trust and reputation when people have to rely on information
from each other.

WHEN CITIZENS PROVIDE THE NEWS

With its strategic location on the Gulf of Mexico, the port of
Veracruz was the gateway for the Spanish conquistadors who

colonized the country in the sixteenth century. With his eleven ships, 508 soldiers and sixteen horses, the Spanish conquistador Hernán Cortés founded the city in 1519. Veracruz went on to become one of the main channels to the riches of the Aztec empire. Spanish galleons laden with Aztec gold, silver, cotton and tobacco sailed from the port to Spain. Today, little remains of the colonial city, but it is still Mexico's most important port.

Some five hundred years later, Veracruz has become a gateway for drugs, and Mexico's criminal cartels are the ones fighting for control. In the summer of 2011, the state of Veracruz caught the attention of criminal gangs. By then, tens of thousands of people had died in five years of clashes between criminals, police and the military since President Felipe Calderón launched an assault on criminal cartels. The violence had been concentrated in the north, along the U.S. border, but in 2011, it started spilling south, and Veracruz was a prized state for the cartels. By September, more than five hundred people had died in drug-related violence, up from 179 in 2010 and 133 in 2009. Bodies were dumped in the street or left to rot in houses, often bound and tortured. Many were the victims of tit-for-tat killings by criminal gangs. But police and civilians had also been caught in the crossfire.

The violence in Mexico is not just about controlling the flow of drugs. The drug cartels also want to control the flow of information. Anyone who reports on the activities of the country's drug lords is in danger. Mexico has become one of the world's most dangerous countries for journalists. Nowhere is more dangerous than Veracruz state, which is one of the world's ten most dangerous places for the media. The drug cartels don't want the attention of the press and seek to silence them in the most brutal ways possible. Among the journalists who fell victim to gangs were Gabriel Huge and Guillermo Luna. They went missing in May 2012. A day later, they were found dismembered, stuffed into garbage bags and dumped in a drainage canal in a wealthy beachfront suburb of the port of Veracruz. Their deaths brought to seven the number of local journalists killed in two years in the city.

The campaign of intimidation by the cartels has had an alarming effect on the media. The press are just too scared to report the gang violence, afraid that they or their families will be grabbed, killed and dumped by the side of the road. The *Vanguardia* newspaper in the northern state of Coahuila even ran an editorial telling its readers that the "absurd, inexplicable and indescribable violence" made it impossible for its journalists to do their jobs. In many areas of Mexico, millions live without reliable and accurate reports from professional journalists of the violence around them.

Citizens have filled the void left by professional media, posting information about the latest violent outbreaks online. "There are cities in Mexico in which people do not go out if they haven't first checked social networks," Jesus Robles Maloof, a human rights activist, told the BBC. In a highly connected country like Mexico, where cell phones are commonplace, Twitter has become one of the main sources of information. By March 2011, Twitter had just under 2.5 million active users in the country, and they pumped out a lot of messages. A study by the Oxford Internet Institute showed that Mexico was the fifth-largest country in terms of information shared on Twitter, behind the U.S., Brazil, Indonesia and the U.K. People check the service before deciding whether it is safe enough to go to the supermarket or pick up their children from school. Real-time information can be a matter of life or death in cities where people fear stumbling into a gun battle between soldiers and criminals. But people are also trying to decide whether they can trust what they are reading.

THE CIVIC MEDIA CURATORS

When a team at Microsoft Research dug into the exchanges on social media in Mexico, they were surprised by the results. The researchers focused on four cities—Monterrey, Reynosa, Saltillo and Veracruz—and analyzed almost 600,000 tweets sent over sixteen months between August 2010 and November 2011. These were all messages related to Mexico's drug conflict. Half the posts were individual messages, while a third were retweets spreading the original message. Violence was a common thread, with words such as "shootings" and "explosions" commonly used. An upsurge in reports of clashes or kidnappings triggered a spike in messages.

At first glance, the volume of information points to a lively exchange. The messages came from 65,082,414 users in the four cities. On average, they posted 9.4 messages each. But that figure is misleading, as it includes many who only ever sent out one tweet. Instead, a handful of people were behind most of the information. In Monterrey, just nine people were responsible for more than a thousand messages associated with events in the city. The results were similar for the other three cities. The research reflects how top-line figures about sharing mask the dynamics of how information circulates. Some people are active some of the time, but only a few are active all of the time. On Twitter, 40 per cent of active users don't share anything— they log in to see what's going on—and a tiny fraction receives most of that attention. This makes it even more important to identify the key Influencers and assess how reliable they are as trusted sources.

One of these trusted sources is Angela. A woman in her twenties, she spends up to fifteen hours a day on Twitter and has amassed twenty-five thousand followers since signing up in 2009. She was one of the few citizens of Mexico identified as civic media curators. Angela is not her real name; revealing her identity would put her life at risk. Usually, we will be suspicious of information coming from someone who wants to remain anonymous; in the information wars in Mexico, anonymity saves lives. In September 2011, the mutilated bodies of a man and woman in their twenties were left hanging from a pedestrian bridge in the border city of Nuevo Laredo. "This will happen to all Internet snitches," said a sign near the bodies, listing the names of blogs that report on the drug trade. The message was signed "Z," a possible reference to the Zetas cartel.

In such an atmosphere of fear, anonymous sources such as Angela establish their credibility over time, by reporting on the location of gunmen, shootings and cartel checkpoints. As they share more and more reliable information, they build up a reputation for dependable and timely information. "They are very influential, powerful people in the Twittersphere in their city," said Andrés Monroy-Hernández of Microsoft Research. "They have a wide reach and people trust them."

For Angela, her work in vetting information and broadcasting details of roads to avoid or of violent clashes in the city is a service to the community. "It is as if I was a war correspondent on social networks of the war we are living in Mexico," she said. Curators like Angela are managing to provide reliable information. Research shows that spikes in reports of violence on Twitter match with attacks later reported in the local media.

SORTING FACT FROM FICTION

The open nature of social media makes it susceptible to deliberate attempts by criminal gangs to spread misinformation or to erroneous reports by citizens who believe they are doing the right thing for their community.

Gilberto Martinez Vera thought he was doing his fellow citizens a service. The schoolteacher considers himself a true resident of Veracruz. He sees himself as a "truth troubadour" who abhors the injustices of the world. One of the ways he did this was by chronicling the latest goings-on in the city on Twitter. On Thursday, August 25, 2011, his attempt to tell the truth and help the people of Veracruz backfired. "I can confirm that at the Jorge Arroyo school in the Carranza district, five children taken, armed group. Total psychosis in the area," he tweeted. The message might have gone unnoticed. But it was picked up by an informal group of locals who follow the Twitter account VerFollow. The account was one of the trusted information hubs on events in Veracruz, so the original message gained additional credibility.

A few minutes later, Martinez gave more details of the supposed attacks. In this message, he said information came from his sister-in-law, and he corrected the name of the school, saying it was Alfonso Arroyo school. Around the same time, a former government official turned radio commentator, Maria de Jesus Bravo Pagola, started posting information on Facebook about other attacks at the city's schools. During the day, she wrote various messages, including that a helicopter had opened fire at one of the schools.

The news about school attacks lit a powder keg. The residents of Veracruz were already on edge after a summer of gunfights between police and drug traffickers. One attack outside the city aquarium had left a tourist dead and maimed his wife and children. On this particular Thursday, some residents thought more violence was imminent after spotting convoys of marines. Parents raced to save their children. There was traffic chaos on the streets of Veracruz. In the ensuing hysteria, there were twenty-six car crashes. Some just gave up on their cars, leaving the vehicles in the middle of the road. Emergency telephone lines were jammed as terrified parents tried to find out whether their children were in danger.

None of the reports of the attacks turned out to be true. Gunmen didn't kidnap any kids. No helicopters fired on schoolchildren. The only "psychosis" on that day was from worried parents, whose worst fears had been fuelled by the erroneous information. The governor of the state of Veracruz, Javier Duarte, was furious. He had tried to correct the misinformation almost as soon as the first report of school attacks broke on Twitter. But his tweet from his personal account that the rumour was false didn't make any difference. Martinez and Bravo Pagola were arrested and charged with terrorism and sabotage. "Those who caused damage are not being punished because they are Twitter users but because of the consequences of their irresponsible acts," Governor Duarte wrote on Twitter.

The terrorism charges against Martinez and Bravo Pagola made headlines across the world. The two Mexicans faced thirty years in prison for passing on what they thought at the time was accurate information. In Mexico, thousands rallied behind the two accused, taking to social networking sites to vent their outrage at the arrests. Amnesty International weighed in, accusing Mexico of violating freedom of expression. The terrorism charges were dropped a month later, but only after the state created a new offence of using social media to spread misinformation that might disturb the public order.

The story of the "Twitter terrorists" is an extreme example of what happens when people try to make sense of the world with limited information. People are not going to stop spreading half-truths or rumours. When a community doesn't have reliable information, it improvises and makes do with what it has. Rumours take hold when details are ambiguous. They gain further traction when people are in a heightened state of anxiety but lack credible sources of information. In Veracruz, a mistrust of local officials and a muzzled press created an environment for the hurried proliferation of half-truths and lies, even when those spreading the information had the best intentions.

Rumours are improvised news. People improvise and make do with what they have when faced with a threatening or ambiguous situation. They add what they have heard to a large pool of unverified information that swirls among social circles where information is contested or confirmed. It may be talk about the death of a well-known figure, a new Apple iPhone or a celebrity couple. The surfeit of speculation, rumour and opinion reflects how people have always managed information. Such information gains far more prominence due to the speed, reach and visibility of digital networks, adding urgency for a combination of verification approaches that considers four areas of credibility: the characteristics of the message, the person who sent it, its topic and how it spread.

DETECTING THE LANGUAGE OF TRUTH

When people talk about Brett Lawrie, it's usually about his performance on the baseball diamond with the Toronto Blue Jays. The third baseman from Langley, British Columbia, made his major league debut in August 2011. He didn't have much time to make an impression. His season ended prematurely when he fractured his right middle finger the following month. During an inconsistent second season with the Jays, Lawrie was in the headlines in May 2012 for his "wild rage" after contesting a call by the umpire. The Blue Jays player made the news again a month later, but not for his performance on the field.

Lawrie was unwinding with his buddy Corey at the Eaton Centre in downtown Toronto on Saturday, June 2, 2012, after an afternoon game against the Boston Red Sox. He was on the way out of the shopping mall when he heard a series of bangs in rapid succession. Lawrie didn't know what was going on, but joined the shoppers rushing to get out of the place. At 6:24 P.M., he sent a message to his more than 125,000 followers on Twitter from his @blawrie13 account: "Pretty sure someone just let off a round bullets in eaton center mall .. Wow just sprinted out of the mall . . . Through traffic . . ." A minute later, he sent out another tweet: "People sprinting up the stairs right from where we just were . . . Wow wow wow."

Lawrie's quick-fire messages were some of the first accounts of a shooting at the shopping mall in which two people were killed and five injured. More than a thousand people passed on his initial tweet. Hundreds shared his photograph of emergency vehicles outside the mall, one of the first images posted online of the turmoil at the scene. Speaking about his improbable stint as an impromptu reporter, Lawrie said he was just trying to help people. "I just thought I'd get it out there to anybody that could have been in the mall or anybody that needed to get there ASAP," he told reporters. "I thought I could give a good piece of information."

On this Saturday, Lawrie became a credible source of news, with his tweets cited as proof of the mall shooting by both media outlets and the public. As a public figure, he would have much to lose if it turned out he was spreading malicious rumours. But his tweets demonstrate how the language used can provide clues as to the veracity of a piece of information. Lawrie's punctuation and grammar was all over the place, adding authenticity. He sounded like someone trying to make sense of the alarming events unfolding around him. The same mistakes in a newspaper story would have the opposite effect, undermining the authority of the publication. People in the middle of a dramatic breaking-news situation tend to focus on specific details of what they are seeing and experiencing, and worry less about dotting all the Is and crossing all the Ts.

Missing from Lawrie's tweets were phrases such as "breaking news." People are not likely to write in journalese, mimicking the media by using terms such as "breaking" or "confirmed." Any such messages need to be treated with a degree of extra caution as they may signal an attempt to hoax the public. When Superstorm Sandy tore through the U.S. eastern seaboard in October 2012, one of the most infamous sources of bogus information was Shashank Tripathi. A New York City hedge fund analyst, he used an anonymous Twitter account under the alias @ComfortablySmug to spread fake news. "BREAKING: Con Edison has begun shutting down ALL power in Manhattan," read one of the missives. Another said: "BREAKING: Confirmed flooding on NYSE. The trading floor is flooded under more than 3 feet of water." The claim of flooding on the floor of the New York Stock Exchange was retweeted 650 times and even made it onto CNN. The use of journalese should have cast doubt on the reliability of the information.

One final indicator of authenticity is the use of swear words. Such language rarely makes it into the daily newspaper, but people tend to swear at times of high stress. Indian researchers analyzed tweets related to fourteen global news events in 2011, including Hurricane Irene, the London riots and the resignation of Steve Jobs. They found that people tended to use profanity when reacting to the news. American software engineer Mike Wilson let off a string of expletives after surviving a plane crash in December 2008. Moments after a Continental Airlines 737 slid off the runway in Denver, he said on his Twitter account @2drinksbehind, "Holy fucking shit I wasbjust in a plane crash!" Wilson even included a typing error for added authenticity.

Sometimes, it is next to impossible to figure out whether a particular snippet that comes across social media is true. We may have no way of judging whether the information is correct. But ignoring the content of the message and instead focusing on the language can help. As a first step, the grammar and punctuation, the use of journalistic clichés and the presence of expletives are clues that can help to evaluate to what extent something may be true. But you should always consider the source and the digital trail left online.

DIGITAL BREADCRUMBS TO THE TRUTH

It is easy to see why people were duped by a fake Twitter account, @AliZiDanPM, purporting to be the Libyan prime minister, Ali Zeidan. There was a photo of the Libyan leader, a link to the government website and the blue checkmark that signals an account verified by Twitter. The messages sounded plausible and gained further credibility as they were quoted in the media. And in case anyone had any doubts, high-profile figures such as British Foreign Secretary William Hague and the U.K. ambassador in Libya followed the account. So far, so credible.

When the real prime minister was caught up in a hostage situation in October 2013, journalists noticed something wasn't quite right with his presumed Twitter account. During his short-lived abduction, Zeidan supposedly tried to persuade a Libyan journalist, Fadwá Gallal, that the Twitter account was genuine. Sky News journalist Tom Rayner dug into earlier messages to find some unlikely statements. "Hmm, @guardian live blog quoting @AliZiDanPM—not convinced it's legit. Aug 16th tweet says he will make all Libyans 'tree hugging hippies.'" @AliZiDanPM was exposed as a hoax.

Checking the credibility of someone's presence on social networks goes beyond just looking at the bio and photo on the account. It involves evaluating digital clues, such as the network of connections, past messages, interactions with others and the account's history. Scrutinizing past messages can help to put together a sense of the person behind the account.

A software consultant in Pakistan, Sohaib Athar, gained worldwide prominence when it turned out he had reported the raid on Osama bin Laden's compound in Abbottabad as it happened in May 2011 on his @ReallyVirtual Twitter account. His past messages about power cuts and hailstorms in Abbottabad suggested he did live in the city, giving his reports greater weight.

One further sign that Athar was genuine was the history behind his account. He had signed up for Twitter as @ReallyVirtual on May 5, 2007, well before the bin Laden raid. An account that has suddenly popped up could signal trouble; the dilemma is that many people join social media immediately after major news events. Some are eyewitnesses; others filter information, adding context and background. Some express support and sympathy while others take advantage of the news to spread falsehood, spam, rumours or phishing attempts. Almost forty thousand new Twitter accounts were opened to comment on the Boston Marathon bombings in the five days after the attack in April 2013. Many were genuine. But many were not. Two months later, 19 per cent of these accounts were deleted or suspended by Twitter.

SEEING THE BIG PICTURE

The hodgepodge of messages offers a trove of information, but it requires taking a bird's-eye view of the overall activity rather than just focusing on individual messages. Charting the conversations around the news shows that the crowd works as a self-correcting machine to elevate the truth. Lies and deceptions tend to be contested far more than credible reports. In the aftermath of the 2010 Chilean earthquake, people living in the capital, Santiago, turned to Twitter. Information from official sources was scarce, creating the ideal conditions for rumours to spread. But the Twitter community functioned as a collaborative filter to confirm reports that were true and cast doubt on those that turned out to be false. Suspect reports were questioned by far more people more often than truthful information. In one example, for every false warning of a tsunami in Valparaiso, there were more than ten updates denying it.

The London riots of August 2011 also showed how social networks can serve to challenge fabrications. Politicians and police were quick to blame social media for helping to incite and organize the disturbances. But an analysis of more than 2.6 million riot-related tweets showed that Twitter was mainly used to mobilize the cleanup rather than to incite violence. During the unrest itself, the network was used to knock down wild rumours of tigers on the loose or of the London Eye on fire. "Despite helping rumours spread at great speed, Twitter has an equal and opposite power to dispel them—often in the space of two or three hours, particularly if the counter-evidence is strong," wrote *Guardian* journalists Jonathan Richards and Paul Lewis.

The bigger the news, the more sensational a story, the more noise there is, the farther it travels and the harder it becomes to detect the truth. There are some events that transcend national boundaries and get everyone talking, such as the Boston Marathon bombings. That's when the limits of the social self-correction machine become all too clear. The story of the bombings unfolded across every media outlet around the world, including social media. Facts competed with speculation, mis-information and rumour. On Twitter alone, there were three thousand tweets per minute at the time of the bombings.

In the days after the marathon bombings, one of the most widespread rumours was the misidentification of the missing Brown University student, Sunil Tripathi, as one of the bombers. The rumours were triggered by the release by the FBI of grainy surveillance photographs of the bombing suspects. A Reddit thread was devoted to discussing whether Tripathi was suspect No. 2. Information taken from the Boston police scanner and spread on Twitter added to the confusion, until the FBI released the names of the suspects: the Tsarnaev brothers.

Even amid the din of misinformation, some tried to stop the speculation. For every five erroneous tweets about Sunil Tripathi, there was one correction. Those 4,485 tweets were initially lost among the 22,819 misleading ones because the wrong informa-tion spread first and at a much faster rate in the initial hours, leaving the truth to catch up later. Others rumours at the time of the bombings, such as the death of an eight-year-old girl, also spread much faster and more widely than corrections. The speed strains our cognitive abilities to detect the patterns pointing to the reliability of a particular piece of information. So in labs across the world, information scientists are working on systems to automatically assess the "truthiness" of social media content, detect fake messages and amplify corrections to reduce the spread of misinformation.

AUTOMATIC DETECTION

"Truthiness" seems to be the right word to describe much of the stuff that floats on social networks. Introduced in October 2005 by satirist Stephen Colbert, it went on to be named the word of the year in 2006 by Merriam-Webster. It inspired a group of scientists at Indiana University, working on ways to separate the truth from misinformation masquerading as facts online, to name their project Truthy. Truthy processes thousands of messages on Twitter, looking for patterns that might lie behind what sometimes seems like a frenzied maelstrom of facts, smears and misinformation. The aim is to develop a truthiness engine to help detect and debunk falsehoods rapidly. "There's a timescale at which things are propagating in social media that's so short," said Filippo Menczer, one of the lead investigators on the project. "We're talking seconds and minutes rather than hours and days."

Scientists have already started noticing some giveaways that messages are fakes or hoaxes by examining the patterns of diffusion of messages. An analysis of close to eight million tweets by 3.7 million users, sent between April 15 and 19, 2013, about the Boston Marathon bombings, highlighted some key trends. Accurate reports tended to be spread at a steady pace from the start. The messages usually came from users with significant numbers of followers. Accounts with small numbers of followers tended to be behind fake messages. The messages spread far more slowly at first, until big-name users passed them on to their networks of fans.

These approaches reveal the order in the apparent chaos of Twitter. The way information circulates through our social circles online can help to assess truthiness. One giveaway is if a handful of accounts churn out a large number of messages and rebroadcast each other's messages. The aim is to give the impression of a groundswell of public outrage over an issue or personality and influence opinions. The tactic is known as "political astroturfing." One of the first documented examples of this type of Twitter-bomb came during the senate race in Massachusetts between Democrat Martha Coakley and Republican Scott Brown. The special election was called after the death of Democratic senator Ted Kennedy in August 2009. In the week leading up to the vote on January 19, 2010, Coakley was on the receiving end of a concerted campaign promoting an anti-Coakley website. Nine fake Twitter accounts, created within thirteen minutes of each other, were behind the 929 tweets sent in 138 minutes. The campaign is estimated to have reached more than sixty thousand Twitter users and resulted in the anti-Coakley website rising in Google search results for the query "Martha Coakley." How far such dirty tricks influence swing voters is hard to say. But in a result widely considered to be an upset, Coakley lost out to Brown by just over 100,000 votes.

Astroturfing campaigns leave telltale signs that scientists can investigate to uncover the political ruses. Rather than analyzing the content of a message to see whether it is true or false, they are using network analysis techniques to look for patterns in how information propagates. Propaganda campaigns tend to share similarities that raise alarm bells: a large number of messages are sent over a short period of time; many of the messages are duplicates, although with slight changes in the wording; they often originate from a handful of accounts that then retweet each other's messages, as in the Coakley case.

"If you hear the same message from many different sources that you think are independent who are saying the same thing, you're much more likely to believe it," explained Bruno Gonçalves, a research associate on the Truthy project. The fire hose of social media messages makes it impossible for an ordinary voter to discern real from fake outbursts of opinion. But it is possible to see how the state-of-the-art algorithms worked on by scientists at Indiana and other universities could be built in to the services and devices used for social media to alert users.

A ready-made system that can help us decode the chatter on social networks, accentuate the good and play down the negative has still to make it out of the lab. Rumours have always been part of the media. So has misinformation. With the development of the Internet and the growth of social networks, there are new avenues for old practices. But the game has changed. In a matter of minutes, a message can reach tens of thousands of people. The powerful communication tools at our fingertips can be harnessed by an oppressed people seeking freedom, as in the Middle East, or by those in power to besmirch opponents. Social media has become a new battlefield for information warfare—above all, when it comes to politics.

a Shared Story
#The Political Power of
a Shared Story
#The Political Power of
a Shared Story
#The Political Power of
a Share

#The Political Power of
a Shared Story

ENRIQUE PEÑA NIETO WAS DRUMMING UP SUPPORT FOR HIS BID TO be Mexico's next president when his carefully orchestrated campaign went off script. During a stop at the Ibero-American University in Mexico City on May 11, 2012, the front-runner in the polls was booed and heckled. On the campus of this elite private university, Peña Nieto was confronted over human rights abuses during his time as a state governor as hundreds of students chanted "Out, out, out." For the students, the suave and telegenic politician was the unacceptable new face of the old authoritarian Institutional Revolutionary Party, the PRI, which had ruled Mexico for seven decades before it was kicked out of office in 2000. Twelve years later, it was making a come-back in the form of Peña Nieto.

What happened next was an eye-opening experience for the students who shouted down the PRI politician. The Mexican media portrayed the protest as the work of a handful of heck-lers. The two dominant TV networks, Televisa and TV Azteca, gave airtime to Peña Nieto officials who argued the trouble-makers were plants, paid by political opponents. The newspapers, which tended to side with the PRI, peddled a similar line. Front-page headlines described Peña Nieto's visit to the university as a "triumph."

Frustrated at the political spin and biased media coverage, 131 students hit back. They recorded short clips of themselves on their laptops and posted the edited video to YouTube. Looking into the camera, the students recited their names and student ID numbers. The simple video was widely shared on Twitter and Facebook with the phrase #YoSoy132, ("I am 132"), amassing more than a million views in ten days. Out of it came Yo Soy 132, a social movement born out of the frustration of an educated youth fed up with entrenched political interests and a media duopoly with business interests closely aligned with those in power.

Yo Soy 132 is one of many recent popular movements that have used social media to take on political elites. From Tahrir Square in Cairo to Gezi Park in Istanbul to Maidan Square in Kiev, protests on the street have been inextricably linked to updates on Twitter, pages on Facebook and videos on YouTube. These resources have been forged into tools of resistance. The very visible role of these new tools has tended to polarize debate. Most noticeably, author Malcolm Gladwell decried the impact of social media, arguing the revolution will not be tweeted. It's too easy to dismiss a like or retweet as inconsequential. Disputing whether social media caused the Arab Spring or arguing whether Occupy Wall Street changed income inequality in the U.S. misses the point. Tweets don't topple governments. But that doesn't mean they don't matter.

Throughout history, popular movements have used the best communication technologies at their disposal to foment revolution—from the telegram to the fax machine and beyond.

At the turn of the century, activists discovered the potential of mobile phones to facilitate and sustain collective action. In the Philippines in 2001, people used text messaging to coordinate five days of protest that resulted in the resignation of President Joseph Estrada. Likewise, text messaging was also used in 2004 in Ukraine to mobilize and organize citizens outraged at fraudulent presidential elections.

Texts, like faxes and photocopiers, have one basic limitation: it is hard to reach and connect with a large, dispersed group of sympathizers. Grassroots movements were always at a disadvantage when faced with the organized machine of established institutions. Social media services don't create movements, but they do help to remove many of the obstacles that make it hard to start a movement, galvanize supporters and publicize aims. Facebook provides a ready-made social network, while Twitter offers an instant broadcast channel.

In Mexico, Twitter was a vital tool for Yo Soy 132. Spanish is the second most common language on Twitter, and some twelve million Mexicans are active on the service. In 2012, Mexico was ranked seventh in the world by the number of Twitter accounts, ahead of Canada, Spain and the Philippines in the top ten. It is one of the main ways that citizens share and receive real-time updates about the ongoing drug violence. Social media made it possible to turn an isolated event into a national movement by making visible a groundswell of opposition to the established elites. The students of Yo Soy 132 were able to tell their story despite being ignored by the media.

CHALLENGING ELITE NARRATIVES

A patch of green in the heart of Istanbul's historic centre seems an unlikely backdrop for revolt. But Gezi Park proved to be the spark that lit simmering discontent with the ruling Justice and Development Party (AKP). In common with those in Tahrir Square in Egypt, Zuccotti Park in New York and Maidan Square in Kiev, the protests in Turkey were synonymous with the physical occupation of a symbolic location. The park was one of the few remaining green spaces in Taksim Square and was due to make way for a replica of an Ottoman-era barracks, with a shopping mall and luxury apartments. A few dozen protesters staged a sit-in at the park at the end of May 2013 to stop bulldozers from uprooting trees. The peaceful protest was met with tear gas and pepper spray as police moved in to clear the area.

A photograph by Osman Orsal of Reuters encapsulated the moment: a police officer in riot gear is pepper-spraying a woman dressed in red who looks like she is simply standing there, her head turned to one side. The picture echoed another one, taken in November 2011, of a police officer at the University of California at Davis pepper-spraying student protesters that became an Internet meme. In Turkey, instead of dampening the revolt, the police action prompted thousands more to turn up in the park. The more police used tear gas and water cannon, the more Gezi Park became a lightning rod, attracting thousands with grievances against the government.

Anyone watching Turkish TV would have little idea of what was unfolding in the centre of Istanbul. The conglomerates that own mainstream Turkish media are cautious about making trouble for a government that can hand out lucrative contracts. As water and tear gas flew in Gezi Park, CNN Türk showed a documentary about penguins. Meanwhile, CNN International was broadcasting live from Taksim Square. CNN Türk's programming choice, as Istanbul turned into a battlefield, seemed too ridiculous to be true, and the story spread like wildfire on social media.

The lack of mainstream media coverage didn't matter; Turks could share accounts, photos and videos on Twitter. Over the first few days of the protest, there were at least two million tweets with hashtags related to Gezi Park. Most of the messages came from within Turkey, and about 50 per cent originated from Istanbul. With virtually no coverage in the mainstream media, the protesters created their own news network on Twitter to tell their story.

The stories from Gezi Park, Occupy Wall Street and Idle No More would have been so different without Twitter or Facebook. When it comes to covering civil disobedience, journalists rely on police and officials to explain what happened. The people who are quoted in a story shape the nature and tone of the coverage. Sometimes, protesters are seen as heroes, as in Egypt. At other times, they are portrayed as villains, as in the G20 protests in Toronto. When the media cover alternative movements, they tend to focus on the clashes between protesters and police. Any political aims are buried by the accounts of violence.

Journalists are understandably perplexed at how to cover movements such as Gezi or Occupy, which seemingly lack identifiable leaders or a set list of demands. Confrontations with the police make for a much clearer narrative. When Occupy started in Manhattan on September 17, 2011, no one seemed to know what to make of the bunch of people at Zuccotti Park. For the first week, nothing appeared in the major newspapers. When *The New York Times* turned its attention to what was happening in its city, the coverage was dismissive in tone, with headlines that read GUNNING FOR WALL STREET, WITH FAULTY AIM and WALL STREET OCCUPIERS, PROTESTING TILL WHENEVER. TV news was worse; there were no mentions on the major networks for ten days.

In Canada, the mainstream media presented "two parallel, rarely intersecting universes," said Donald Gutstein, adjunct professor at Simon Fraser University's School of Communication. Some newspapers, such as the *Toronto Star*, presented Occupy as a worldwide movement demanding greater economic equality. But others—above all, the right-leaning *National Post*—tended to portray Occupy as "little more than a rag-tag bunch of ne'er-do-wells with vague but nevertheless invalid goals."

At the same time, a different narrative was being created through social media. It told the story of citizens concerned about the gap between the rich and the poor. Some activists provided blow-by-blow accounts of police attempts to disband the camps. Others selected stories from the media, adding their own headlines to place them in the context of the aims of Occupy. For yet others, it was a way to challenge the views of opponents. Twitter provided a framework for a geographically dispersed group of people to express a common message of resistance: "We are the 99 per cent." In the mainstream media, Occupy was largely dismissed or marginalized. In social media, it was applauded, analyzed and argued over.

The same pattern of two narratives vying for attention played out in Canada over the Idle No More movement. Over

December 2012 and January 2013, indigenous groups, environmental activists and critics of the Conservative government came together to stage mass protests across Canada. On Twitter, there was a lively discussion with the hashtag #Idlenomore. But as with Occupy, much of the mainstream media first ignored the movement and then either dismissed or criticized it. NATIVES NEED TO TONE DOWN THE ANGER was the headline on an op-ed by one of Canada's most prominent journalists, Rex Murphy, for the *National Post*. In the parallel media universe of Twitter, people instead shared stories from Al Jazeera and *The Guardian* that presented the movement as Canada's own Arab Spring, dubbed its Native Winter.

Changing the tone and focus of the debate does not, by itself, change the outcome. But it can influence how we think of an issue. In June 2009, headlines in the West started to talk about a Twitter revolution in Iran. As Iranians took to the streets to make their anger felt over contested presidential elections, it was hard not to come across a piece in the media extolling Twitter as "the medium of the movement." Iran was one of the first major examples of Twitter taking centre stage as the platform for revolt. The hashtag #IranElection was a major trending topic on Twitter. The number of tweets related to the disputed election result in Iran in June 2009 peaked at 221,774 in one hour, from an average flow of between 10,000 and 50,000 an hour. Seeing the events in Iran through the lens of social media, it appeared as though an irresistible popular movement demanding democracy was sweeping the country.

With enough tweets, it seemed as though the Islamic regime would fall and democracy would come to Iran. Yet at the time of the June 2009 elections, there were only 19,235

Twitter accounts registered in the country, with most of them located in Tehran. As the protests grew in the days after polling, the number of messages coming from inside Iran dropped from half before the election to less than a quarter. In reality, most of the tweets from people talking about the Iran elections came from Europe or North America. The pattern of the messages was in line with waking patterns in North America. People outside of Iran, particularly the large Iranian dispora in the U.S., rather than people in Iran, were the ones behind most of the activity. Twitter was used mainly by concerned citizens watching from abroad to draw attention to the struggle for democracy, rather than as a tool for activists inside Iran to organize and mobilize.

Despite headlines in the West about a Twitter revolution in Iran, the euphoria was short-lived. The protests over a fraudulent presidential election were silenced by a regime ready to use force to stay in power. Tweets were no match for police truncheons and tear gas. But awareness was raised in the West about the internal politics of Iran. For a couple of weeks in June, Americans were paying as much attention to news from Iran as they were to reports about the troubled U.S. economy. Similarly, the Occupy Wall Street movement of 2012 might have failed to bring about any change in the financial system, but it did succeed in getting Americans and the media talking about issues of equality and wealth redistribution.

Governments, businesses and advocacy have always tried to influence public discussion, largely through newspapers, radio and television. Moreover, authoritarian regimes rely on controlling information to isolate and dissuade potential agitators while punishing those who disobey. But the exponential advance in our capacity to share and connect allows for nascent movements to flower, take shape and multiply much more easily and rapidly than ever before.

Social media is the connective tissue of the new body politic. Connective tissue is the most common form of tissue in the body. It keeps everything together, providing support and cohesion. Social media has made feasible new movements that rise quickly, seemingly ad hoc, without clear leaders or established institutional structures. For movements from Egypt to Ukraine to Canada, social media has provided the connective tissue to identify like-minded individuals, rally supporters, draw strength from allies and tell their stories.

SHARED AWARENESS, SHARED POWER

Pluralistic ignorance has been one of the greatest barriers for embryonic social movements. The term, first coined in the 1930s by American psychologists Floyd H. Allport and Daniel Katz, refers to a person's notion that he or she is the only one who holds a particular belief or opinion, even though there are others who feel the same way. The phenomenon is common in many social situations. During a poor lesson, students may hesitate to raise their hands to ask a question because they assume they are the only ones who don't understand the material. Individual gang members may be privately uneasy about extreme violence, but go along with it because they incorrectly assume that most others accept it. Everything changes when it becomes easy to find that you are not alone and to connect to others who share your views, as happened in Egypt.

In June 2010, two plainclothes police officers seized Khaled Said in an Internet café in Egypt's second-largest city, Alexandria. Witnesses recalled how the officers dragged the twenty-eight-year-old Egyptian into a nearby building and then beat him to death, smashing his head against an iron gate, punching him in the face and gut and kicking him. The police denied accusations of brutality, claiming that Said had choked to death while trying to swallow drugs.

Reports of police beatings were far from unusual in Egypt. During thirty years of rule by Hosni Mubarak, police and security services were known for resorting to excessive force to quash anyone questioning their authority. State censorship of media meant such abuses of power went unreported. The Internet was creating a space for dissent. Egyptian bloggers turned to the web to write about such frowned-upon issues as workers' or women's rights. Harassed and intimidated by the police, these bloggers tended to be read by other activists. Then came the death of Khaled Said.

A few days after his death, the now-famous Facebook page We Are All Khaled Said appeared. It showed cell phone photos taken by Said's brother when he visited the morgue. Behind the memorial page was an Egyptian-born Google marketing executive, Wael Ghonim, who was living in Dubai at the time. The images of Said's battered face, broken nose and shattered jaw struck a chord with Ghonim and others like him. Tens of thousands of people joined the page to report accounts of police brutality and human rights abuses in Egypt.

Facebook didn't create the outrage, but it helped to provide an outlet for Egyptians to connect with like-minded individuals and draw strength from the numbers who had had enough of

Mubarak and his cronies. There were four million people in Egypt on Facebook by 2010. Unlike political blogs, which tended to be read mostly by activists, the social network included all sorts of people. "Prior to the murder of Khaled Said, there were blogs and YouTube videos that existed about police torture, but there wasn't a strong community around them," said Jillian C. York of the OpenNet Initiative at the Berkman Center for the Internet and Society at Harvard University. Facebook was the connective tissue for individuals to synchronize their actions and realize their collective power.

Social media was even more important in undermining pluralistic ignorance in Tunisia. The administration of Zine El Abidine Ben Ali was a far more authoritarian regime, one that tolerated no dissent. During my time as a foreign correspondent for the BBC in the early 1990s, I personally attracted the ire of the government for reporting on democracy activists and on human rights abuses and was expelled from the country. One of the ways the aging autocrat had held on to power since 1987 was through a tightly controlled media. No one much liked Ben Ali, but it was hard to get a sense of the scale of the discontent. The government's approach was to isolate and quash protests quickly, before news of them could spread. The strategy worked when demonstrations were held in Gafsa and nearby towns in the interior in 2008. Even Facebook was blocked for a while, although only a few thousand Tunisians were on it at the time.

By the time a street vendor doused himself with petrol and set himself alight in Sidi Bouzid in December 2010, Ben Ali's strategy of containment no longer worked. Within hours, the actions of Mohamed Bouazizi sparked protests in the town that were documented in videos posted to Facebook, which was far more popular by then—even Ben Ali had 223,000 "friends" on Facebook. Activists outside of Tunisia repackaged the footage for international audiences and Al Jazeera broadcast it to millions of Tunisians. A small protest turned into a nationwide revolt as the news spread online and on TV.

There is power in the knowledge that there are others who are willing to take a stand. It is a common thread in movements such as Occupy Wall Street. The activists who gathered in Zuccotti Park near Wall Street in New York used the hashtag #occupywallstreet as a rallying call. For them, Twitter was a way to bring people together and feel part of something. "It's the first time that it's very common and supportive for so many different kinds of people to just sort of mesh together," said a demonstrator called Erica. "But being able to be in contact, and you meet people in New York who feel the same way you do. It can be really liberating and satisfying, and encouraging."

Imagine being one of a handful of people who turn up for a demonstration. Fear of taking part in an unsuccessful protest and the potential consequences are a significant deterrent to action—more so in repressive regimes, where the cost of public dissent can be a beating, detention or worse. In Egypt, the message of resistance shared by thousands across social networks was to be a powerful catalyst for action. Facebook didn't cause tens of thousands of Egyptians to take to the streets and risk a brutal reaction from the police, but it did play a critical role in encouraging many to take a stand.

Zeynep Tufekci of the University of North Carolina at Chapel Hill teamed up with Christopher Wilson of the civic advocacy group the Engine Room to investigate how social media shaped the protests. During four days in February 2011, the team surveyed just under 1,200 people who had taken to Tahrir Square. The interviews took place less than two weeks after the resignation of President Mubarak, against a backdrop of continuing street violence and political uncertainty.

Egyptians tuned in to Al Jazeera via their satellite dishes and read the newspapers for general information. But more interpersonal forms of media, like Facebook and email, were vital in organizing, mobilizing and amplifying the protests. Egyptians who turned to Facebook, Twitter and blogs to talk about the planned action were far more likely to have attended the first day, on January 25. The odds were much lower for those following events on satellite TV. Making a public stand in the first demonstration takes courage. It is when an opposition movement is at its most vulnerable. No one can be sure how many people are going to attend or how the regime will react. The connections people made, both face to face and via social media, forged ties that emboldened individuals to take action.

A click to "like" a Facebook page cannot be dismissed as mere slacktivism. Even something as simple as a like can be a compelling signal that others share the same values and beliefs. Just as in Egypt, social media served as a catalyst in the student-led protests in Chile in 2011. The people who used social media frequently were nearly eleven times more likely to take to the streets than those who ignored Twitter or Facebook. Social media does not replace taking to the streets, but it can encourage and motivate people to take action. Once the initial spark has been lit, the way people use social media can help to fan the flames of resistance.

MAKING CONNECTIONS

The students who sparked the Yo Soy 132 movement made for unlikely revolutionaries. Ibero-American was one of Mexico's most select private universities, where students were often stigmatized as privileged, clueless kids. Student activism has traditionally sprung out of Mexico's public universities; private institutions were places for the sons and daughters of the country's rich. Little over a week after the students' video was posted to YouTube, rallies were held in seventeen cities across the country, largely organized via Facebook and Twitter. From 150 university students in Cancun to 1,500 protesters in Guadalajara to 46,000 in Mexico City, the message was "No more PRI."

For the protesters in Mexico, using the label #YoSoy132 on Twitter helped the movement spread beyond just university students. Researchers Andrés Monroy-Hernández and Gilad Lotan analyzed who was sending out messages with the hashtag. People from different educational backgrounds, from both the left and the right, coalesced around the #YoSoy132 message of dissent. Movements such as Yo Soy 132 are at a significant disadvantage compared with older, better-established social movements. They don't have the formal structures of more traditional organizations such as trade unions or NGOs. The hashtag makes up in part for this organizational deficit.

Using a hashtag signals a desire to join a conversation and tell everyone your reaction, on subjects as diverse as #RIPMandela, #RoyalBaby and #sharknado. For loose social movements such as Yo Soy 132, it serves as a social and cultural bridge through which individuals from diverse backgrounds come together in loosely knit groups on an ad hoc basis—no formal membership required. The hashtag has helped movements get beyond their immediate base and foster a shared awareness among people fed up with mainstream politics, indignant at corporate greed and frustrated with a lack of jobs and opportunities. The use of the hashtag reveals whether protesters are trying to connect with a national or international audience.

For the first few weeks of the uprising in Egypt and in the days after the fall of Mubarak, there were hundreds of thousands of tweets with the hashtag #egypt. It gave the impression of a nation rising up after years of repression and expressing a collective cry for freedom. The reality is somewhat different. In these early, heady days of the revolution, the majority of messages were in English, and only a third came from Egypt. Among those on the ground who rose to prominence were young Egyptians Gigi Ibrahim and Mona Seif. But alongside the voices from Cairo was a parallel stream of opinion leaders outside of the country who served to bridge cultural differences between East and West.

The Mauritanian-American activist Nasser Weddady, known on Twitter as @weddady, was one such cultural bridge. The son of a Mauritanian diplomat, he left his homeland in 1999 and moved to the U.S. Wedaddy emerged as one of the four most influential people on Twitter during the Arab Spring. From his office in Boston, Weddady acted as a clearinghouse for tweets from the region, passing them on to his network of journalists, policy makers, experts and the public. Another such bridge was the Egyptian-American writer and journalist Mona Eltahawy. She became a familiar name on TV screens and on Twitter as she filtered and interpreted events in Egypt for Western audiences. Such voices took a message of revolution and made it understandable for the West, helping to kindle sympathy and support for the demonstrators.

In the weeks following the fall of Mubarak on February 11, 2011, there was a change in the conversation on #egypt. The number of tweets in English tapered off and the conversation shifted to rebuilding a political system. From March, an average of 75 per cent of tweets were not in English. Instead of reaching out to the West, Egyptians were using Twitter to exchange news, views and aspirations about the future of their country. The conversation continues to this day.

THE LIMITS OF A SHARED STORY

In Mexico, the Yo Soy 132 movement could not stop the PRI from returning to power after an absence of twelve years. After various recounts, Peña Nieto was confirmed as the new president on July 6, 2012. The forty-six-year-old won with 38 per cent of the vote, just six points ahead of his nearest rival. Since his victory at the ballot box, the Mexican president has become one of the most influential heads of state on Twitter, coming in ninth out of 123 world leaders who are on the network. Through his account on Twitter, @EPN, Peña Nieto regularly shares information and photos of his daily activities and meetings with his more than 1.5 million followers.

The supporters of Yo Soy 132 have the consolation of knowing that Peña Nieto faces checks and balances that did not exist when the PRI was last in power. His party did not win a majority in either of the legislative houses. Twelve of the thirty-one states are in the hands of other parties, as is the federal district of Mexico City. As with other grassroots movements, such as Gezi Park, it is difficult to gauge the immediate impact of social media. The AKP remained in power in Turkey, but the protests showed that the party could be challenged.

The principal strength of social media for new social movements is also its main weakness. Facebook, Twitter and YouTube allow people to share their views and connect with others, without the need for an institutional structure or even a name. In the past, mounting any sort of campaign was hard and time-consuming. Social media accelerates the pace of rebellion. A small event, be it a video by Mexican students or a protest camp in Istanbul, can quickly spiral into a national protest movement, drawing in supporters from all walks of life. It is then documented in real time by the people in the middle of it all.

The velocity of protest is unprecedented. But velocity is both friend and foe. Movements gain momentum but lack staying power. Movements from Gezi Park to Occupy to Idle No More faced the same challenge: how to tap the burst of energy and enthusiasm before it fizzles out. The lack of clear leadership, hierarchy or direction emerge as weaknesses, as these are key elements in transitioning from a vibrant movement of the now to an organization of tomorrow. The unity created by a shared cry of "no" has to be translated into a positive proposal of change. Twitter is very good at spreading a message of opposition. It is much harder to use it to work out an agenda for change.

#The Way Ahead
#The Way Ahead
#The Way Ahead
#The Way Ahead
#The Way Ahead
#The Way Ahead
#The Way Ahead

CHAPTER TEN

#The Way Ahead

THE EXPLOITS OF A WORLD WAR I ACE CAN TEACH US A LOT ABOUT navigating social media. A hundred years ago, the skies buzzed with men in rickety biplanes in fast-paced dogfights. When Europe went to war in 1914, aerial warfare was a new phenomenon. This was a time of experimentation, during which planes went from being slow, unarmed reconnaissance platforms to fast and deadly flying weapons. Over the four years of war, more than 100,000 aircraft and more than 55,000 air crewmen were lost. For the first two years, air combat was unplanned and erratic, until one German pilot came up with a novel approach that revolutionized aerial warfare.

Oswald Boelcke flew his first combat mission on September 1, 1914, and downed his first enemy plane ten months later, on July 4, 1915. The son of a teacher, Boelcke was not the top German ace of the war, but he was a master tactician who set the tone for aerial combat for decades to come. Boelcke wasn't physically strong and was susceptible to asthma attacks. But during the first two years of the Great War, he was the scourge of the Allied air forces and celebrated as a German hero. At just twenty-five years of age, he was recognized by the German emperor with the highest honour for war services, the Blue Max.

What made Boelcke remarkable is that he was the first to try to understand this new form of fighting in the skies. He noticed that individual German aircraft, flying without any coordination, were easy pickings for Allied fighters. He drew on his aptitude for mathematics and physics to develop the concept of situational awareness in aerial combat. He figured out that it was not enough for pilots to be aware of what was in their immediate vicinity; they needed to understand the big picture so that they could anticipate what might happen next.

In the skies above Europe, pilots had to be always vigilant, monitoring the rudimentary instruments in the cockpit while remaining on the alert for the dot on the periphery of their vision that could signal the approach of an enemy. A hundred years later, we find ourselves in a similar position: our digital skies are filled with news and information, coming at us via television, radio, newspapers, magazines, computers, cell phones, tablets, e-readers, and even game consoles. Keeping up with the news is no longer a discrete activity that takes place first thing in the morning or in the evening. It is an activity that takes place throughout the day via different formats, devices and technologies, shared by journalists, bloggers, experts, friends or family.

By 2014, the average American adult was spending eleven hours per day watching TV, listening to the radio, checking their smartphone or going online on their computer. The figure is even higher for millennials: they're spending up to eighteen hours a day skimming the web, using social media, watching TV, playing video games and more, doing several of these things all at the same time. Media is ever-present and ubiquitous.

The basis for situational awareness is knowing what is happening around you and understanding what the information means to you, now and in the future. Boelcke realized that in order to win in the air, a pilot had to be able to keep tabs on dogfights all around. He brought discipline and order to the chaotic skies by pioneering the idea of fighter squadrons and tactics training, coming up with the "Dicta Boelcke," a set of basic principles for aerial combat that have guided fighter pilots ever since. The rules were designed to improve the situational awareness of his squadron in a rapidly changing environment. In the summer of 1916, he picked the most promising pilots, organized them into squadrons and trained them in his new tactics. The effect was immediate and dramatic. Over the two months of September and October 1916, Boelcke's squadrons accounted for the majority of the 211 Allied aircraft shot down. The Germans lost only thirty-nine planes.

In a media environment that seems to be always on, always buzzing with information, the lament from many is that there is no time to think because of what the veteran British TV journalist Nik Gowing has called the "tyranny of real time." Past generations felt the same way as new communication technologies altered flows of information. In 1621, the English scholar Richard Burton griped about "new news" he heard every day of "war, plagues, fires, inundations, thefts, murders, massacres, meteors, comets, spectrums, prodigies, apparitions" and more. Burton was writing during the explosion in publishing that came in the wake of the development of the Gutenberg printing press. The outcome was a rethink in how to cope with the abundance of published information, the results of which led to the development of tools such as indices and a realization that not every book needs to be read.

People living through the surge in cheap dailies and weeklies in the late nineteenth century felt similarly challenged by the speed and volume of information. Some U.S. cities had a dozen or more daily newspapers, where news jostled with a miscellany of tidbits, from household hints to historical factoids. An editorial in *Harper's Magazine* in 1892 complained that people "cannot afford a quarter of an hour a day to glance at a newspaper, and to reflect for five minutes more upon the meaning of the intelligence of the whole planet which is daily spread before them."

Grumblings about new media technologies turning us into a generation of skimmers are nothing new. Every generation finds a way of coping with what seems like a sudden leap in the amount of news and information around us. In response to the information overload of the late nineteenth and early twentieth centuries, scrapbooks became the Google and blogging of the day. Thousands made scrapbooks of news clippings to save and create their own record of events, often passing those books on to family and friends.

Facebook, Twitter and YouTube are just the latest media technologies to accelerate the pace of news and information. As with previous generations, we need new ways to cope with the tapestry of media of the twenty-first century. The pilots of World War I faced a comparable scenario and turned to situational awareness techniques to make sense of the whirlwind around them.

While situational awareness came out of aviation, it has spread to other fields in which individuals operate in a complex environment, from air traffic controllers to nuclear power plant operators. It has even surfaced in video games. In the third-person shooter *Spec Ops: The Line*, players are rewarded with a situational awareness trophy when they stun approaching enemies by shooting a skylight and dumping sand on their heads. At a time when we are seemingly immersed in media during every waking moment, situational awareness can help to conquer the seemingly torrential streams of news and information all around us.

MAKING SENSE OF SITUATIONAL AWARENESS

We humans have always needed to be mindful of our surroundings. Our prehistoric ancestors, eking out a living in a hostile and violent land, would have needed to watch out for and recognize vital cues to stay alive. The longer someone managed to survive, the better they became at situational awareness. In the industrial age, the need for situational awareness became ever more pressing as machines replaced people to perform simple physical tasks. The workplace became more complicated, requiring people to monitor, understand and assess information to make sure everything ran smoothly.

Power plant operators are a good example of a job where people have to keep track of multiple factors. Every day, they scrutinize charts, meters and gauges to monitor voltage and electricity flows, checking equipment and indicators to ensure that we can switch on the kettle in the morning, heat up our lunch and watch TV in the evening. The work is not physically strenuous, but workers have to pay attention all the time. The

U.S. Department of Labor describes it as a job for people who are attentive and detail-oriented, with strong problem-solving skills. In other words, they need to be good at situational awareness—taking in a great deal of information, understanding what it means and foreseeing future consequences.

The presence of complex information systems in the workplace has been mirrored by the use of similar systems in our social spheres. Every day, people are exposed to streams of words, images, sound and video demanding attention and interpretation. "The problem with today's systems is not a lack of information, but finding what is needed when it is needed," wrote the renowned expert in situational awareness, Mica Endsley, in 2000. Endsley, with more than two hundred scientific articles and reports to her credit, made these comments before the dawn of social media. But her work on situational awareness can help in navigating these endless streams of information.

Situational awareness offers a framework to know what's going on at any particular time. It is how people like pilots or power plant operators develop and maintain an idea of their sophisticated and dynamic workplace in order to be able to plan ahead and make good decisions. Endsley defines situational awareness as "the perception of elements in the environment within a volume of time and space, the comprehension of their meaning and the projection of their status in the near future."

There are three basic levels to situational awareness. Level one is being aware of what is happening around you, monitoring, detecting and recognizing actions and events. Level two is making sense of what is happening around you by taking what might be disjointed elements and putting them together to see the bigger picture. Level three involves taking that understanding to anticipate what might happen next so that you can make the best decisions.

The experience of pilots of commercial airliners illustrates the three levels of situational awareness. First, they have to be aware of the details of the flight plan, weather conditions along the way, the state of the onboard systems and the location of other aircraft, as well as a myriad of other details such as fuel reserves. The safety of the flight depends on how the flight crew deciphers all this information. Second, crew members have to understand how changes in the route may affect the flight. Will the plane have to climb to a higher altitude to avoid stormy weather, deviating from the flight plan? How will that affect fuel reserves? Pilots make sense of information by applying their knowledge and experience to create an accurate mental model of their environment. And third, the flight crew then needs to think ahead and anticipate future developments based on its members' perception and understanding of the environment. Has the estimated time of arrival changed? Should the pilots burn more fuel to make up for a delay? If the aircraft misses its landing slot, how long will it need to fly in a holding pattern until another one opens up? All these considerations go into achieving the final goal of getting travellers safely to their destination.

Despite all the training, almost 90 per cent of accidents among major airlines involving human error could be attributed to a loss of situational awareness. An analysis of errors taken from U.S. safety reports found a heavy workload, a breakdown in communications, time pressures, weather or inexperience all undermined situational awareness. Planes deviated off course, changed altitude or came too close to another aircraft.

Given the importance of constantly knowing what is happening around you, flight crew members are trained to spot the factors that chip away at situational awareness. There are numerous factors that constantly undermine the perception level of situational awareness, such as tunnel vision. For someone driving a car, this might entail concentrating on a forthcoming turn-off and not noticing that other vehicles are coming up fast from behind. Other things include complacent behaviour or distracted driving. On long, boring journeys, it can be awfully tempting to reach out for the smartphone and just check messages. When it comes to sending and receiving information, obsessing about one message could result in failure to see the wider context.

The danger is compounded at the comprehension level of situational awareness. An informed interpretation of a situation depends on reliable information. The problem is exacerbated by scant knowledge or experience. The end result is misunderstanding a situation and drawing the wrong conclusions. Sometimes it is due to confirmation bias, when people interpret information to confirm what they already believe is the problem, in spite of evidence to the contrary. For a business, it could mean dismissing negative comments on social media as inconsequential, with potentially damaging results for a brand.

THE VALUE OF EXPERIENCE

We can improve our situational awareness, given the will and discipline to do so. Anyone who has trained for a job that requires them to assimilate and process large volumes of data knows that the starting point is developing knowledge and experience. A power plant operator needs to know what all the dials and displays do in order to understand what it all means and work out what might happen. The more time you spend at the controls, the more familiar you'll be with the system and the better able you will be to make good decisions. In the workplace, a new employee would expect to be trained and supervised. Power plant operators, for example, go through a program of rigorous on-the-job instruction and have to take more training courses regularly. Knowledge of the system is reinforced by experience, resulting in expertise in an initial level of situational awareness.

When it comes to sharing, it is all too easy to send an ill-advised quip that could land someone in court or an embarrassing photo that could backfire at work. A misunderstanding of Facebook or Twitter is often behind such a slip-up. Such services are deceptively simple to use, and this ease of use hides how social media blurs established boundaries between the personal and professional, the private and public. Using Twitter is child's play. Sign up, write a message of no more than 140 characters and hit "Tweet." Cue anything from photos of food and cute kittens to links to news stories and graphic videos of unrest in the Middle East. Sharing is so simple that it is easy to misstep, even for experienced journalists.

On the evening of February 5, 2009, Peter Horrocks, then head of the BBC newsroom, sent a tweet to another senior editor, Richard Sambrook. They were discussing senior newsroom appointments. The conversation had been taking place in private by using the direct message function in Twitter. But Horrocks clicked the wrong button, sending one of his messages out in a public reply. "It's a very embarrassing cock-up and everyone in the newsroom has been having a lot of fun at my expense," he said at the time. It was a rookie mistake, but one that is all too easy to make in the instant exchange of messages on Twitter.

The more we experience these tools, the more we develop our expertise in understanding them. The ostensibly shambolic and erratic torrent of seemingly random details on Twitter can be bewildering to someone who has just signed up. The information is all mixed up, with no apparent order, hierarchy or coordination. Part of the reason it seems so messy is that it is novel and very different to past forms of media, such as the newspaper. A newspaper front page makes sense to us, as most people have years of knowledge and experience in reading print. It has order and structure. Headline size serves as a pointer to work through the words on the page and decide where to allocate attention. It is a reassuringly familiar format.

In contrast, social media is in its infancy, and its forms shift from year to year. As more people use Facebook or Twitter for longer periods of time, their levels of knowledge and experience increase. What seemed mystifying becomes familiar. What seemed novel becomes a habitual part of the everyday. And the more people are immersed in social media, the more comfortable they are with getting news and information on these services.

Something novel places a heavy burden on our short- and long-term memory, affecting how much brainpower we have left to dedicate to observing and assessing a situation. Perception is shaped by our working and long-term memory stores. Working memory is where we process and keep information for a short period of time. Experience allows the development of long-term memory structures that can help to overcome the shortcomings of our working memory by providing shortcuts to quickly assess a situation. New information simply requires more of our human processing power. Expertise frees up mental resources to devote to figuring out what we need to know, when to seek it and where to find it.

Familiarity matters when it comes to situational awareness. Mental models help to process information quickly. For example, our mental model of how email works may be that we click to create a new message, type in an address, write a short note and then hit Send. The model helps us use email without having to figure out the steps every time we want to send a message. Mental models serve as cognitive shortcuts that allows us to allocate attention, integrate new information and project ahead without overload our working memory. Some of the burden of making sense of a situation is offloaded to long-term recall, leaving more working memory to turn information into knowledge.

FOCUSING ATTENTION

Anyone who commutes by car to work is already applying techniques of situational awareness. Driving is a complex undertaking. We have to figure out the route, look ahead at road signs and signals, keep an eye on the vehicles and pedestrians around us and monitor the dashboard. There might be music playing or a radio host babbling on about the latest celebrity gossip. Driving engages the three levels of situational awareness. We observe the road to see what is happening around us, interpret the information and then project what might happen and make decisions. If we see a traffic light turning orange, we understand that the light will turn red, so we make plans to stop—or, sometimes, to speed up, hoping to make it through just in time.

To be a good driver means not paying attention, at least not to everything all at once. Instead, it involves being selective with limited mental resources. Psychology professor Leo Gugerty of Clemson University in South Carolina tested the idea with twenty-six experienced motorists in a simulator. For half of the experiment, the drivers were asked to remember the position of as many cars as possible. For the other half, they just had to recall cars in their immediate vicinity.

On average, drivers could only keep track of five vehicles, and then only for about fourteen seconds. Most concentrated on the cars closest to them. But there was a significant difference between those asked to remember as much as possible and those asked to limit their recall to the location of the closest cars. Drivers prompted to focus their attention on their immediate vicinity were better at remembering the position of the traffic. Motorists who tried to take in as much information as possible did far worse at remembering the location of cars behind them or farther in front. Striving for total recall worsens situational awareness. Focusing our attention on the most immediate hazards—in this case, the closest vehicles—improves situational awareness.

The value of partial recall was first stressed by cognitive psychologist George Sperling in the 1960s. He tested how many letters people could remember after briefly seeing an array of twelve in rows of four each. Sperling found that people could usually only remember three or four letters. But when he asked them to recall a particular row, the participants could accurately remember any set.

Cognitive training techniques can help allocate attention to the right thing at the right time. Psychology researchers Kerry O'Brien and David O'Hare tested one technique with students at the University of Otago in New Zealand. The students took on the role of an air traffic controller using a simulator called the Wombat Situational Awareness and Stress Tolerance Test. For the experiment, students were told to focus their attention on one plane at a time, while still being aware of what the others were doing. They were instructed to prioritize their attention by considering which was the next aircraft to deal with. Narrowing the priorities of the task, while maintaining a peripheral awareness of the bigger picture, helped weaker students allocate attention, process information and make better decisions.

In an information-rich environment, the temptation is to try to take it all in. There are constant cries for attention from email alerts, Facebook status updates or Twitter messages popping up on myriad devices. Ignoring them can prompt feelings of anxiety. Fear of missing out (FOMO) is a state of mind that has always existed. But social media has fuelled the compulsion to be continually connected with what others are doing. It is worse among millennials, a generation who have grown up against a backdrop of Facebook, Twitter and YouTube. Trying to keep up with everything is counterproductive. Instead, don't respond to every chime or ping. Adopt partial recall strategies and allocate attention to the most pressing and relevant elements at any given time. The result will be an improved awareness and understanding of the environment.

AWARENESS WITH PURPOSE

Knowledge and focus are of limited use in situational awareness without one more vital ingredient: purpose. Identifying goals is central to situational awareness. Defining specific goals helps to allocate attention and select relevant information. As goals change, so do the selection, interpretation and integration of information. In battle, clear goals can mean the difference between life and death. Officers face a barrage of information on the battlefield. They have to decide what to pay attention to, what it means and what might happen next. The volume of information is rising as the U.S. Army develops wearable computer systems that provide a nonstop stream of data, from the location of friendly and enemy forces to constant voice communications with other soldiers.

The aim of a mission will determine what sort of situational awareness the soldiers need at different stages of an operation. To avoid casualties, an infantry unit will try to avoid being detected by the enemy. To accomplish this goal, platoon leaders need to be aware of the enemy location, numbers and weapons, type of terrain, time of day and weather conditions. The officers then need to interpret the data, assessing enemy strengths and weaknesses, the immediacy and severity of the threat and the platoon's ability to avoid it, and potential cover or exposure along a route. Based on the perception and understanding of the enemy presence, the platoon leaders can project the likelihood of enemy contact, the risk of being detected, the actions required to counter a threat and the likely outcomes of an enemy encounter.

The same strategy can be applied to sorting through the volume of information on social media. Before going to

Facebook, stop and consider the purpose. It might be to check in on friends, for entertainment or just to pass the time. Defining goals can help you to decide what information to gather, how to understand it and what to do with it. Procrastinating on Facebook requires a very different level of attention than seeking specific information.

The same applies whenever someone hits that Share button. There is often a specific reason behind posting a status update or photo, even if people are explicitly aware of it. Sharing is a way of defining who we are, signalling what we care about and nurturing relationships. Sometimes we give little thought to how a shared story or photo will be interpreted by others. A mental exercise to improve awareness of the potential outcome involves running though a series of "what if" scenarios. The idea is to consider how the unexpected might affect initial assumptions and to think about how to adapt to changing circumstances. What if my friends don't get my jokey tweet? What if my boss sees the photo of me passed out on the couch? What if a journalist quotes my comment in a story? Such an approach can mitigate the potential fallout for both individuals and businesses.

THE TECHNOLOGIES OF SITUATIONAL AWARENESS

The layout of a cockpit or a car dashboard is designed to take some of the heavy lifting out of maintaining situational awareness. The setup of dials and displays is intended to reduce the cognitive workload and free up more resources to interpret and make good decisions. For pilots, the flight deck of an aircraft is meant to promote situational awareness by providing the appropriate data at the appropriate time in the appropriate format. The design of such interfaces is critical in roles where people have to keep an eye on multiple and variable sources of information. With the speed and volume of disorganized data on social media, the same techniques are now being applied in business to turn the plethora of tweets, likes and shares into actionable information.

Baseball, free food and a natural disaster came together a couple of years ago to highlight how technology can be used to improve situational awareness on social media. In October 2012, Taco Bell offered its popular Doritos Locos Taco for free if a player stole a base in the World Series between the San Francisco Giants and the Detroit Tigers. During the second game, Giants out-fielder Ángel Pagán stole second base in the eighth inning, triggering the Taco Bell promotion. When the company announced details about when to get the beef and cheese crunchy taco, there was an immediate jump in positive feedback on social media.

As Taco Bell geared up to hand out free snacks, it suddenly looked like the PR win might turn sour. There was another massive spike in buzz about the company on social media, from approximately 1,000 to more than 800,000 messages in two hours. This time, the comments were from people along the northeast coast, which was being battered by Hurricane Sandy. In the midst of high winds, torrential rains and flooding, fans were worried that they wouldn't be able to get their free tacos.

Fortunately, Taco Bell had in place a system to monitor social media buzz in real time and a team on hand to interpret the data. The company quickly issued a statement, saying it would honour its promise of free tacos in areas affected by the hurricane. The result was another big spike in social media talk about the brand, most of it positive. Taco Bell averted a PR crisis by practising situational awareness. It proactively monitored the opinions and emotions of consumers by keeping an eye on social chatter. When it noticed something was going on, it investigated and interpreted the feedback, allowing it to take action before the promotion backfired. It could do this by using one of the new social media analytical tools developed in response to the speed and volume of data.

Over the past few years, tools to monitor and evaluate what people are talking about on Twitter or Facebook have become big business. Companies and organizations from Dell to Salesforce to the American Red Cross have set up social media command centres: dedicated areas with large TV screens displaying live streams of tweets, heat maps of sentiment, and more, monitored by staff trained in social media. With 1.5 billion people on social media, there is a potential treasure trove of information. Social media analytical tools offer ways to analyze and decipher the data so that businesses can make more informed and timely decisions.

Listening to what consumers say can show that there are more important things than taste when U.K. consumers choose between a KitKat and a Galaxy chocolate bar. Twitter chatter about both snacks showed similarly positive comments. Delving deeper into a year's worth of tweets showed why people chose Galaxy—known as Dove outside the U.K. Marketing the Galaxy bar as a more sophisticated and special type of chocolate bar seems to have resonated with consumers. As many people talked about the chocolate as an indulgence as they did about its taste. Galaxy was considered much more of a treat than KitKat, at least according to Twitter users in the U.K. And two-thirds of those tweeting about Galaxy were women, compared with a third who talked about KitKats.

At other times, as was the case with Taco Bell, having systems and people in place can prevent feedback and criticism from turning into a crisis. By January 2014, almost two-thirds of marketing organizations were using social media analytics to track campaigns, monitor brands and gain insights into the competition. With social media less than ten years old and new tools and services springing up all the time, many companies are struggling to keep up. Two-thirds of business leaders admitted that their companies were unprepared to handle social media, given the fast pace of change.

Their bewilderment is understandable. When it comes to social media, current systems are incunabula—a term usually applied to early books printed before 1501 but that also means the first traces of something. When historians look back at the turn of the twenty-first century, they may consider current social media tools and services as incunabula. They are at the earliest stages of development. The German ace Oscar Boelcke would be bewildered by the complexity of the displays needed to handle the speed, agility and firepower of today's fighter jets. In much the way that the cockpit of an aircraft has evolved since the early days of aerial combat, so too will the systems to navigate an open, vibrant and diverse information ecosystem.

IN FLOW WITH THE FUTURE

On the afternoon of Saturday, October 28, 1916, Boelcke was on patrol over the Somme with his squadron when they encountered two British fighters. Boelcke, known as an aggressive pilot, set his sights on one of them. Manfred von Richthofen, better known as the Red Baron, went after the other. As the planes dashed across the cloudy skies, Richthofen saw that his friend was gunning for his target. But so was another member of the German squadron, Boelcke's wingman, Erwin Böhme. In his memoirs, Richthofen recalled how he thought the British plane would be shot down at any moment as the two German pilots closed in on it.

Then tragedy struck. Boelcke's wing hit Böhme's undercarriage. "The two machines merely touched one another," wrote Richthofen. "However, if two machines go at the tremendous pace of flying machines, the slightest contact has the effect of a violent concussion." The midair collision left Boelcke struggling to make an emergency landing. Buffeted by violent gusts, the German ace died when his fighter crashed into the ground. In the cut and thrust of the dogfight, Boelcke had failed to notice that his wingman was quite so close to his plane. For a few fatal seconds, he lost situational awareness.

Pilots in those early days of aerial warfare had to invent new ways to deal with a new reality. Changes in the methods and weapons of war changed the nature of conflict. Today, changes in the world of information are transforming the nature of communication. News and information have gone from being scarce to abundant commodities. They have become like the air we breathe—literally ambient, all around us all the time, coming in the shape of updates from friends, photos of cute animals or links to funny videos.

The sheer amount of stuff coming at us from friends, family and colleagues may seem overwhelming, and that's without considering all the news from media outlets. A novice mistake is to try to be on top of it all. The goal is not to take in everything, paying perfect attention to every tweet or like; neither is it to be passive and let information simply wash over you. Techniques of situational awareness can help consumers reach equilibrium. In practice, it means being peripherally aware of information as it flows in the background, paying attention when something important and relevant, or pleasing and entertaining, pops up.

Social media requires a different mindset from the way we approached things like the newspaper. The daily paper was finite. It had a set number of pages, column inches and words. And even then, most didn't read every single story and perhaps ignored some sections altogether. Social media is the ambient music of the everyday. Much of what is shared consists of the mundane details of life, the small talk and casual exchanges that are important in fostering societal bonds. It is flowing in the periphery of our awareness and doesn't demand much attention. Like ambient music, we know is it there, but it is unobtrusive. Changes in the volume, speed and tone signal that something requires attention, much like a sudden change in background music catches our attention.

There is always a degree of fear and apprehension that comes with change. A century ago, the telephone was the new method of communication. An AT&T advertisement in the May 1916 edition of the Boy Scouts' magazine *Boys' Life* reflected the hopes and fears of the time. It heralded the telephone network as "the kingdom of the subscriber" and sought to reassure customers that "the telephone cannot think or talk for you, but it carries your thought where you will." The ad attempted to reassure Americans that they were in control of the newfangled device they were letting into their homes. "It is yours to use," it read. One hundred years later, the same ad could be applied to the myriad new and evolving ways we have to connect and communicate. Today's constant flow of information is ours to use.

Alfred Hermida, PhD, is an award-winning author, online news pioneer and digital media scholar. He is an associate professor and director of the School of Journalism at the University of British Columbia, Vancouver, where he focuses on digital journalism and social media. Recognized as one of Canada's leading social media experts, Hermida is regularly featured in national and international news outlets. He is the recipient of numerous awards, including the 2015 National Business Book Award and the 2011 UBC President's Award for Public Education Through Media. Hermida was a BBC journalist for sixteen years, including four as a correspondent in North Africa and the Middle East.

http://alfredhermida.com/
@Hermida
www.facebook.com/TellEveryoneBook
http://www.telleveryone.ca/

NOTES AND SOURCES

INTRODUCTION

2   *Even in ancient Greece* Thomas G. West, *Thinking Like Einstein* (New York: Prometheus Books, 2004).

3   *In the Middle Ages* M.T. Clanchy, *From Memory to Written Record: England 1066–1307* (Oxford: Blackwell, 1993).

3   *A hundred hours* YouTube statistics, http://www.youtube.com/yt /press/en-GB/statistics.html; Raffi Krikorian, "New Tweets per second record, and how!" *Engineering Blog,* Twitter, August 16, 2013, https://blog.twitter.com/2013/new-tweets-per-second-record-and-how; "Our Mission," *Company Info: Facebook Newsroom,* http://newsroom .fb.com/company-info/.

7   *The twenty-four-year-old was prolific on* On Twitter, Jessica went by Redfield, the maiden name of her grandmother. Jessica Redfield, Twitter profile page, https://twitter.com/JessicaRedfield.

7   *A few days before* Jessica Redfield, Twitter post, July 16, 2012, https://twitter .com/JessicaRedfield/status/224909972822171649.

7   *This picture is proof* Jessica Redfield, Twitter post, June 14, 2012, https:// twitter.com/JessicaRedfield/status/213343036086824960/photo/1.

7   *One video on YouTube* "STSA Fun with Hockey," YouTube video, posted by Ticket760, December 2, 2010, http://www.youtube.com/watch ?v=SY8IigZTPoA&.

7   *Even more disconcerting* Jessica Redfield, "Late Night Thoughts on the Eaton Center Shooting," *A Run On of Thoughts* (blog), June 5, 2012, http://jessicaredfield.wordpress.com/2012/06/05/late-night -thoughts-on-the-eaton-center-shooting/.

7   *Her Twitter account documented* Jessica Redfield, various Twitter posts, July 20, 2012, https://twitter.com/JessicaRedfield.

8   *After her death* Jessica Redfield Foundation Facebook page, https://www.facebook.com/JessicaRedfieldFoundation.

CHAPTER 1: THE NEWS NOW

10   *The oldest was The Denver Post* profiled the 12 people who died in the shooting. http://www.denverpost.com/news/ci_21129876/lives-that -ended-an-aurora-theater-were-full.

10   *Morgan provided a meticulous* The timeline by Integ3r on Reddit, http://www.reddit.com/r/news/comments/wv8t1/comprehensive _timeline_aurora_massacre/.

10   *I stayed up all* Quoted in John Herman, "How 18-year-old Morgan Jones told the world about the Aurora shooting," *Buzzfeed*, July 20, 2012, http://www.buzzfeed.com/jwherrman/how-18-year-old-morgan -jones-told-the-world-about.

11   *In the hours and* Mark Coddington examined the reporting on mainstream media and social media for the Nieman Journalism Lab, April 19, 2013, http://www.niemanlab.org/2013/04/this-week-in-review-verification -online-and-off-in-bostons-wake-and-an-underdogs-pulitzer-win/.

11   *As tends to happen* His tweet is at https://twitter.com/Boston_to_a_T /status/323871088532668416.

12   *However, though it started with* Erik Martin, "Reflections on the Recent Boston Crisis," *Reddit*, April 22, 2013, http://www.redditblog.com /2013/04/reflections-on-recent-boston-crisis.html.

13   *It sold for just* Anthony Fellow, *American Media History* (Boston, MA: Wadsworth Publishing, 2009).

14   *"The object of this . . ."* Quoted in Shirley Biagi, *Media/Impact: An Introduction to Mass Media* (Belmont, CA: Thomson Higher Education, 2007).

14   *It was accused of* Edwin Emery and Michael Emery, *The Press and America: An Interpretative History of the Mass Media* (Englewood Cliffs, NJ: Prentice Hall, 1978).

15   *It's just that the* Journalism, Satire or Just Laughs? "The Daily Show with Jon Stewart," Examined, Pew Research, March 8, 2008, http://www.journalism.org/2008/05/08/journalism-satire-or-just -laughs-the-daily-show-with-jon-stewart-examined/.

15   *And when Americans* Ibid.

17   *News existed before* Mitchell Stephens, *A History of News*. 3rd ed. (New York: Oxford University Press, 2006).

17   *Being aware of what* Harvey Molotch and Marilyn Lester, "News as Purposive Behavior: On the Strategic Use of Routine Events, Accidents, and Scandals," *American Sociological Review* 39, no. 1 (February 1974).

18   *We were all* The site is no longer active. The post is quoted in Stuart Allan, *Online Journalism* (Maidenhead, Berkshire: Open University Press, 2006).

19   *The BBC alone received* Richard Sambrook, "Citizen Journalism and the BBC," Nieman Reports, Winter 2005, http://www.nieman.harvard .edu/reportsitem.aspx?id=100542.

19   *Within ninety minutes of* Quoted in Allan.

19   *At the BBC, an* Sambrook.

20   *Scientists have found that* Fei Xiong and Yun Liu, "Opinion Formation on Social Media: An Empirical Approach," *Chaos: An Interdisciplinary Journal of Nonlinear Science* 24 (2014), http://dx.doi.org/10.1063 /1.4866011.

21   *Within twenty-four hours, there* The number of tweets is based on my analysis of the hashtag using Crimson Hexagon social media analytics.

23   *Anyone turning to Google* The article is available at http://scallywagmagazine .blogspot.ca/2012/11/scallywag-magazine-article-on-lord.html.

23   *I looked up Lord* The messages that have since been deleted were accessed using the social media monitoring company Topsy Pro.

24   *Author and researcher* danah boyd, "How 'Context Collapse' was Coined: My Recollection," December 8, 2013, http://www.zephoria.org/thoughts /archives/2013/12/08/coining-context-collapse.html.

25   *But his account was* Paul Chambers's Twitter account, https://twitter .com/pauljchambers.

25   *People might picture an* danah boyd, "Social Network Sites as Networked Publics: Affordances, Dynamics, and Implications," in *Networked Self: Identity, Community, and Culture on Social Network Sites,* ed. Zizi Papacharissi (New York and Abingdon, U.K.: Routledge, 2010), 39–58.

27   *Privacy used to mean* Beate Rossler, *The Value of Privacy* (Cambridge, U.K.: Polity, 2004).

27   *It's like being at* The example comes from danah boyd, "Facebook's Privacy Trainwreck: Exposure, Invasion, and Social Convergence," *Convergence: The International Journal of Research into New Media Technologies* 14, no. 1 (2008): 13–20, http://www.danah.org/papers /FacebookPrivacyTrainwreck.pdf.

28   *What one person sees* Microsoft researcher Nancy Baym raised this issue at an MIT conference in 2013. https://twitter.com/nancybaym /status/330365382965751808.

29   *The renowned communications* James Carey, "A Short History of Journalism for Journalists," *The Harvard International Journal of Press/Politics* 12, no. 3 (2007).

CHAPTER 2: WHY WE SHARE

32   *Two million people registered* Tom Hespos, "BMW Films: The Ultimate Marketing Scheme," *iMedia Connection,* July 10, 2002, http://www .imediaconnection.com/content/546.asp.

32   *More important for the carmaker* Horatiu Boeriu, "Video Collection:

BMW Films—The Hire," *BMW Blog*, August 25, 2009, http://www
.bmwblog.com/2009/08/25/video-collection-bmw-films-the-hire/.

33   *"Man is by nature a political animal . . . "* Aristotle, *Politics*, bk. 1, part II: 3,
trans. Benjamin Jowett (New York: Viking Press, 1957).

33   *"Sharing has probably been . . . "* John A. Price, "Sharing: The
Integration of Intimate Economies," *Anthropologica* (1975): 3–27, 17,
no. 1. http://www.jstor.org/stable/25604933.

33–34   *Early humans needed* Robert Boyd, Peter J. Richerson and Joseph
Henrich, "The Cultural Niche: Why Social Learning Is Essential for
Human Adaptation," in *Proceedings of the National Academy of Sciences
of the United States of America* 108, no. S2 (June 28, 2011): 10918–
10925, http://www.pnas.org/content/108/Supplement_2/10918.full,
doi: 10.1073/pnas.1100290108.

34   *According to anthropologists* Ibid., p. 10918.

34   *News is driven by an innate need* P.J. Shoemaker, "Hardwired for News:
Using Biological and Cultural Evolution to Explain the Surveillance
Function," *Journal of Communication* 46, no. 3 (September 1996):
32–47.

35   *The idea of social capital* Robert Putnam, *Bowling Alone: The Collapse
and Revival of American Community* (New York: Simon & Schuster,
2000).

35   *The 229 children* Ernst Fehr, Helen Bernhard and Bettina Rockenbach,
"Egalitarianism in Young Children," *Nature* 454, no. 7208 (August 28,
2008): 1079–1083, http://www.nature.com/nature/journal/v454/n7208
/abs/nature07155.html, doi:10.1038/nature07155.

36   *Children learn to be more egalitarian* Nancy Eisenberg and Paul H.
Mussen, *The Roots of Prosocial Behavior in Children* (Cambridge:
Cambridge University Press, 1989).

36   *The French sociologist* Pierre Bourdieu, *Distinction: A Social Critique of
the Judgment of Taste* (London: Routledge, 1984).

38   *In the early 2000s* Jennifer Stromer-Galley, "Diversity of Political
Conversation on the Internet: Users' perspectives," *Journal of Computer-
Mediated Communication* 8, no. 3 (April 2003), onlinelibrary.wiley.com
/doi/10.1111/j.1083-6101.2003.tb00215.x/full, doi: 10.1111/j.1083-6101
.2003.tb00215.x.

38   *Unsurprisingly, people liked* Jennifer Stromer-Galley, "New Voices in
the Public Sphere: A Comparative Analysis of Interpersonal and
Online Political Talk," *Javnost—The Public* 9, no. 2 (2002): 23–42.

38   *A quick glance at the comment section* Na'ama Nagar, "The Loud Public:
The Case of User Comments in Online News Media", Doctoral dissertation, SUNY Albany (2011).

38   *The role of sharing* "The Psychology of Sharing," *The New York Times
Insights*, http://nytmarketing.whsites.net/mediakit/pos/.

38   *Social psychologists define such actions* S. D. Gosling, S. J. Ko, T.
Mannarelli and M. E. Morris, "A Room with a Cue: Personality

Judgments Based on Offices and Bedrooms," *Journal of Personality and Social Psychology* 83, no. 3 (2002): 379–398.

39   *Clothing has long been a medium* Marjorie Garber explores sumptuary laws in her book *Vested Interests: Cross-dressing and Cultural Anxiety* (New York: Routledge, 1992).

39   *When Rutgers University researchers* Mor Naaman, Jeffrey Boase and Chih-Hui Lai, "Is It Really About Me? Message Content in Social Awareness Streams," in *Proceedings of the 2010 ACM Conference on Computer-supported Cooperative Work* (Savannah, GA: February 6–10, 2010): 189–192.

40   *Everyday conversation is a dynamic mix* Jerome R. Sehulster analyzes what men and women talk about in "Things We Talk About, How Frequently, and to Whom: Frequency of Topics in Everyday Conversation as a Function of Gender, Age, and Marital Status," *American Journal of Psychology* 119, no. 3 (Fall 2006): 407–432.

40   *Harvard scientists* Diana I. Tamir and Jason P. Mitchell, "Disclosing Information about the Self is Intrinsically Rewarding," in *Proceedings of the National Academy of Sciences of the United States of America* 109, no. 21 (May 22, 2012): 8038–8043.

40   *Psychologists have looked* Ibid.

40   *People who talk politics online* Stromer-Galley, "Diversity of Political Conversation."

41   *For some, it's about having a right old ding-dong* Nagar, "The Loud Public."

41   *An analysis of comments* Lily Canter, "The Misconception of Online Comment Threads," *Journalism Practice* 7, no. 5 (2013): 604–619, http://www.tandfonline.com/doi/abs/10.1080/17512786.2012.74017 2, doi: 10.1080/17512786.2012.740172.

42   *The success of French tennis player* Rebecca Guest, "When Women Look Strong: Marion Bartoli and the Sexism at Wimbledon," *Christian Science Monitor,* July 10, 2013, http://www.csmonitor.com/The-Culture/Family /2013/0710/When-women-look-strong-Marion-Bartoli-and-the -sexism-at-Wimbledon.

42   *For some, Bartoli was* Some messages were captured by the website Public Shaming, http://publicshaming.tumblr.com/post/54864863081 /womens-wimbledon-champion-marion-bartoli-deemed.

42   *The higher visibility of* For example, in the BBC documentary "Blurred Lines: The New Battle of the Sexes." http://www.bbc.co.uk/programmes /b0436qlw."

42   *The statement by U.S. Justice* Louis Dembitz Brandeis, "What Publicity Can Do," *Harper's Weekly,* December 20, 1913, 10–13. The text is available at http://www.law.louisville.edu/library/collections/brandeis /node/196.

43   *Journalists themselves worry* Quoted in Canter, "The Misconception of Online Comment Threads."

43   *They tend to think* See Canter, "The Misconception of Online Comment Threads" and Nagar, "The Loud Public."

43   *Offensive remarks tend to* Canter, "The Misconception of Online Comment Threads."

44   *"My feeling is it doesn't matter . . . "* Quoted in Stromer-Galley, "New Voices in the Public Sphere."

44   *For 84 per cent, sharing* "The Psychology of Sharing."

44   *Regardless of the size* Nagar, "The Loud Public" and Stromer-Galley, "New Voices in the Public Sphere" and "Diversity of Political Conversation."

44   *The video, made by the U.S.–based* Andrew Page, "Kony 2012," *Know Your Meme*, http://knowyourmeme.com/memes/events/kony-2012.

44   *Within four days of its release* Josh Kron and David Goodman, "Online, a Distant Conflict Soars to Topic No. 1," *The New York Times*, March 9, 2012, http://www.nytimes.com/2012/03/09/world/africa/online -joseph-kony-and-a-ugandan-conflict-soar-to-topic-no-1.html.

44   *Its critics said it simplified* Ethan Zuckerman, "Unpacking Kony 2012," *My Heart's in Accra* (blog), March 8, 2012, http://www.ethanzuckerman .com/blog/2012/03/08/unpacking-kony-2012/.

45   *The study by The New York Times* "The Psychology of Sharing."

46   *Instead, it shifted its focus* Sue Robinson, "Journalism as Process: The Organizational Implications of Participatory Online News," *Journalism & Communication Monographs* 13, no. 3 (Fall 2011): 138–210.

46   *For Robinson, "these citizens . . . "* Ibid., p. 174.

46   *Pioneering research by UCLA* Emily B. Falk, Sylvia A. Morelli, B. Locke Welborn, Karl Dambacher and Matthew D. Lieberman, *Psychological Science* 24, no. 7 (July 2013):1234–1242, http://pss.sagepub.com/content /24/7/1234.full, doi: 10.1177/0956797612474670.

46–47 *"We wanted to explore . . . "* Quoted in Stuart Wolpert, "How the Brain Creates the 'Buzz' that Helps Ideas Spread," Stuart Wolpert, *UCLA Newsroom*, July 5, 2013, http://newsroom.ucla.edu/portal/ucla/how -the-brain-creates-buzz-247204.aspx.

47   *"You might expect people . . . "* Ibid.

48   *The academies of scholars* Jane Everson, "Intellectual Networks," *History Today* 62, no. 9 (September 2012), http://www.historytoday .com/jane-everson/intellectual-networks.

48   *In Stuart England in the 1600s* Brian Cowan, "The Social Life of Coffee: Commercial Culture and Metropolitan Society in Early Modern England, 1600–1720," PhD dissertation, Princeton University (2000).

48   *In the early days of the republic* Qin Shao, "Tempest over Teapots: The Vilification of Teahouse Culture in Early Republican China," *Journal of Asian Studies* 57, no. 4 (November 1998): 1009–1041.

48–49 *Madame Doublet's salon* For a discussion on the role of the salon, see Félix-Sebastien Feuillet de Conches, *Les salons de conversation au dix-huitième siècle* (Paris: Charavay Frères, 1882).

50   *Among the places they would go* The historian Robert Darnton charts this period in "An Early Information Society: News and the Media in Eighteenth-Century Paris," *American Historical Review* 105, no. 1 (February 2000): 1–35.

50   *A Parisian turning up* Biz Stone, "What's Happening?" *Twitter Blogs*, November 19, 2009, https://blog.twitter.com/2009/whats-happening.

50   *Madame Doublet herself* Feuillet de Conches tells the story in *Les salons de conversation*, 115–116.

50–51 *In the words of historian* Darnton, "An Early Information Society."

51   *They want to enrich* Robinson, "Journalism as Process."

CHAPTER 3: OMG! I HAVE TO TELL YOU

53   *Gas attacks on civilians* Liam Corcoran, "The Month in Social News Sharing—August 2013," *NewsWhip*, September 19, 2013, http://blog.newswhip.com/index.php/2013/09/infographic-1.

54   *Variety's story on the casting* The *Variety* story is at http://variety.com/2013/film/news/ben-affleck-is-the-new-batman-1200586881/.

55   *It was the brainchild of Adolph S. Ochs*, "Adolph S. Ochs Dead at 77: Publisher of Times Since 1986," *The New York Times*, April 9, 1935, http://www.nytimes.com/learning/general/onthisday/bday/0312.html.

55   *When Ochs acquired the paper* W. Joseph Campbell, a professor at the School of Communication at American University in Washington, explores the meaning of the phrase in a column for the *BBC News* website: "Story of the Most Famous Seven Words in U.S. Journalism," *BBC News*, February 9, 2012, http://www.bbc.co.uk/news/world-us-canada-16918787.

55   *What started as an advertising slogan* Ibid.

55   *As well as emotion, editors assess* The list of news values is taken from an introductory textbook for journalism students: Jerry Lanson and Mitchell Stephens, *Writing and Reporting the News*, 3rd ed. (New York: Oxford University Press, 2008). The list of news values is widely debated by scholars.

56   *In 2010, readers were sending out* Jacob Harris, "How Often Is The Times Tweeted," *The New York Times*, April 15, 2010, http://open.blogs.nytimes.com/2010/04/15/how-often-is-the-times-tweeted/.

56   *By 2010, almost half of all people* Kristen Purcell, Lee Rainie, Amy Mitchell, Tom Rosenstiel and Kenny Olmstead, "Understanding the Participatory News Consumer; Part 5: News Gets Personal, Social and Participatory," *Pew Research Internet Project*, March 1, 2010, http://www.pewinternet.org/Reports/2010/Online-News/Part-5/2-News-as-a-social-activity.aspx.

56   *Facebook alone accounted for* Kenneth Olmstead, Amy Mitchell and Tom Rosenstiel, "Navigating News Online: Facebook Is Becoming

Increasingly Important," *Pew Research Journalism Project*, May 9, 2011, http://www.journalism.org/analysis_report/facebook_becoming _increasingly_important.

56   *For The New York Times* Ibid.

56   *By January 2014, the official* Facebook page of *The New York Times*, https://www.facebook.com/nytimes.

57   *When Wharton business professors* Jonah Berger, "Crafting Contagious," *Google Think Insights*, July 2012, http://www.thinkwithgoogle.com /quarterly/play/crafting-contagious.html.

57   *Similarly, a British study found* Nic Newman, *Mainstream Media and the Distribution of News in the Age of Social Discovery* (Oxford: Reuters Institute for the Study of Journalism, October 6, 2011), http://reutersinstitute .politics.ox.ac.uk/about/news/item/article/mainstream-media-and-the -distributi.html.

57   *The stories that pop up* Quoted in Ibid., p. 24.

59   *The message carried a photograph* Barack Obama, Twitter post, November 6, 2012, http://twitter.com/BarackObama/status/266031293945503744; and "Timeline Photos," Barack Obama Facebook page, https://www.facebook .com/photo.php?fbid=10151255420886749&set=a.53081056748 .66806.6815841748.

60   *The message of hope and change* Kevin Wallsten, "Many Sources, One Message: Political Blog Links to Online Videos During the 2008 Campaign," *Journal of Political Marketing* 10 (2011), 88–114.

60   *In six years, the video* Jake Heller and Patrice Howard, "YouTube's 10 Most-Watched Videos Ever," *The Daily Beast*, April 23, 2013, http:// www.thedailybeast.com/articles/2013/04/23/youtube-s-10-most -watched-videos-ever.html.

60   *Such videos are shared* Karen Nelson-Field, Erica Riebe and Kellie Newstead, "The Emotions That Drive Viral Video," *Australasian Marketing Journal* 21, no. 4 (November 2013): 205–211.

60   *In the late 1990s* Jonathan Keats wrote about the Gates email in "Copy This Article & Win Quick Cash!" *Wired*, July 2004, http://www.wired .com/wired/archive/12.07/hoax.html.

60   *The message was started as a joke* Ibid.

60   *"I have ab-so-smurfly . . . "* Quoted in "Bill Gates Has $1,000 (and a Virus) Just for You!," *About.com Urban Legends*, August, 30, 1998, http://urbanlegends.about.com/library/blgates.htm.

61   *Most people feel good* Lee Rainie, Amanda Lenhart, and Aaron Smith, "The Tone of Life on Social Networking Sites," *Pew Research Internet Project*, February 9, 2012, http://pewinternet.org/Reports/2012 /Social-networking-climate.aspx.

61   *A doctoral student at Michigan State University* Sonya Song, "Proto-analysis of Boston Globe Traffic on Facebook," *Sonya's Thoughts on Media and Tech*, July 14, 2013, http://sonya2song.blogspot.ca/2013/07 /proto-analysis-of-boston-globe-traffic.html.

61   *Even for discerning readers* Jonah Berger and Katherine L. Milkman, "What Makes Online Content Viral?," *Journal of Marketing Research,* 49, no. 2 (April 2012): 192–205.

61   *Television is still the leading source* "In Changing News Landscape, Even Television Is Vulnerable," *Pew Research Center for the People & the Press,* September 27, 2012, http://www.people-press.org/2012/09/27 /in-changing-news-landscape-even-television-is-vulnerable/.

62   *According to psychology researchers* Kim Peters, Yoshihisa Kashima and Anna Clark, "Talking About Others: Emotionality and the Dissemination of Social Information," *European Journal of Social Psychology* 39, no. 2 (March 2009): 207–222.

62   *They analyzed thousands* Berger and Milkman, "What Makes Online Content Viral?"

63   *In January 2014* Jill Foster, "Freddie's Mum Is Dying but Her Love Will Live Forever," *MailOnline,* January 15, 2014, http://www.dailymail.co.uk /femail/article-2540162/Freddies-mum-dying-love-live-forever-Cancer -kill-months-shes-written-cards-celebrate-birthdays-21-wedding.html.

64   *Sonya Song spotted* Song, "Proto-analysis of Boston Globe Traffic on Facebook."

64   *On ViralNova, Rowena's* "Her Little Boy Has No Idea His Mother Is About to Die," *ViralNova,* January 17, 2014, http://www.viralnova .com/dying-mother-gift/.

65   *The truth, though* Lydia Saad, "Most Americans Believe Crime in U.S. Is Worsening," *Gallup Well-Being,* October 31, 2011, http://www .gallup.com/poll/150464/americans-believe-crime-worsening.aspx.

65   *Researchers Kim Peters* Peters, Kashima and Clark, "Talking About Others."

65–66 *The results contradicted* Chip Heath, "Do People Prefer to Pass Along Good or Bad News? Valence and Relevance of News as Predictors of Transmission Propensity," *Organizational Behavior and Human Decision Processes* 68, no. 2 (November 1996): 79–94.

66   *The Canadian musician* Dave Carroll tells the story on his website http://www.davecarrollmusic.com/music/ubg/.

68   *Most people will have heard* Gary Alan Fine examines the reasons for these types of urban legends in an academic paper, "The Kentucky Fried Rat: Legends and Modern Society," *Journal of the Folklore Institute* 17, no. 2/3 (May–December 1980): 222–243, http://www .jstor.org/stable/3813896.

69   *Researchers Chip Heath* Chip Heath, Chris Bell and Emily Sternberg, "Emotional Selection in Memes: The Case of Urban Legends," *Journal of Personality and Social Psychology* 81, no. 6 (2001): 1028–1041.

69   *Psychologists who have studied* Paul Rozin, Jonathan Haidt and Clark McCauley, "Disgust," In *The Handbook of Emotions,* 3rd ed., eds. M. Lewis, J.M. Haviland-Jones and L.F. Barrett (New York: Guilford Press, 2008), 756–776.

70   *Yet it was also one* Rosanna E. Guadagno, Daniel M. Rempala, Shannon Murphy and Brandon M. Okdie, "What Makes a Video Go Viral? An Analysis of Emotional Contagion and Internet Memes," *Computers in Human Behavior* 29, no. 6 (November 2013): 2312–2319.

70   *But according to researchers* Olivier Luminet IV, Patrick Bouts, Frédérique Delie, Antony S. R. Manstead and Bernard Rimé, "Social Sharing of Emotion Following Exposure to a Negatively Valenced Situation," *Cognition & Emotion* 14, no. 5 (2000): 661–688, http://dx.doi.org /10.1080/02699930050117666, doi: 10.1080/02699930050117666.

70   *The scene looks real enough* Brian Hickey, "'Cut Back to a Wide Shot. Open the Skull': The Faces of *Death Guy* Looks Back," *Deadspin*, February 2, 2012, http://deadspin.com/5855402/cut-back-to-a-wide -shot-open-the-skull-the-faces-of-death-guy-looks-back.

71   *"It had not been re-published . . . "* Adam Curtis, "Just Kidding," *BBC: The Editors*, September 18, 2006, http://www.bbc.co.uk/blogs/theeditors /2006/09/just_kidding.html.

71   *The clue lay in the headline* "Sudan man forced to 'marry' goat," *BBC News*, February 24, 2006, http://news.bbc.co.uk/2/hi/4748292.stm.

71   *The article told the story* Curtis, "Just Kidding."

71-72 *Curtis wasn't sure whether* Ibid.

72   *Eating scraps on the streets* "Sudan's famous goat 'wife' dies," *BBC News*, May 3, 2007, http://news.bbc.co.uk/2/hi/6619983.stm.

72   *The BBC carried a mock obituary* "R.I.P. Sudan's married goat," *BBC News*, May 4, 2007, http://news.bbc.co.uk/2/hi/uk_news/magazine /6623895.stm.

CHAPTER 4: THE DAILY WE

77   *By 2013, a third of Americans* Rasmus Kleis Nielsen and Kim Christian Schrøder, "The Relative Importance of Social Media for Accessing, Finding and Engaging with News," *Digital Journalism*, doi: 10.1080/21670811.2013.872420.

79   *An estimated twenty million* Bart Barnes and Joe Holley, "America's Iconic TV News Anchor Shaped the Medium and the Nation," *Washington Post*, July 18, 2009, http://www.washingtonpost.com /wp-dyn/content/article/2009/07/17/AR2009071703345.html ?sid=ST2009071703376.

79   *When President Dwight Eisenhower* Paul J. Deutschmann and Wayne A. Danielson studied how news spread at the time in the study "Diffusion of Knowledge of the Major News Story," *Journalism Quarterly* 37, no. 3 (September 1960): 345–355.

79   *For decades thereafter* An exception was the assassination of President John F. Kennedy in 1963. One study found that half of Americans first heard the news from another individual. Researcher Bradley

Greenberg concluded that news spread by word of mouth under very special and unique circumstances in his paper, "Person-to-Person Communication in the Diffusion of News Events," *Journalism & Mass Communication Quarterly* 41, no. 4 (December 1964): 489–494.

80   *While President Obama* A 2012 study collected 614,976 tweets mentioning "Laden" over two hours on the night. Mengdie Hu, Shixia Liu, Furu Wei, Yingcai Wu, John Stasko and Kwan-Liu Ma, "Breaking News on Twitter," in *CHI '12: Proceedings of the SIGCHI Conference on Human Factors in Computing Systems* (Austin, TX: May 5–10, 2012): 2751–2754, doi: 10.1145/2207676.2208672.

80   *Most of the tech-savvy readers* Ben Parr, "How Did You Hear About Osama bin Laden's Death?," *Mashable.com,* May 2, 2011, http://mashable.com/2011/05/02/osama-bin-laden-death/.

80   *Researchers Barbara Kaye* Barbara K. Kaye and Thomas J. Johnson, "The Shot Heard Around the World Wide Web: Who Heard What Where About Osama bin Laden's Death," *Journal of Computer-Mediated Communication* 19, no. 3 (April 2014): 643–662, doi:10.1111/jcc4.12055.

81   *Others, like Lauren Mary Gotimer* Lauren Mary Gotimer, "Where Were You When Osama Bin Laden Died?" May 2, 2011, http://lamargoti.com/2011/05/02/where-were-you-when-osama-bin-laden-died/.

81   *Twitter CEO Dick Costolo* Quoted in Ina Fried, "Dick Costolo Says Twitter Is an 'Indispensable Companion' That Can Meet Growth Targets," *Re/code,* February 13, 2014, http://recode.net/2014/02/13/dick-costolo-says-twitter-is-an-indispensable-companion-that-can-meet-growth-targets/.

82   *Two-thirds of voters* Scott Keeter, Juliana Horowitz and Alec Tyson, "Young Voters in the 2008 Election," *Pew Research Center,* November 13, 2008, http://www.pewresearch.org/2008/11/13/young-voters-in-the-2008-election/.

82   *Surveys and interviews* Brian Stelter, "Finding Political News Online, the Young Pass It On," *The New York Times,* March 27, 2008, http://www.nytimes.com/2008/03/27/world/americas/27iht-27voters.11460487.html.

82   *"If the news is that important . . . "* Ibid.

82   *A year later* "Maybe Media Will Be a Hobby Rather Than a Job," *Der Spiegel,* July 28, 2009, http://www.spiegel.de/international/zeitgeist/0,1518,638172,00.html.

83   *The Pew Internet and American Life Project* Kristen Purcell, Lee Rainie, Amy Mitchell, Tom Rosenstiel and Kenny Olmstead, "Understanding the Participatory News Consumer," *Pew Internet and American Life Project,* March 1, 2010, http://www.pewinternet.org/Reports/2010/Online-News.aspx.

83   *An online survey* Alfred Hermida, Fred Fletcher, Darryl Korell and Donna Logan, "Share, Like, Recommend: Decoding the Social Media News Consumer," *Journalism Studies* 13, no. 5–6 (2012): 815–824.

83   *In other countries* Nielsen and Schrøder, "The Relative Importance of Social Media."

83–84 *"Why have to turn . . . "* Megan Doyle, "Students Use Twitter, Facebook to Connect with Current Events," *The Observer*, September 2, 2011, http://www.ndsmcobserver.com/news/students-use-twitter-facebook-to-connect-with-current-events-1.2573069.

84   *When Pew Research* Amy Mitchell, Jocelyn Kiley, Jeffrey Gottfried and Emily Guskin, "The Role of News on Facebook: Common Yet Incidental," *Pew Research Journalism Project*, October 24, 2012, http://www.journalism.org/2013/10/24/the-role-of-news-on-facebook/.

84   *Something becomes news when it is widely shared* Eric Holthaus, "No, New York City Will Not Get 30 Inches of Snow This Weekend," *Slate*, February 5, 2014, http://www.slate.com/blogs/future_tense/2014/02/05/nyc_blizzard_hoax_new_york_won_t_get_30_inches_of_snow_this_weekend.html.

84   *New Yorkers learned* Caity Weaver, "NYC Will Get Either 3 or 30 Inches of Snow This Weekend," *Gawker*, February 6, 2013, http://gawker.com/5982121/nyc-will-get-either-3-or-30-inches-of-snow-this-weekend.

86   *The most common type* Ibid.

87   *A study of 138 daily newspapers* Jane B. Singer, "User-generated Visibility: Secondary Gatekeeping in a Shared Media Space," *New Media & Society* 16, no. 1 (February 2014): 55–73, first published on March 15, 2013, doi:10.1177/1461444813477833.

87   *Journalists and researchers are* A good starting point on algorithms and the media is Nick Diakopoulos, "Algorithmic Accountability Reporting: On the Investigation of Black Boxes," *Tow Center for Journalism*, 2013, http://towcenter.org/algorithmic-accountability-introduction/.

87   *The question is how* Mitchell, Kiley, Gottfried and Guskin, "The Role of News on Facebook."

87–88 *Research in the U.S.* Ibid.

88   *In Canada, too* Hermida, Fletcher, Korrell and Logan, "Share, Like, Recommend."

88   *American sociologist* Leon Festinger, *A Theory of Cognitive Dissonance*, (Stanford, CA: Stanford University Press, 1957).

88–89 *Through selective exposure* Dolf Zillmann and Jennings Bryant, eds., *Selective Exposure to Communication* (Hillsdale, NJ: Lawrence Erlbaum, 1985).

89   *In modern society* Ibid., p. 3.

89   *In his 2007 book* Cass Sunstein, *Republic.com 2.0* (Princeton, NJ: Princeton University Press, 2007).

90   *Taking as his starting point* Nicholas Kristof, "The Daily Me," *The New York Times*, March 18, 2009, http://www.nytimes.com/2009/03/19/opinion/19kristof.html.

90   *Social media does reinforce homophily* Miller McPherson, Lynn

Smith-Lovin and James M. Cook, "Birds of a Feather: Homophily in Social Networks," *Annual Review of Sociology* 27 (2001):415–444.

90 *Whenever the conversation turns* Marc A. Smith, Lee Rainie, Ben Shneiderman and Itai Himelboim, "Mapping Twitter Topic Networks: From Polarized Crowds to Community Clusters," *Pew Research Center*, February 20, 2014, http://www.pewinternet.org /2014/02/20/mapping-twitter-topic-networks-from-polarized -crowds-to-community-clusters/; and Sarita Yardi and danah boyd, "Dynamic Debates: An Analysis of Group Polarization Over Time on Twitter," *Bulletin of Science, Technology and Society* 30, no. 5 (October 2010): 316–327.

91 *Twitter helps to reinforce* Smith, Rainie, Shneiderman and Himelboim.

91 *Researchers at the School of Information* Eytan Bakshy, Itamar Rosenn, Ceron Marlow and Lada Adamic, "The Role of Social Networks in Information Diffusion," in *WWW '12: Proceedings of the 21st International Conference on World Wide Web* (Lyon, France, April 16–20, 2012): 519–528.

92 *Here's the math* Eytan Bakshy, "Rethinking Information Diversity in Networks," *Facebook Data Science*, January 17, 2012, https://www.facebook .com/notes/facebook-data-team/rethinking-information-diversity-in -networks/10150503499618859.

92 *"Since these distant contacts . . . "* Ibid.

93 *A team at Beihang University in Beijing* A study by Jichang Zhao, Junjie Wu and Ke Xu, "Weak Ties: Subtle Role of Information Diffusion in Online Social Networks," also points to the importance of weak ties in the diffusion of information on social networks (in *Physical Review E* 82, no. 1 [July 2010]).

93 *The importance of weak ties* Mark Granovetter, "The Strength of Weak Ties," *American Journal of Sociology* 78, no. 6 (May 1973): 1360–1380.

93 *Out of the 229 "friends"* Keith Hampton, Lauren Sessions Goulet, Lee Rainie and Kristen Purcell, "Social Networking Sites and Our Lives," *Pew Research Internet Project*, June 16, 2011, http://www.pewinternet .org/Reports/2011/Technology-and-social-networks.aspx.

93–94 *"The findings suggest . . . "* Ibid.

94 *The Evening Post of August 10, 1710* Roy M. Wiles, *Freshest Advices: Early Provincial Newspapers in England* (Columbus: Ohio State University Press, 1965).

94 *One newspaper referenced this* Ibid.

95 *In his 1998 book* Michael Schudson, *The Good Citizen: A History of American Civic Life* (1998; repr. New York: The Free Press, 2011).

95 *A minority of people* Nielsen & Schrøder, "The Relative Importance of Social Media."

CHAPTER 5: VOICES THAT RISE ABOVE THE NOISE

98   *Back in 1996* John Perry Barlow, *A Declaration of the Independence of Cyberspace*, February 9, 1996, https://projects.eff.org/~barlow /Declaration-Final.html.

98   *In an interview* Robert Mackey, "Interview with an Egyptian Blogger," *The Lede* (blog), *The New York Times*, January 27, 2011, http://thelede .blogs.nytimes.com/2011/01/27/interview-with-an-egyptian-blogger/.

99   *She was one of the group of bloggers* Zizi Papacharissi and Marie de Fatima Oliveira, "Affective News and Networked Publics: The Rhythms of News Storytelling on #Egypt," *Journal of Communication* 62, no. 2 (April 2012): 266–282.

99   *Sociologists Paul Lazarsfeld* Paul F. Lazarsfeld, Bernard Berelson and Hazel Gaudet, *The People's Choice: How the Voter Makes Up His Mind in a Presidential Campaign*, 3rd ed. (New York: Columbia University Press, 1968).

100   *Marketing experts Ed Keller* Edward Keller and Jonathan Berry, *The Influentials: One American in Ten Tells the Other Nine How to Vote, Where to Eat, and What to Buy* (New York: The Free Press, 2003).

102   *A rare bunch of cool* Duncan Watts and his research were featured in an article in *Fast Company* by Clive Thompson, "Is the Tipping Point Toast?" *Fast Company*, February 1, 2008, http://www.fastcompany.com/641124 /tipping-point-toast.

102   *During his time* Sharad Goel, Duncan J. Watts and Daniel G. Goldstein, "The Structure of Online Diffusion Networks," in *EC '12: Proceedings of the 13th ACM Conference on Electronic Commerce* (Valencia, Spain, June 4–8, 2012): 623–638.

102   *For another study* Eytan Bakshy, Jake M. Hofman, Winter A. Mason and Duncan J. Watts, "Everyone's an Influencer: Quantifying Influence on Twitter," in *WSDM '11: Proceedings of the Fourth ACM International Conference on Web Search and Data Mining* (Hong Kong, February 9–12, 2011): 65–74.

103–104 *The AP message* The social analytics company Topsy examined the spread of the news of Whitney Houston's death on Twitter in a blog post on February 12, 2012, by rishab http://topsylabs.com/2012/02/12/2-5 -million-tweets-an-hour-as-news-of-whitney-houstons-death-spreads/.

104   *In the first hour* Ibid.

104   *When he looked at the data* "Timing, Network and Topicality: A Revealing Look at How Whitney Houston Death News Spread on Twitter," *SocialFlow* (blog), February 17, 2012, http://blog.socialflow .com/post/7120244763/timing-network-and-topicality-a-revealing -look-at-how-whitney-houston-death-news-spread-on-twitter.

104   *Indiana University researchers created* L. Weng, A. Flammini, A. Vespignani and F. Menczer, "Competition Among Memes in a World with Limited Attention," *Scientific Reports* 2 (2012), http://www

.nature.com/srep/2012/120329/srep00335/full/srep00335.html, doi: 10.1038/srep00335.

105 *When something goes viral* Quoted in David F. Carr, "Science Probes Why Tweets Go Viral," *Information Week Network Computing*, April 5, 2012, http://www.informationweek.com/infrastructure/networking/ science-probes-why-tweets-go-viral/d/d-id/1103738?.

106 *Mackey wrote a blog* Robert Mackey, "Egyptian Blogger's Account of a Vigil in Cairo," *The Lede* (blog), *The New York Times*, January 7, 2011, http://thelede.blogs.nytimes.com/2011/01/07/egyptian-bloggers -account-of-a-vigil-in-cairo/.

106 *When the uprising started* Robert Mackey, "YouTube Video of Protests in Egypt," *The Lede* (blog), *The New York Times*, January 25, 2011, http://thelede.blogs.nytimes.com/2011/01/25/video-of-protests-in -egypt-on-youtube/.

106–107 *In February, the flagship* The documentary is available on the PBS *Frontline* website, http://www.pbs.org/wgbh/pages/frontline/revolution -in-cairo/video-gigis-revolution/.

107 *Around the same time* The video of her appearance on *Newsnight* can be seen on YouTube, http://www.youtube.com/watch?v=9Ptu7rnk2IQ.

108 *Almost three-quarters* Using the social media analytical tool Topsy Pro, I analyzed tweets for the time period that featured the #Jan25 and #Egypt hashtags and were identified as coming from Egypt. I compared the number sent in all languages with those sent in English. The same ratio applied when considering all tweets, and not just those coming from Egypt.

108 *Activists tweeting in English* Alfred Hermida, Seth Lewis and Rodrigo Zamith, "Sourcing the Arab Spring: A Case Study of Andy Carvin's Sources on Twitter During the Tunisian and Egyptian Revolutions," *Journal of Computer-Mediated Communication* 19, no. 3 (April 2014): 479–499.

109 *The Guardian and the Internarional Herald Tribune*, "Newspaper Coverage of the 2011 Protests in Egypt," *International Communication Gazette* 74, no. 4 (June 2012): 342–366.

110 *Individuals like Gigi* Yale University professor Ellen Lust and Jakob Wichmann of JMW Consulting dissect the causes behind the 2011 uprisings in "Three Myths About the Arab Uprisings," *YaleGlobal Online*, July 24, 2012, http://yaleglobal.yale.edu/content/three-myths- about-arab-uprisings.

111 *"When this critical mass existed. . ."* Duncan Watts, *Everything Is Obvious* *Once You Know the Answer* (New York: Crown Business, 2011): 96–97.

112 *On the other hand* News sourcing is one of the key areas of research in media studies. There is a large body of research that points to the dominance of elite sources in news reporting. Some of the main studies include Simon Cottle, *News, Public Relations and Power* (London: Sage,

2003); Paul Manning, *News and News Sources: A Critical Introduction* (London: Sage, 2001); and Gaye Tuchman, *Making News: A Study in the Construction of Reality* (New York: Free Press, 1978).

112   *How the protests are* A major study into the selection of sources by journalists was published in 1978: Stuart Hall, Chas Critcher, Tony Jefferson, John N. Clarke and Brian Roberts, *Policing the Crisis: Mugging, the State, and Law and Order* (London: Macmillan, 1978).

112   *At the height* Candis Callison and Alfred Hermida, "Dissent and Resonance: #Idlenomore as an Emergent Middle Ground," under review at the *Canadian Journal of Communication*.

113   *Sociologist Zeynep Tufekci* Zeynep Tufekci, "'Not This One': Social Movements, the Attention Economy, and Microcelebrity Networked Activism," *American Behavioral Scientist* 57, no. 7 (July 2013): 848.

114   *Outside of the country* This is based on my analysis, using Topsy Pro, of a database of tweets sent with the hashtag #Jan25 on the first day of the protests.

114   *She was part of a group* Papacharissi and de Fatima Oliveira, "Affective News and Networked Publics."

CHAPTER 6: A NERVOUS SYSTEM FOR THE PLANET

118   *With fires raging across* Jamie Williams, a journalism graduate from the University of British Columbia, compiled a timeline of Shinya Takatori's messages and translated them for a course assignment, *Through the Eyes of Shinya Takatori, Local DJ and Twitterer*, http://storify.com/urbanjamie/a-twitter-response-to-the. Takatori goes by the handle of @RANKandFILErec on Twitter (https://twitter.com/RANKandFILErec).

118   *In the hours* Abdur Chowdhury, "Global Pulse," *Twitter Blogs*, June 29, 2011, https://blog.twitter.com/2011/06/global-pulse.html.

118   *By the end of the day* Not all the messages would have been about Japan, but the figure provides an indication of how much information was flowing on the network. "#numbers," *Twitter Blogs*, March 14, 2011, https://blog.twitter.com/2011/03/numbers.html.

119   *One of the few contemporary* Mark Molesky, "The Vicar and the Earthquake: Conflict, Controversy, and a Christening During the Great Lisbon Disaster of 1755," *E-Journal of Portuguese History* 10, no. 2 (Winter 2012): 76–94, http://www.brown.edu/Departments/Portuguese_Brazilian_Studies/ejph/html/issue20/pdf/v10n2a04.pdf.

119   *The worst was far* Alexander E. Gates and David Ritchie, *Encyclopedia of Earthquakes and Volcanoes*, 3rd ed. (New York: Facts On File, 2007): 151.

120   *First accounts of the* T. D. Kendrick explores how news spread in *The Lisbon Earthquake* (New York: J. P. Lippincott, 1955): 213–245.

120   *Even three weeks after* Ibid., p. 213.

120 *By the turn of* Quoted in Ana Cristina Araujo, "European Public Opinion and the Lisbon Earthquake," *European Review* 14, no. 3 (July 2006): 313–319.

121 *No one is sure* Alvaro S. Pereira examines the figures for the death toll in his paper "The Opportunity of a Disaster: The Economic Impact of the 1755 Lisbon Earthquake," *Journal of Economic History* 69, no. 2 (June 2009): 466–499.

121 *By the end of* David K. Chester examined the impact of the disaster in "The 1755 Lisbon Earthquake," *Progress in Physical Geography* 25, no. 3 (September 2001): 363–383.

122 *A team of researchers* Takeshi Sakaki, Makoto Okazaki and Yutaka Matsuo, "Earthquake Shakes Twitter Users: Real-time Event Detection by Social Sensors," in *WWW '10: Proceedings of the 19th International Conference on World Wide Web* (Raleigh, N.C., April 26–30, 2010): 851–860.

122 *People can either follow* The U.S. Geological Survey's Tweet Earthquake Dispatch (TED) is on Twitter at https://twitter.com/USGSted.

122 *In one of its* Paul S. Earle, Daniel C. Bowden and Michelle Guy, "Twitter Earthquake Detection: Earthquake Monitoring in a Social World," *Annals of Geophysics* 54, no. 6 (2011), http://www.annalsofgeophysics .eu/index.php/annals/article/view/5364, doi: 10.4401/ag-5364.

123 *In the case of* The response of the USGS to the Tohoku earthquake is analyzed in Gavin P. Hayes, Paul S. Earle, Harley M. Benz, David J. Wald, Richard W. Briggs and the USGS/NEIC Earthquake Response Team, "88 Hours: The U.S. Geological Survey National Earthquake Information Center response to the 11 March 2011 Mw9.0 Tohoku Earthquake," *Seismological Research Letters* 82, no. 4 (July–August 2011): 481-493, doi: 10.1785/gssrl.82.4.481.

123 *When there was an earthquake* Sophia B. Liu, Beau Bouchard, Daniel C. Bowden, Michelle Guy and Paul Earle, "S21A-2431: USGS Tweet Earthquake Dispatch (@USGSted): Using Twitter for Earthquake Detection and Characterization," poster presented at the fall meeting of the American Geophysical Union, San Francisco, December 2012, http://fallmeeting.agu.org/2012/eposters/eposter/s21a-2431/.

124 *In those first few* Lewis MacLeod, "New Media Vital in Breaking Haiti Earthquake Story," *BBC World Service World Agenda*, January 22, 2010, http://www.bbc.co.uk/worldservice/worldagenda/2010/01/100122 _worldagenda_haiti_monitoring.shtml.

124 *"Without information sharing . . . "* Quoted in Harvard Humanitarian Initiative, *Disaster Relief 2.0: The Future of Information Sharing in Humanitarian Emergencies* (Washington, D.C., and Berkshire, U.K.: United Nations Foundation and Vodafone Foundation Technology Partnership, 2011), http://www.unfoundation.org/disaster-report.

125 *On the timeline* Ibid.

125 *A handful of residents* Jeannette Sutton, Leysia Palen and Irina Shlovski, "Backchannels on the Front Lines: Emergent Uses of Social Media in

the 2007 Southern California Wildfires," in *Proceedings of the 5th International Conference on Information Systems for Crisis Response and Management* (Washington, D.C., May 2008).

125 *Far more were tweeting* Amanda Lee Hughes and Leysia Palen, "Twitter Adoption and Use in Mass Convergence and Emergency Events," in *Proceedings of the 6th International Conference on Information Systems for Crisis Response and Management* (Gothenburg, Sweden, May 10–13, 2009).

125 *Many came from family* Harvard Humanitarian Initiative, *Disaster Relief 2.0.*

126 *Tweets from Miyagi* Adam Acar and Yuya Muraki, "Twitter for Crisis Communication: Lessons Learned from Japan's Tsunami Disaster," *International Journal of Web Based Communities* 7, no. 3 (2011): 392–402.

127 *During Superstorm Sandy, such* Emily Guskin and Paul Hitlin, "Hurricane Sandy and Twitter," *Pew Research Journalism Project*, November 6, 2012, http://www.journalism.org/2012/11/06/hurricane-sandy-and-twitter/.

127 *When storms battered Memphis* Carrie Brown-Smith, "#Memstorm: Twitter as a Community-driven Breaking News Reporting Tool," *#ISOJ: The Official Research Journal of the International Symposium on Online Journalism* 2, no. 2 (Fall 2012): 5–28, http://online.journalism.utexas.edu/ebook.php.

127 *During Sandy, the second* Guskin and Hitlin, "Hurricane Sandy and Twitter."

128 *At the time of the floods* Axel Bruns, Jean Burgess, Kate Crawford and Frances Shaw, *#qldfloods and @QPSMedia: Crisis Communication on Twitter in the 2011 South East Queensland Floods* (Brisbane: ARC Centre of Excellence for Creative Industries and Innovation, 2012).

128 *People come together* The idea of a transient news crowd is proposed by Janette Lehmann, Carlos Castillo, Mounia Lalmas and Ethan Zuckerman in "Transient News Crowds in Social Media," in *ICWSM '13: Proceedings of the 7th International Conference on Weblogs and Social Media* (Boston, July 8–11, 2013), http://chato.cl/papers/lehmann_castillo_lalmas_zuckerman_2013_transient_news_crowds.pdf.

128 *Some 14 per cent* Guskin and Hitlin, "Hurricane Sandy and Twitter."

129 *"We share storie . . . "* Quoted in Brown-Smith, "#Memstorm."

130 *The upshot is disaster myths* There is a substantial body of academic work into the topic of disaster myths. A key study is "When Disaster Strikes: It Isn't Much Like What You've Heard and Read About," by E. L. Quarantelli and Russell R. Dynes, *Psychology Today* 5, no. 9 (1972): 66–70. Amanda Ripley explores the topic in *The Unthinkable: Who Survives When Disaster Strikes and Why* (New York: Three Rivers Press, 2009). The textbook *Pathways: Disaster Response and Recovery* by David A. McEntire (Hoboken, NJ: Wiley, 2007) offers a good academic overview.

130 *A seminal study in the* Dennis E. Wenger, James D. Dykes, Thomas D. Sebok and Joan L. Neff, "It's a Matter of Myths: An Empirical Examination of Individual Insight into Disaster Response," *Mass Emergencies* 1, no. 1 (October 1975): 33–46, http://www.massemergencies.org/VIN1/Wenger_VIN1.pdf.

131 *An official report into* Virginia Tech Review Panel, *Mass Shootings at Virginia Tech: Report of the Review Panel,* http://www.washingtonpost.com/wp-srv/metro/documents/vatechreport.pdf.

132 *"This place is in . . . "* Quoted in Christine Hauser and Anahad O'Connor, "Virginia Tech Shooting Leaves 33 Dead," *The New York Times,* April 16, 2007, http://www.nytimes.com/2007/04/16/us/16cnd-shooting.html?pagewanted=all.

132 *Rather than panicking* The team have written several papers on the shootings, including Leysia Palen, Sarah Vieweg, Sophia B. Liu and Amanda Lee Hughes, "Crisis in a Networked World: Features of Computer-Mediated Communication in the April 16, 2007, Virginia Tech Event," *Social Science Computer Review* 27, no. 4 (November 2009): 467; and Sarah Vieweg, Leysia Palen, Sophia B. Liu, Amanda L. Hughes and Jeannette Sutton, "Collective Intelligence in Disaster: Examination of the Phenomenon in the Aftermath of the 2007 Virginia Tech Shooting," in *Proceedings of the 5th International Conference on Information Systems for Crisis Response and Management* (Washington, D.C., May 2008).

134 *If someone from Sendai* The message was in Japanese, so it fit within the 140-character limit of Twitter (Shinya Takatori, Twitter post, March 11, 2011, https://twitter.com/RANKandFILErec/status/46425137318330368).

135 *Instead they are taking* The idea of distant witnesses is referenced by Lehmann, Castillo, Lalmas and Zuckerman, "Transient News Crowds in Social Media."

136 *The remaining 80 per cent* Based on my own research using the social media analytical tool Topsy Pro.

CHAPTER 7: WHEN CONSUMERS STRIKE BACK

137 *McKinsey consultants* Michael Chui, James Manyika, Jacques Bughin, Richard Dobbs, Charles Roxburgh, Hugo Sarrazin, Geoffrey Sands and Magdalena Westergren, *The Social Economy: Unlocking Value and Productivity Through Social Technologies,* McKinsey & Company Insights and Publications, July 2012, http://www.mckinsey.com/insights/high_tech_telecoms_internet/the_social_economy.

138 *She took a photo* The post "My mistake sir, I'm sure Jesus will pay for my rent and groceries," attracted thousand of comments: http://www.reddit.com/r/atheism/comments/17i382/my_mistake_sir_im_sure_jesus_will_pay_for_my_rent.

138   *It sparked a social media backlash* Quoted in Chris Morran, "Waitress Who Posted No-tip Receipt from 'Pastor' Customer Fired from Job," *Consumerist*, January 31, 2013, http://consumerist.com/2013/01/31/waitress-who-posted -no-tip-receipt-from-pastor-customer-fired-from-job/.

139   *Two Domino's Pizza employees* The videos have been removed from YouTube but are available at http://www.goodasyou.org/good_as _you/2009/04/video-let-the-dominoes-appall.html.

140   *"Any idiot with a camera . . . "* Quoted in "Consumerist Sleuths Track Down Offending Domino's Store," *Consumerist*, April 14, 2009, http://consumerist.com/2009/04/consumerist-sleuths-track-down -offending-dominos-store.html.

140   *When the company* Amy Jacques provides a detailed account in "Domino's Delivers During Crisis: The Company's Step-by-step Response after a Vulgar Video Goes Viral," *The Public Relations Strategist*, August 17, 2009, http://www.prsa.org/Intelligence /TheStrategist/Articles/view/8226/102/Domino_s_delivers _during_crisis_The_company_s_step.

141   *Computer scientists in South Korea* Jaram Park, Meeyoung Cha, Hoh Kim and Jaeseung Jeong, "Managing Bad News in Social Media: A Case Study on the Domino's Pizza Crisis," paper presented at the 6th International AAAI Conference on Weblogs and Social Media, June 4, 2012.

141   *"What we missed . . . "* Quoted in Jacques, "Domino's Delivers During Crisis."

141   *A survey just after* HCD Research, "Domino's Brand Takes a Hit after YouTube 'Prank' Video," *MediaCurves.com*, April 17, 2009, http://www .mediacurves.com/NationalMediaFocus/J7329-Dominos/Index.cfm.

142   *And Old Spice saw* Robin Grant, "Wieden+Kennedy's Old Spice Case Study," *We Are Social*, August 10, 2010, http://wearesocial.net /blog/2010/08/wieden-kennedys-spice-case-study/.

143   *How O2 handled* Jonathan Lyon and Alex Georgiou wrote about the issue in "Calming a Twitstorm: O2's Masterclass in Dealing with 'Outrage Outrage,'" *Wired U.K.*, July 17, 2012, http://www.wired .co.uk/news/archive/2012-07/17/o2-outage-social-media-masterclass.

145   *The computer scientists* Sitaram Asur and Bernardo A. Huberman, "Predicting the Future with Social Media," in *WI-IAT '10: Proceedings of the 2010 IEEE/WIC/ACM International Conference on Web Intelligence and Intelligent Agent Technology*, vol. 1: 492–499.

146   *The prices for movie* The prices of stocks in Oscar, Emmy and Grammy Awards correlate well with the outcome of award ceremonies, and the costs of movie stocks accurately predict real box office results. See David M. Pennock, Steve Lawrence, C. Lee Giles and Finn Årup Nielsen, "The Real Power of Artificial Markets," *Science 291*, no. 5506 (February 9, 2001):987–988.

146   *Word of mouth helps* Yong Liu, "Word-of-mouth for Movies: Its Dynamics and Impact on Box Office Revenue," *Journal of Marketing 70*, no. 3

(July 2006): 74–89, http://ssrn.com/abstract=1949819. Also David Godes and Dina Mayzlin, "Using Online Conversations to Study Word-of-mouth Communication," *Marketing Science* 23, no. 4 (Fall 2004), http://ssrn.com/abstract=980060.

146   *Its fans took to Twitter* Asur and Huberman, "Predicting the Future with Social Media."

147   *Variety now includes* http://variety.com/t/social-media-buzz/.

148   *It was the first film* Searle Kochberg, "Institutions, Audiences and Technology," in *An Introduction to Film Studies*, ed. Jill Nelmes (London: Routledge, 1996).

148   *"With Jaws, we didn't . . ."* Quoted in Dade Hayes, "Tentpoles Face Fast After Opening Blast," *Variety*, August 4, 2002.

150   *Similarly, approximately 50 per cent* Thorsten Hennig-Thurau, Caroline Wiertz and Fabian Feldhaus, "Does Twitter Matter? An Investigation of the Impact of Microblogging Word of Mouth on Consumers' Adoption of New Products," working paper, March 5, 2012, http://ssrn.com/abstract=2016548.

151   *The team analyzed* Ibid.

151   *"We found that sentiment . . ."* Quoted in Cass Business School, "'Twitter Effect' Is No Hollywood Myth, Study Shows," news release, March 13, 2012, http://www.cass.city.ac.uk/__data/assets/pdf_file/0014/130523/Twitter_Final.pdf.

151   *Almost three-quarters* Chris Godley, "THR's Social Media Poll: How Facebook and Twitter Impact the Entertainment Industry," *The Hollywood Reporter*, March 21, 2012, http://www.hollywoodreporter.com/gallery/facebook-twitter-social-media-study-302273.

152   *Movie moguls can take* Ibid.

152   *Super 8 went on* "Super 8 (2011)," *Box Office Mojo*, http://boxofficemojo.com/movies/?page=main&id=super8.htm.

153   *Timothy published a photo* Timothy Oldham's detention note on Tumblr: http://alwaystheherooftimerealornotreal.tumblr.com/post/20324985794.

153   *It went viral when* "Timeline Photos," *The Hunger Games* official Facebook page, June 14, 2012, https://www.facebook.com/photo.php?fbid=491225374227452&set=a.288998967783428.89832.159746560708670&type=1.

154   *It set a new record* "Top March Opening Weekends at the Box Office," *Box Office Mojo*, http://boxofficemojo.com/alltime/weekends/month/?mo=03&p=.htm.

154   *It empowered fans* Marcus Andersson and Per Ekman, "Ambassador Networks and Place Branding," *Journal of Place Management and Development* 2, no. 1 (2009): 41–51.

154   *In 1999, the university student* "The Subway Diet: Jared Fogle Becomes a Celebrity by Losing Weight," *CBS News 48 Hours*, March 2, 2004, http://www.cbsnews.com/news/the-subway-diet-02-03-2004/.

155 *Lionsgate's campaign to mobilize* Mike Girard, "The Hunger Games' Social Media Campaign: A Case Study in Content Marketing," *The ExactTarget Blog*, March 26, 2012, http://www.exacttarget.com/blog /the-hunger-games-social-media-campaign-a-case-study-in-content -marketing/.

155 *"We felt that this . . . "* Quoted in Ari Karpel, "Inside 'The Hunger Games' Social Media Machine," *Co.Create*, http://www.fastcocreate.com /1680467/inside-the-hunger-games-social-media-machine.

156 *Every Friday, the* "Fan of the Week," *The Hunger Games* official Facebook page, https://www.facebook.com/photo.php?fbid=499639656719357 &set=a.491383774211612.27803783.159746560708670&type=1 and https://www.facebook.com/photo.php?fbid=511005045582818 &set=a.288998967783428.89832.159746560708670&type=1.

156 *The lucky fans* The Cleveland Indians case is examined in Avery Holton and Mark Coddington, "Recasting Social Media Users as Brand Ambassadors: Opening the Doors to the First 'Social Suite,'" *Case Studies in Strategic Communication* 1 (2012): 4–24, http://cssc.uscannenberg .org/wp-content/uploads/2013/10/v1art2.pdf.

157 *Team officials thought* Ibid.

CHAPTER 8: TRUTHS, LIES AND RUMOURS

159 *Sometimes all it takes* AP journalist Margie Mason wrote about the fortieth anniversary of the photo in "Photo of 'Napalm Girl' from Vietnam War Turns 40," *Yahoo! News*, June 4, 2012, http://news.yahoo.com /ap-napalm-girl-photo-vietnam-war-turns-40-210339788.html.

159 *The BBC was alerted to the photograph* The BBC story does not mention the use of the photograph. "Syria Massacre in Houla Condemned as Outrage Grows," *BBC News*, May 27, 2012, http://www.bbc.co.uk /news/world-middle-east-18224559.

160 *"Efforts were made to track down . . . "* Chris Hamilton, "Houla Massacre Picture Mistake," *BBC News: The Editors*, May 29, 2012, http://www .bbc.co.uk/blogs/theeditors/2012/05/houla_massacre_picture _mistake.html.

160 *In 1835, the* New York Sun "The Great Moon Hoax of 1835," *Museum of Hoaxes*, http://www.museumofhoaxes.com/hoax/archive/permalink /the_great_moon_hoax.

162 *With his eleven ships, 508 soldiers* Encyclopaedia Britannica Online, s.v. "Hernán Cortés, Marqués del Valle de Oaxaca," http://www.britannica .com/EBchecked/topic/138839/Hernan-Cortes-marques-del-Valle-de -Oaxaca/1555/The-expedition-to-Mexico.

162 *But it is still Mexico's most important port* Administración Portuaria Integral de Veracruz (Veracruz Port Administration), *Who We Are*, http://www.apiver.com/apiver/en/who-we-are.

162   *By September, more than five hundred people had died* "Who Is Behind Mexico's Drug-related Violence?" *BBC News*, October 9, 2012, http://www.bbc.co.uk/news/world-latin-america-10681249.

162   *Nowhere is more dangerous* "The 10 Most Dangerous Places for Journalists," *Reporters Without Borders*, December 21, 2011, http://en.rsf.org/annualoverview-21-12-2011,41582.html.

163   *A day later, they were found* Dudley Althaus, "More Journalists Murdered in Mexico," *Houston Chronicle*, May 3, 2012, http://www.chron.com/news/houston-texas/article/More-journalists-murdered-in-Mexico-3533501.php.

163   *The Vanguardia newspaper* "Entre Ombras [Between Shadows]," *Vanguardia*, November 13, 2010, http://www.vanguardia.com.mx/entresombras-589883-editorial.html.

163   *"There are cities in Mexico . . . "* Julian Miglierini, "'Twitter terrorism' charges cause uproar," *BBC News*, September 6, 2011, http://www.bbc.co.uk/news/world-latin-america-14800200.

163   *By March 2011, Twitter* Guillermo Perezbolde, "Twitter en México 2011," *MenteDigital.com*, March 6, 2011, http://mentedigital.com/site/?p=14.

163   *A study by the Oxford Internet Institute* Mark Graham and Monica Stephens, "A Geography of Twitter," *Visualizing Data at the Oxford Internet Institute*, June 19, 2012, http://www.oii.ox.ac.uk/vis/?id=4fe09570.

164   *When a team at* Andrés Monroy-Hernández, danah boyd, Emre Kiciman, Munmun De Choudhury and Scott Counts, "The New War Correspondents: The Rise of Civic Media Curation in Urban Warfare," in *CSCW '13: Proceedings of the 2013 Conference on Computer Supported Cooperative Work* (San Antonio, TX, February 23–27, 2013): 1443–1452, doi:10.1145/2441776.2441938.

165   *On Twitter, 40 per cent of active users* "One Hundred Million Voices," *Twitter Blogs*, September 8, 2011, https://blog.twitter.com/2011/one-hundred-million-voices.

165   *She was one of the few citizens* Monroy-Hernández et al., "The New War Correspondents."

165   *In the information wars in Mexico* Mariano Castillo, "Bodies Hanging from Bridge in Mexico Are Warning to Social Media Users," *CNN.com*, September 15, 2011, http://edition.cnn.com/2011/WORLD/americas/09/14/mexico.violence/index.html?hpt=hp_t2.

165   *"They are very influential . . . "* Monroy-Hernández, talk at the Berkman Centre for Internet and Society, Harvard University, 2012.

166   *"It is as if I was a war correspondent . . . "* Quoted by Monroy-Hernández in his Berkman talk.

166   *Research shows that spikes in reports* Ibid.

166   *He sees himself as a "truth troubadour"* Gilberto Martinez Vera, Twitter profile (in Spanish), https://twitter.com/gilius_22.

166   *But it was picked up by an informal group* The original message was in Spanish: "#Verfollow confirmo en la Esc. 'Jorge Arroyo' de la Col.

Carranza se llevaron 5 niños, grupo armado, Psicosis total en la zona."
Gilberto Martinez Vera, Twitter post, August 25, 2011, https://twitter.
com/gilius_22/status/106757025983246336.

166 *"I can confirm that at the Jorge Arroyo school . . . "* VerFollow, Twitter
profile, https://twitter.com/verfollow.

166 *In this message, he said* The original in Spanish can be found at https://
twitter.com/gilius_22/status/106760996860870656.

167 *During the day, she wrote various messages* Most have been removed. One
is available on her Facebook account: https://www.facebook.com/
maruchi.bravopagola/posts/10150262053336408. CNN Mexico put
together an account of her messages in Spanish: Rodrigo Soberanes,
"Los mensajes que causaron psicosis en escuelas de Veracruz," *CNN
México*, September 1, 2011, http://mexico.cnn.com/nacional/2011/09
/01/los-mensajes-que-causaron-psicosis-en-escuelas-de-veracruz.

167 *Emergency telephone lines* The incident was widely covered in the U.S.
and U.K. media. For two good accounts, see Miglierini, "Mexico
'Twitter terrorism' charges cause uproar;" and Associated Press, "2
Mexicans Face 30 Years in Prison for Tweets that Caused Panic in
Violence-wracked City," *New York Daily News*, September 4, 2011,
http://articles.nydailynews.com/2011-09-04/news/30136979_1_
tweet-panic-private-schools.

167 *"Those who caused damage . . . "* The message was in Spanish: "El castigo
para los q ocasionaron daños no es por ser usuarios del twitter es por
las consecuencias q causaron sus actos irresponsables." Javier Duarte,
Twitter post, September 3, 2011, https://twitter.com/Javier_Duarte
/status/110055632303951872.

168 *The terrorism charges were dropped* "Mexico 'Twitter terrorism' charges
dropped," *BBC News*, September 21, 2011, http://www.bbc.co.uk/
news/world-latin-america-15010202.

168 *Rumours take hold* Gordon W. Allport and Leo J. Postman, *The
Psychology of Rumor* (New York: Henry Holt, 1947).

168 *They gain further traction* Susan Anthony, "Anxiety and Rumor,"
Journal of Social Psychology 89, no. 1 (1973): 91–98.

168 *Rumours are improvised news* Tomatsu Shibutani, *Improvised News: A
Sociological Study of Rumor* (Indianapolis: Bobbs-Merrill, 1966).

168–169 *Such information gains far more prominence* Carlos Castillo, Marcelo
Mendoza and Barbara Poblete, "Predicting Information Credibility in
Time-sensitive Social Media," *Internet Research* 23, no. 5 (2013): 560–
588, http://dx.doi.org/10.1108/IntR-05-2012-0095, doi:10.1108/IntR
-05-2012-0095.

169 *His season ended prematurely* Canadian Press, "Blue Jays' Lawrie Out for
Remainder of Season," *CBC Sports*, September 21, 2011, http://www
.cbc.ca/sports/baseball/story/2011/09/21/sp-lawrie-scratch.html.

169 *During an inconsistent second season* Associated Press, "Brett Lawrie
Ejected after Wild Rage," *ESPN*, May 16, 2012, http://espn.go.com/mlb

/story/_/id/7936517/toronto-blue-jays-brett-lawrie-hits-ump-thrown -helmet-gets-ejected.

169 *"Pretty sure someone just let off a round . . ."* Brett Lawrie, Twitter post, June 2, 2012, https://twitter.com/blawrie13/status/209047958304468992.

169 *A minute later, he sent out another tweet* Brett Lawrie, Twitter post, June 2, 2012, https://twitter.com/blawrie13/status/209048242187538432.

170 *Hundreds shared his photograph* Brett Lawrie, Twitter post, June 2, 2012, https://twitter.com/blawrie13/status/209051675640594433.

170 *"I just thought I'd get it out there . . ."* Jennifer Pagliaro, "Blue Jays' Brett Lawrie breaks news of Eaton Centre Shooting," *Toronto Star*, June 2, 2012, http://www.thestar.com/news/article/1205057.

171 *"BREAKING: Con Edison"* ComfortablySmug (Shashank Tripathi), Twitter post, October 29, 2012, https://twitter.com/ComfortablySmug /status/263075838340251648.

171 *"BREAKING: Confirmed flooding . . . "* ComfortablySmug (Shahank Tripathi), Twitter post, October 29, 2012, https://twitter.com /ComfortablySmug/status/263083953152466947.

171 *The claim of flooding on the floor* Julie Moos, "CNN, Weather Channel Inaccurately Report that New York Stock Exchange Is under 3 Feet of Water," *Poynter*, October 29, 2012, http://www.poynter.org/latest -news/mediawire/193564/cnn-weather-channel-inaccurately-report -that-new-york-stock-exchange-is-under-3-feet-of-water/.

171 *But people tend to swear* Aditi Gupta and Ponnurangam Kumaraguru, "Credibility Ranking of Tweets During High Impact Events," in *PSOSM '12: Proceedings of the 1st Workshop on Privacy and Security in Online Social Media*, article no. 2 (Lyon, France, April 17, 2012), http:// doi.acm.org/10.1145/2185354.2185356, doi: 10.1145/2185354.2185356.

171 *Moments after a Continental Airlines 737* Steve Buttry, "How to Verify Information from Tweets: Check it Out," *The Buttry Diary*, January 21, 2013, http://stevebuttry.wordpress.com/2013/01/21/how-to-verify -information-from-tweets-check-it-out/.

172 *During his short-lived abduction* Fadwá Gallal, Twitter post, October 10, 2013, https://twitter.com/Douuu/statuses/388249169250746368.

172 *"Hmm, @guardian live blog quoting . . . "* Markham Nolan, "Ticked Off by a Fake Libyan Twitter Account," *Storyful Blog*, October 10, 2013, http://blog .storyful.com/2013/10/10/ticked-off-by-a-fake-libyan-twitter-account/.

173 *Almost forty thousand new Twitter accounts* Aditi Gupta, Hemank Lamba and Ponnurangam Kumaraguru, "$1.00 per RT #BostonMarathon #PrayForBoston: Analyzing Fake Content on Twitter," accepted at IEEE APWG eCrime Research Summit (eCRS), 2013, http://precog.iiitd.edu .in/Publications_files/ecrs2013_ag_hl_pk.pdf

174 *But the Twitter community functioned* Marcelo Mendoza, Barbara Poblete and Carlos Castillo, "Twitter under Crisis: Can We Trust What We RT?" in *SOMA '10: Proceedings of the First Workshop on Social Media Analytics* (Washington, D.C., July 25, 2010): 71–79.

174   *But an analysis of more than 2.6 million* James Ball and Paul Lewis, "Twitter and the Riots: How the News Spread," *The Guardian*, December 7, 2011, http://www.guardian.co.uk/uk/2011/dec/07/twitter -riots-how-news-spread.

174   *"Despite helping rumours spread . . . "* Rob Procter, Farida Vis and Alex Voss, "How Riot Rumours Spread on Twitter," *The Guardian*, December 7, 2011, http://www.guardian.co.uk/uk/interactive/2011 /dec/07/london-riots-twitter.

175   *On Twitter alone, there were three thousand* Kate Starbird, "Crises, Crowds & Online Convergence: Crowdsourcing in the Context of Disasters," presentation at the National Academy of Engineering Frontiers of Engineering Symposium, September 18, 2013, Wilmington, DE, http://www.naefrontiers.org/File.aspx?id=41201.

175   *A Reddit thread was devoted* Reddit Boston, "Is the missing student Sunil Tripathi Marathon Bomber #2?" http://www.reddit.com/r/ boston/comments/1cn9ga/.

175   *For every five erroneous tweets* Kate Starbird, Jim Maddock, Mania Orand, Peg Achterman and Robert M. Mason, "Rumors, False Flags, and Digital Vigilantes: Misinformation on Twitter after the 2013 Boston Marathon Bombings," in *iConference 2014 Proceedings* (Berlin, March 4–7, 2014), doi:10.9776/14308.

176   *It inspired a group of scientists* Indiana University, "Truthy: Information Diffusion Research at Indiana University," http://truthy.indiana.edu/.

176   *"There's a timescale . . . "* Craig Silverman, "Misinformation Propagation," *Columbia Journalism Review*, November 4, 2011, http://www.cjr.org /behind_the_news/misinformation_propagation.php?page=all.

176   *An analysis of close to eight million tweets* Gupta, Lamba and Kumaraguru, "$1.00 per RT."

177   *One of the first documented examples* Eni Mustafaraj and Panagiotis Metaxas, "From Obscurity to Prominence in Minutes: Political Speech and Real-time Search," in *Proceedings of the WebSci10: Extending the Frontiers of Society Online* (Raleigh, NC, April 26–27, 2010): 317.

177   *Propaganda campaigns tend to share similarities* Two academic papers investigated astroturfing: Cristian Lumezanu, Nick Feamster and Hans Klein, "#bias: Measuring the Tweeting Behavior of Propagandists," *International AAAI Conference on Weblogs and Social Media*, http://www.aaai.org/ocs/index.php/ICWSM/ICWSM12/ paper/view/4588; and Jacob Ratkiewicz, Michael Conover, Mark Meiss, Bruno Gonçalves, Snehal Patil, Alessandro Flammini and Filippo Menczer, "Detecting and Tracking the Spread of Astroturf Memes in Microblog Streams," in *Proceedings of the 20th International Conference Companion on World Wide Web* (Hyderabad, India, March 28–April 1, 2011): 249–252, http://arxiv.org/abs/1011.3768, doi:10.1145/1963192.1963301.

178   *"If you hear the same message . . . "* Quoted in Kurt Kleiner, "Bogus

Grass-roots Politics on Twitter," *MIT Technology Review*, November 2, 2010, http://www.technologyreview.com/news/421506/bogus-grass-roots-politics-on-twitter/.

CHAPTER 9: THE POLITICAL POWER OF A SHARED STORY

179 *On the campus of* A video of the event was posted to YouTube on May 11, 2012: http://www.youtube.com/watch?v=ACGAIxceH78.

180 *Front-page headlines described* Photos of some front pages are included in Roman Cotera, "LGVPLE: El Muñeco Sin Cabeza [The Headless Doll]," *Vice*, May 16, 2012, http://www.vice.com/es_mx/read/la-gua-vice-para-las-elecciones-el-mueco-sin-cabeza.

180 *Looking into the camera* RECREO, "131 Alumnos de la Ibero Responden [131 Students at Ibero-America Respond]," YouTube, May 14, 2012, http://www.youtube.com/watch?v=P7XbocXsFkI&.

180 *Most noticeably* Malcolm Gladwell, "Small Change: The Revolution Will Not Be Tweeted," *The New Yorker*, October 4, 2010, http://www.newyorker.com/reporting/2010/10/04/101004fa_fact_gladwell?currentPage=all.

181 *In 2012, Mexico was* Rachel Glickhouse, "Explainer: Twitter in Latin America," *Americas Society / Council of the Americas*, January 18, 2013, http://www.as-coa.org/articles/explainer-twitter-latin-america.

182 *A photograph by Osman Orsal* Max Fisher, "The Photo that Encapsulates Turkey's Protests and the Severe Police Crackdown," *The Washington Post*, June 3, 2013, http://www.washingtonpost.com/blogs/worldviews/wp/2013/06/03/the-photo-that-encapsulates-turkeys-protests-and-the-severe-police-crackdown/.

182 *The picture echoed one* "Casually Pepper Spray Everything Cop," *Know Your Meme*, http://knowyourmeme.com/memes/casually-pepper-spray-everything-cop.

183 *Over the first few* Joshua Tucker, "A Breakout Role for Twitter? Extensive Use of Social Media in the Absence of Traditional Media by Turks in Turkish in Taksim Square Protests," *The Monkey Cage*, June 1, 2013, http://themonkeycage.org/2013/06/01/a-breakout-role-for-twitter-extensive-use-of-social-media-in-the-absence-of-traditional-media-by-turks-in-turkish-in-taksim-square-protests/.

184 *For the first week* Media coverage was studied by Kevin M. DeLuca, Sean Lawson and Ye Sun in "Occupy Wall Street on the Public Screens of Social Media: The Many Framings of the Birth of a Protest Movement," *Communication, Culture & Critique* 5, no. 4 (December 2012): 483–509.

184 *In Canada, the mainstream* Donald Gutstein, "How Canada's Corporate Media Framed the Occupy Movement," *Vancouver Observer*, December 1, 2011, http://www.vancouverobserver.com/politics/commentary/2011/12/01/how-canadas-corporate-media-framed-occupy-movement.

184   *It told the story* Joel Penney and Caroline Dadas, "(Re)Tweeting in the Service of Protest: Digital Composition and Circulation in the Occupy Wall Street Movement," *New Media & Society* 16, no. 1 (February 2014): 74–90.

185   *Natives need to tone* Rex Murphy, "Natives Need to Tone Down the Anger," *National Post*, January 12, 2013, http://fullcomment.nationalpost .com/2013/01/12/rex-murphy-natives-need-to-tone-down-the-anger/.

185   *As Iranians took to* Lev Grossman, "Iran Protests: Twitter, the Medium of the Movement," *Time*, June 17, 2009, http://www.time.com/time /world/article/0,8599,1905125,00.html#ixzz2JPMNgk3e.

185   *The number of tweets* Ben Parr, "Mindblowing #IranElection Stats: 221,744 Tweets Per Hour at Peak," *Mashable,* June 17, 2009, http:// mashable.com/2009/06/17/iranelection-crisis-numbers/.

185   *Yet at the time* Mark Evans, "A Look at Twitter in Iran," *Sysomos Blog,* June 21, 2009, http://blog.sysomos.com/2009/06/21/a-look-at-twitter -in-iran/.

185   *Twitter was used mainly* Devin Gaffney, "#iranElection: Quantifying Online Activism," in *Proceedings of the WebSci10: Extending the Frontiers of Society Online* (Raleigh, N.C., April 26–27, 2010): http:// journal.webscience.org/295/.

186   *For a couple of* "Strong Public Interest in Iranian Election Protests," *Pew Research Center for the People and the Press*, June 24, 2009, http://www .people-press.org/2009/06/24/strong-public-interest-in-iranian -election-protests/.

187   *The term, first coined* Daniel Katz and Floyd H. Allport, *Students' Attitudes: A Report of the Syracuse University Reaction Study* (Syracuse, NY: Craftsman Press, 1931): 1–8.

188   *Witnesses recalled how* The café owner, Haytham Hassan Hanafi, gave details of the assault in his testimony to the authorities. Ahmed Shalaby and Mostafa El-Marsfawy, "Al-Masry Al-Youm Exclusive: Khaled Saeed Case Investigation," *Egypt Independent*, December 7, 2010, http://www.egyptindependent.com/news/al-masry-al-youm -exclusive-khaled-saeed-case-investigation.

188   *A few days after* The We Are All Khaled Said Facebook page is at https://www.facebook.com/ElShaheeed.

189   *"Prior to the murder . . . "* Quoted in Jennifer Preston, "Movement Began with Outrage and a Facebook Page that Gave It an Outlet," *The New York Times*, February 5, 2011, http://www.nytimes.com/2011/02/06/world /middleeast/06face.html?pagewanted=all&_r=0.

190   *Activists outside of Tunisia* Ethan Zuckerman, "Cute Cats to the Rescue? Participatory Media and Political Expression," *My Heart's in Accra*, April 29, 2013, http://ethanzuckerman.com/papers/cutecats2013.pdf.

190   *"But being able . . . "* Penney and Dadas, "(Re)Tweeting in the Service of Protest."

190   *Zeynep Tufekci of the University* Zeynep Tufekci and Christopher Wilson, "Social Media and the Decision to Participate in Political

Protest: Observations from Tahrir Square," *Journal of Communication* 62, no. 2 (April 2012): 363–379, doi: 10.1111/j.1460-2466.2012.01629.x.

191   *A click to "like"* Evgeny Morozov is one of the leading critics of the use of social media for political dissent. See *The Net Delusion: The Dark Side of Internet Freedom* (New York: Public Affairs, 2011).

191   *The people who* Sebastián Valenzuela, "Unpacking the Use of Social Media for Protest Behavior: The Roles of Information, Opinion Expression, and Activism," *American Behavioral Scientist* 57, no. 7 (July 2013): 920–942.

192   *From 150 university students* CNN Mexico reported on the protests. "Jóvenes participan en marcha Anti-Peña en al menos 17 ciudades," *CNN México*, May 19, 2012, http://mexico.cnn.com/nacional/2012/05/19/jovenes-participan-en-marcha-anti-pena-en-al-menos-17-ciudades.

192   *People from different educational* Andrés Monroy-Hernández outlined the results of the study in a panel discussion on Yo Soy 132 in September 2012, hosted by Microsoft Research New England, in collaboration with the Center for Civic Media: http://civic.mit.edu/blog/natematias/mexicos-networked-social-movements-yosoy132.

193   *In these early, heady* Kate Starbird and Leysia Palen, "(How) Will the Revolution Be Retweeted?: Information Diffusion and the 2011 Egyptian Uprising," in *CSCW '12: Proceedings of the ACM 2012 Conference on Computer Supported Cooperative Work* (Seattle, February 11–15, 2012): 7–16, http://doi.acm.org/10.1145/2145204.2145212, doi:10.1145/2145204.2145212.

193   *The Mauritanian-American activist* Nasser Weddady is profiled in Karen Leigh, "Behind the Arab Revolts, an Activist Quietly Pulling Strings from Boston," *The Atlantic*, January 25, 2012, http://www.theatlantic.com/international/archive/2012/01/behind-the-arab-revolts-an-activist-quietly-pulling-strings-from-boston/251786/?single_page=true.

194   *In the weeks following* Axel Bruns, Tim Highfield and Jean Burgess, "The Arab Spring and Social Media Audiences: English and Arabic Twitter Users and Their Networks," *American Behavioral Scientist* 57, no. 7 (July 2013): 871–898.

194   *Since his victory at* Digital Policy Council, *Research Note: World Leaders on Twitter—Ranking Report*, December 2012, http://www.digitaldaya.com/admin/modulos/galeria/pdfs/69/156_biqz7730.pdf.

CHAPTER 10: THE WAY AHEAD

197   *For the first two* James L. Stokesbury, *A Short History of Air Power* (New York: William Morrow, 1986).

198   *Keeping up with the* "The Personal News Cycle: How Americans Choose to Get Their News," *American Press Institute*, March 17, 2014,

http://www.americanpressinstitute.org/publications/reports/survey
-research/personal-news-cycle/.

198 *By 2014, the average* "An Era of Growth: The Cross-platform Report,"
Nielsen, March 5, 2014, http://www.nielsen.com/us/en/reports/2014/
an-era-of-growth-the-cross-platform-report.html.

198 *The figure is even* "Data Point: How Many Hours Do Millennials Eat
Up a Day?" *Digits: Tech News & Analysis from the Wall Street Journal*
(blog), March 13, 2014, http://blogs.wsj.com/digits/2014/03/13/data
-point-how-many-hours-do-millennials-eat-up-a-day/.

199 *The tyranny of real time* Nik Gowing, *Skyful of Lies and Black Swans:
The New Tyranny of Shifting Information Power in Crisis* (Oxford:
Reuters Institute for the Study of Journalism Challenges, 2009),
https://reutersinstitute.politics.ox.ac.uk/fileadmin/documents
/Publications/Skyful_of_Lies.pdf.

199 *In 1621, the English* Robert Burton, *The Anatomy of Melancholy,* 6th ed.
(London: Hen. Crips and Lodo Lloyd, 1652), http://www.gutenberg
.org/ebooks/10800.

200 *Some U.S. cities had* Ellen Gruber Garvey, *Writing with Scissors:
American Scrapbooks from the Civil War to the Harlem Renaissance,*
(Oxford: Oxford University Press, 2012).

200 *An editorial in Harper's* Henry Mills Alden, ed., *Harper's New Monthly
Magazine* 85 (June–November 1892): 639. Available on Google books at
http://books.google.ca/books?id=H4k7AQAAMAAJ&pg=PA639
&lpg=PA639&dq=harpers+monthly+magazine+in+a+generation+that
+must+run+as+it+reads+take+the+place+of+a+book&source=bl&ots
=sibn_j6zaL&sig=D1pnRiv_WY7O2NAU1PyEalg20Z4&hl=en&sa=X
&ei=DdYsU5LbFo6EogSAqoDIBg&ved=0CCoQ6AEwAA#v
=onepage&q=scrap-books&f=false.

200 *In response to the* Garvey, *Writing with Scissors.*

201 *In the third-person* Ferry Groenendijk, "Spec Ops the Line:
Achievements and Trophies Guide," *Video Games Blogger,* June 28,
2012, http://www.videogamesblogger.com/2012/06/28/spec-ops-the
-line-achievements-trophies-guide.htm.

201–202 *The U.S. Department of Labor describes* Bureau of Labor Statistics, U.S. Department of Labor, *Occupational Outlook Handbook: 2014–15 Edition—Power
Plant Operators, Distributors, and Dispatchers,* http://www.bls.gov/ooh
/production/power-plant-operators-distributors-and-dispatchers.htm#tab-4.

202 *"The problem with today's . . . "* Mica Endsley, "Theoretical Underpinnings
of Situation Awareness: A Critical Review," in *Situation Awareness
Analysis and Measurement* eds. Mica R. Endsley and Daniel J. Garland
(Mahwah, N.J.: Lawrence Erlbaum Associates, 2000): 3–28.

202 *Endsley defines situational awareness* Mica R. Endsley, "Design and
Evaluation for Situation Awareness Enhancement," in *Proceedings of
the Human Factors Society 32nd Annual Meeting* (Santa Monica, CA,
Human Factors Society, 1988): 97–101.

203 *Almost 90 per cent* Mica R. Endsley, "A Taxonomy of Situation Awareness Errors," in *Human Factors in Aviation Operations: Proceedings of the 21st Conference of the European Association for Aviation Psychology* eds. Ray Fuller, Neil Johnston and Nick McDonald (Aldershot, U.K.: Ashgate Publishing, 1995): 287–292.

203 *An analysis of errors* J. Gibson, J. Orasanu, E. Villeda and T. Nygren, "Loss of Situation Awareness: Causes and Consequences," *Proceedings of the Ninth International Symposium on Aviation Psychology* eds. Richard S. Jensen and Lori A. Rakovan, (Columbus: Ohio State University Department of Aerospace Engineering, Applied Mechanics and Aviation, 1997): 1417–1421.

205 *They were discussing* Peter Horrocks, Twitter post, February 4, 2009, https://twitter.com/PeterHorrocks1/status/1178320407.

206 *"It's a very embarrassing . . . "* Quoted in Judith Townend, "Accidental Tweet Announces Senior BBC Appointments (but Are Now Official), *Journalism.co.uk,* February 5, 2009, http://blogs.journalism .co.uk/2009/02/05/accidental-bbc-tweet/.

206 *And the more people* Alfred Hermida, Fred Fletcher, Darryl Korell and Donna Logan, "Share, Like, Recommend: Decoding the Social Media News Consumer," *Journalism Studies* 13, no. 5–6 (2012): 815–824.

206 *Perception is shaped* For example, Mica. R. Endsley, "Designing for Situation Awareness in Complex Systems," in *Proceedings of the Second International Workshop on Symbiosis of Humans, Artifacts and Environment* (Kyoto, Japan, 2001).

208 *Psychology professor Leo* Leo Gugerty, "Evidence from a Partial Report Task for Forgetting in Dynamic Spatial Memory," *Human Factors: The Journal of the Human Factors and Ergonomics Society* 40, no. 3 (September 1998): 498–508.

208 *The value of partial* George Sperling, "The Information Available in Brief Visual Presentations," *Psychological Monographs* 74, no. 2 (1960): 1–29, http://aris.ss.uci.edu/HIPLab/staff/sperling/PDFs/Sperling_ PsychMonogr_1960.pdf.

209 *Psychology researchers* Kerry S. O'Brien and David O'Hare, "Situational Awareness Ability and Cognitive Skills Training in a Complex Real-world Task," *Ergonomics* 50, no. 7 (2007): 1064–1091, http://dx.doi.org /10.1080/00140130701276640, doi:10.1080/00140130701276640.

209 *It is worse among* Andrew K. Przybylski, Kou Murayama, Cody R. DeHaan and Valerie Gladwell, "Motivational, Emotional, and Behavioral Correlates of Fear of Missing Out," *Computers in Human Behavior* 29, no. 4 (July 2013): 1841–1848.

210 *The aim of a mission* Michael D. Matthews, Laura D. Strater and Mica R. Endsley, "Situation Awareness Requirements for Infantry Platoon Leaders," *Military Psychology* 16, no. 3 (2004): 149–161.

211 *A mental exercise* O'Brien and David O'Hare did this with their students as air traffic controllers.

212   *As Taco Bell geared* Lisa Joy Rosner, "4 Tips for Real-time Social Media Monitoring," *Online Marketing Institute,* May 30, 2012, http://www .onlinemarketinginstitute.org/blog/2013/05/social-media-monitoring -best-practices/.

213   *Companies and organizations* Salesforce compiled an eBook with ten examples of social media command centres. It can be found at http:// www.salesforcemarketingcloud.com/resources/ebooks/10-examples-of -social-media-command-centers/.

213   *With 1.5 billion people* "Social Networking Reaches Nearly One in Four Around the World," *eMarketer,* June 18, 2013, http://www.emarketer. com/Article/Social-Networking-Reaches-Nearly-One-Four-Around -World/1009976.

213   *Listening to what* Max Fabricant, "What Could Matter as Much as Taste When It Comes to Chocolate?" *Crimson Hexagon,* http://www.crim- sonhexagon.com/blog/brand-management/social-intelligence-reveals -consumer-perception-two-uk-treats.

214   *By January 2014* "Marketers Adopt Social Media Analytics Tools: Optimizing Campaign Tracking Is the Top Use of Social Media Analytics Tools," *eMarketer,* March 4, 2014, http://www.emarketer.com /Article/Marketers-Adopt-Social-Media-Analytics-Tools/1010644.

214   *Two-thirds of business leaders* Larry Barrett, "CMOs: Analytics, Social Media Key to Business Strategy, but We're Too Swamped," *ZDNet,* March 17, 2014, http://www.zdnet.com/cmos-analytics-social-media -key-to-business-strategy-but-were-too-swamped-7000027387/.

215   *In his memoirs* Manfred von Richthofen, *The Red Battle Flyer* (New York: Robert M. McBride, 1918).

215   *"However, if two . . . "* Ibid., p. 117.

216   *An AT&T advertisement* "The Kingdom of the Subscriber" (AT&T advertisement) in *Boys' Life: The Boy Scouts' Magazine* 6, no. 3 (May 1916): 17, http://books.google.ca/books?id=1Ny-krpq6YIC.

INDEX

ACKNOWLEDGEMENTS

This book draws on countless studies and acres of commentary and discussion in the media, as well as my own professional experience as a journalist and my own research. I am thankful for the work of those who, like me, are trying to figure out the meaning of this phenomenon called social media.

Tell Everyone would not exist in its current form without the sage counsel of my colleague at the University of British Columbia, Mary Lynn Young. When I talked with her about writing about this subject, she suggested I write a book for the general public, rather than an academic text. I am grateful for her insights, wisdom and friendship. I am fortunate to be surrounded by talented and supportive colleagues at the UBC Graduate School of Journalism—Candis Callison, Kathryn Gretsinger, Peter Klein and Kirk LaPointe.

I am indebted to my literary agent, Sally Harding, for her guidance and advice. She saw the potential in my original ideas for the book and helped to take them further. I am very grateful to Sally and the entire team at The Cooke Agency.

I have been fortunate to work with the wonderful people at

Doubleday Canada. My editor, Tim Rostron, motivated me to improve and refine the manuscript. I recall our first meeting with him and publishing director Lynn Henry, and their unbridled enthusiasm for the book. Thank you.

The seeds of this book were nurtured at the offices of Samara in Toronto, helped along by superb companionship, conversation and coffee. Thank you to Alison Loat and Michael MacMillan for providing me with a space to think and write. Thank you to my friends at Samara for their warmth, friendship and hospitality—Kendall Anderson, Ruth Ostrower, Heather Bastedo, Wayne Chu and Jane Hilderman.

I would also like to acknowledge the support for my academic research on social media from the Social Sciences and Humanities Research Council, the Canadian Media Research Consortium and the Peter Wall Institute for Advanced Studies.

I would be remiss not to thank dance DJ Armin van Buuren and his radio show, *A State of Trance*, for serving as the soundtrack to hours of writing.

No acknowledgements would be complete without special thanks to my companion in life, Rachel. She is the first person to read everything I write, my toughest and most supportive reviewer.